Games, Sports
and Cultures

Games, Sports and Cultures

Edited by
Noel Dyck

Oxford · New York

First published in 2000 by
Berg
Editorial offices:
150 Cowley Road, Oxford, OX4 1JJ, UK
70 Washington Square South, New York, NY 10012, USA

Berg is the imprint of Oxford International Publishers Ltd.

Library of Congress Cataloguing-in-Publication Data

A catalogue record for this book is available from the Library of
Congress.

British Library Cataloguing-in-Publication Data

A catalogue record for this book is available from the British Library.

ISBN   1 85973 312 3 (Cloth)
        1 85973 317 4 (Paper)

Printed in the United Kingdom by Biddles Ltd, Kings Lynn

Contents

Part IV: Sport as Cultural Performance

Notes on Contributors

Joseph S. Alter is Assistant Professor of Anthropology at the University of Pittsburgh. A medical anthropologist who has done research on Indian wrestling and physical culture, sexuality, and celibacy, he is currently examining the historical development of yoga as a form of modern medicine in India. He is the author of The Wrestler's Body: Identity and Ideology in North India (1992).

Susan Brownell competed in national and international events in track and field (heptathlon) in the US before representing Beijing City in the 1986 Chinese National College Games. Her experience resulted in her book, Training the Body for China: Sports in the Moral Order of the People's Republic (1995). She is Associate Professor of Anthropology at the University of Missouri, St. Louis.

Noel Dyck is Professor of Social Anthropology at Simon Fraser University in Canada. The author of several books on relations between Aboriginal peoples and governments, he was drawn to the anthropology of sport through his children's participation and his own subsequent involvement as a coach in youth soccer and track and field. He is currently completing a book on adults and the social construction of children's sport.

Yngve Georg Lithman is Professor of International Migration and Ethnic Relations at the University of Bergen, and is Research Director of IMER Norway/Bergen. A social anthropologist by training, he has taught in universities in Sweden, Canada and Norway. He has published extensively in Swedish on historical and contemporary issues in sport, including a study of future trends commissioned by the Swedish Sports Federation.

George Mentore is Associate Professor of Anthropology at the University of Virginia. He has worked with the Waiwai of southern Guyana and northern Brazil for three decades. In addition to teaching and research on lowland South American peoples, his work includes Caribbean studies and the anthropology of the body and power. He is currently working on a book about "Waiwai Social Being".

Philip Moore is Senior Lecturer in Anthropology in the School of Social Sciences at Curtin University of Technology in Perth, Western Australia. He has conducted research in Canada and Australia, and his research interests include the ethnography of work, the anthropology of sport and the practice of anthropological consultancy. For over ten years he has taught a class dealing with sport and contemporary culture.

Charles Fruehling Springwood is Assistant Professor of Anthropology at Illinois Wesleyan University. His research interests include race, gender, sport, and museums, with regional concentrations in Japan and the United States. He is the author of Cooperstown to Dyersville: A Geography of Baseball Nostalgia (1996), co-editor of Team Spirits: The History and Significance of Native American Mascots (forthcoming) and co-author of In Red, White, and Black: Power, Resistance, and the Spectacle of Race in American Collegiate Athletics (forthcoming).

Synthia Sydnor is Associate Professor of Kinesiology, Criticism and Interpretative Theory at the University of Illinois at Urbana-Champaign. In addition to teaching a course on the anthropology of play, her research focuses upon metaphoric, aesthetic, and symbolic representations of sport and play.

Melford S. Weiss received his Ph.D. from Michigan State University in 1971. He is currently Professor of Anthropology at California State University in Sacramento. His research interests and publications include elite women's international gymnastics, the social fabric of schools and schooling, overseas Chinese communities, and contemporary American culture and the American military.

Introduction

Noel Dyck

Why would anthropologists turn their attention to games, sports and cultures? What fresh insights would they seek to bring to an already massive web of local, national and global discourse on games and sport fuelled by zealous sports fans, media commentators and, latterly, sports scholars from a range of other disciplines? Indeed, are games and sports matters that warrant serious intellectual inquiry?

This volume responds to these and other questions by employing anthropological perspectives to examine the intricately interconnected activities, relationships and purposes that inform the organization, performance, discursive construction and consumption of games and sports in a range of contemporary cultural settings. It seeks to extend the literature of sport studies to incorporate wholeheartedly ethnographic accounts of a diverse range of games and sports and the social, cultural and political issues that surround and interpenetrate them. The ten chapters in this volume endeavour to demonstrate the merits of some distinctive investigative and analytical approaches brought to this field of interdisciplinary scholarship by anthropologists. At the same time, the volume aims to provide a larger anthropological audience with tangible evidence of the ethnographic opportunities and theoretical challenges that arise when fieldworkers give systematic and serious attention to games and sports as salient and instructive aspects of everyday life.

The past experience of most of the contributors to this volume, as well as that related to us by other anthropologists of games and sports, would seem to indicate that the second of our objectives will be the more difficult one to accomplish. Social and cultural anthropologists who investigate and write about games and sports have been, not to put too fine a point on it, far better received outside their discipline than within it. Why anthropology has, for the most part, tended to eschew intellectual engagement with games and sports that enlist the passionate involvement of so many of the people whom we study is one of the matters addressed in this volume. What is to be gained by anthropologists abandoning this unspoken but abiding avoidance of the study of games and sports and the myriad ways in which these are played, celebrated and used in everyday life is explored in each of the chapters of this book.

The traditional consignment of sport to the margins of academic interest and respectability is by no means confined to anthropology. Nevertheless, anthropologists who have been persuaded of the benefits to be realized by taking games and sport as legitimate and important matters for study have learned much about how best to link this field to the central core of their discipline's analytical concerns by observing the travails of our compatriots in other disciplines. For instance, in the mid-1980s John MacAloon, an anthropologist who had written (and who continues to write) elegantly and perceptively about the modern Olympic Games, was invited to address a sport sociology conference. His comments, subsequently published in a provocative and frequently cited article (MacAloon 1987), chided sports scholars for too readily and defensively explaining away the slow progress of their field in terms of a general cultural unwillingness to take sport seriously. In MacAloon's view, sport sociologists had yet to take sport as seriously as did the world around them. Sport scholars must, he opined, 'stop perceiving ourselves as *Quixotes* if we are ever to cease acting and writing as *Sancho Panzas*' (MacAloon 1987: 105). MacAloon proposed an ethnographically oriented research agenda for the field that, he argued, would rescue it from some of its practitioners' outmoded structuralist preoccupations or, worse, from others' outright abandonment of theoretical preoccupations: namely, the relocation of sport sociology to the more promising and productive terrain of the sociology of culture.

Not the least interesting aspect of this encounter[1] was the manner in which MacAloon initially introduced himself as an anthropological interloper but proceeded to wrap himself in the garb of a sociologist of sport, a tactic subsequently adopted by more than a few anthropologists of games and sports. This situational re-identification of MacAloon's work as a form of sport sociology detracted not at all from its insights and worth, but it did serve to sustain an impression that nominally leaves the study of games and sport outside the confines of anthropological concern. Alternatively, anthropologists' accounts of games and sports have appeared in volumes and special issues of journals that have focused on more acceptable, 'mainstream' anthropological concerns such as fieldwork (Dyck 2000), cultural performance (MacAloon 1984), gender identities (Brownell 1996) and morality (Archetti 1997). This is, of course, entirely appropriate, for sport is an aspect of contemporary life that speaks to and about fundamental matters of anthropological concern. Nevertheless, the authors of these articles and chapters would appear to have taken special care to establish the theoretical rigour and pertinence of their analyses and to have limited the amount of ethnographic detail provided about the sporting activities in question, not to mention the number of references to other anthropological analyses of sport. Readers are afforded relatively scant indication of the extent of published anthropological scholarship on games and sports and the range of topics and issues that have been examined by anthropological students of athletic forms and activities. Arguably, this outcome is less the result of authorial neglect than a circumspect response to the prejudices of anthropological readers. Sport if necessary, but not necessarily sport. In effect, the anthropology of games and sports has been a field of inquiry that dared not speak its name.

But the time for such reticence, as well as the studied disinterest within anthropology that prompted it, has passed. During the last decade a series of outstanding ethnographies of sport have been published, including those by Alter (1992), Brownell (1995), Klein (1991, 1993, 1997) and Armstrong (1998). These have been joined by volumes that address sport and identity (MacClancy 1996) and world football (Armstrong and Giulianotti 1997), a revised introductory text on the anthropology of sport (Blanchard 1995), and a substantial number of articles that have shown that the products of the anthropology of games and sports can comprise not only welcome contributions to the interdisciplinary field of sport studies but also fine pieces of anthropological work in their own right. This volume is, thus, constructed upon an intellectual foundation that deserves to be named and accorded recognition as a growing and exciting field of anthropological inquiry. What is sought is simple acknowledgement that games, sports and athletic competitions of all manner are frequently encountered or, to put it another way, often inescapable features of contemporary existence around the world. While the degree to which communities and their individual members may be preoccupied with playing, watching or following the performance of these athletic forms may differ substantially from place to place and from one time to another, the organization, performance, contemplation and utilization of these activities warrants anthropological attention - no more and no less than other familiar objects of ethnographic inquiry.

Three implicit props of the lingering anthropological disinclination to discuss games and sports are addressed directly by this volume. First, the assumption that contemporary sport is primarily a North American and European addiction that clutters our newspapers and television broadcasts is belied by chapters that examine games, sports and their cultural consequences in ethnographic settings ranging from India, China, Japan, Australia, Canada, the US to Sweden. Moreover, the athletic forms reported here include indigenous archery contests in the jungles of South America and *kabaddi* (an Indian game of touch-tag), as well as the sports of soccer (football), ice hockey, track and field, gymnastics and baseball. Second, the notion that sport is essentially (and conveniently) separable from other aspects of social life is flatly contradicted by chapters that investigate games and sport in the context of family relations, child rearing, transnationalism, state governance, multiculturalism, nationalism, tourism, business and international politics. Finally, the presumption that, given its physicality, little more can be said about sports than to report the scores to those who care to hear them is disproved in this volume. The analyses presented here apply theoretical approaches - including social constructionism, postcolonial studies, feminism, transnationalism, structuralism, existential and symbolic anthropology, the anthropology of the body, and the study of nostalgia, celebrity, liminality and social drama - that both draw from and, in turn, contribute to larger intellectual concerns within contemporary anthropology.

This volume does not presume to set the boundaries or fix the appropriate subject matter of 'the' anthropology of sport. Rather, the volume seeks to provide a sample of some of the substantive concerns, theoretical perspectives and investigative approaches that can usefully be brought to the anthropological study of games, sports and cultures and made part of a broader interdisciplinary discourse on sport. Nor does this volume represent an attempt to colonize for anthropology 'remote' or 'exotic' corners of the world that have yet to be 'discovered' by other students of sport study. Such an undertaking would be fundamentally wrong headed, even if it was not already too late to mount such a campaign. Many places and peoples whom anthropologists once tended to label as their own have by now been studied by practitioners of other disciplines who have given serious attention to non-Western play, games and sports. What is more, anthropology today acknowledges the realities of globalization and the need to study 'us' as well as 'them'.

In short, our purpose is neither to reduce the study of sport to anthropology[2] nor to produce yet another anthropological subfield where the anthropology of sport can be hermetically sealed off from the rest of the discipline. The chapters in this volume recognize the varied and vital relationships, activities, beliefs and processes that comprise sport and the ways in which these run through, reflect and influence other aspects of social and cultural life. Accepting the inherent interdisciplinarity of sport studies, what is needed is a rapprochement between anthropology and sport scholarship. This is unlikely to entail a simple reconciliation that prompts anthropologists to adopt uncritically the theoretical assumptions, methodological practices, definitions and substantive concerns preferred by various non-anthropological contributors to sport scholarship. But neither is there any wish on our part to erect partisan disciplinary boundaries that would prevent us from engaging with and learning from the work of non-anthropological colleagues. Instead, we reserve the right to transgress disciplinary boundaries freely while searching for and profiting from the similarities and differences in our respective approaches to a field of common and compelling interest.

Overview of the Volume

The volume is organized in four sections. The chapters in the first section explore a variety of theoretical frames and methodological issues that have concerned anthropologists of games and sports. Dyck's initial chapter, which considers the prospects for anthropological engagement with the study of sport, identifies some distinctive ontological, methodological and theoretical contributions that anthropologists are positioned to make to the interdisciplinary field of sport studies. Anthropology's characteristic use of ethnography as a mode of inquiry and analysis places a premium upon contextualization, specificity and comparison as powerful means for shaping substantive accounts and eliciting theoretical insights that complement those generated by other disciplinary approaches. Dyck also examines various aspects of sports activity and involvement - glossed here in terms of 'games, bodies, celebrations and boundaries' - that speak in intriguing ways to broader anthropological concerns. Marshalling the findings of existing ethnographic writings on games and athletic competitions, Dyck argues that anthropologists of sport have rendered and will continue to render a valuable service to their discipline by bringing the study of complexly constructed, subtly nuanced, passionately pursued and intellectually fascinating sets of activities, relationships, beliefs and purposes from the margins into the mainstream of anthropological concern.

Brownell's chapter asks why an anthropologist should study sport and how an appreciation of this field might contribute to our understanding of China. Her response to the first of these questions identifies the persistent problem that anthropologists of sport have encountered in convincing other anthropologists that what could be learned about sports could be of general interest to a theoretically driven discipline. Brownell goes on to outline recent theoretical developments within anthropology, including postcolonial studies, practice theory, feminism, transnational theory and an interest in the body, which have created a more favourable set of conditions for pulling sport studies into 'the larger fold of the discipline'. The insights that each of these approaches enables her to make with respect to Chinese involvement in the Olympic Games provide an instructive example of the capacity of ethnographic studies of sport to speak to large and pressing issues including the emergence of Chinese nationalism within the context of increasing transnational sporting involvement.

Mentore's chapter examines a formalized archery contest among the Waiwai, a people who live in the forests of southern Guyana and northern Brazil, and raises the larger question of how a society takes persuasive hold of its individual members through sport. Grounding his inquiry in a detailed ethnographic account of the body techniques of Waiwai archery and the social and cosmological context within which archery contests occur, Mentore concludes that the determination of winners and losers in these competitions is less significant than the placement of the hunter as athlete at the centre of the social gaze. Arguing that the elements that produce socially valued differences are essentially the same in Waiwai archery as in the Olympic Games, he traces the ways in which this society retrieves through the athlete's body the substances for celebrating its own existence. In examining an indigenous competitive form that lies well outside the boundaries of 'modern' sport, Mentore demonstrates how comparisons drawn between ostensibly 'separate' areas of study can be employed to the benefit of each.

The chapters in the second part of the volume focus upon the politics of identity that often figure prominently in sport. Alter's chapter on *kabaddi*, a national sport of India, surveys the historical transformation or 'sportization' of a traditional game of touch-tag into a highly organized and regulated sport that has become a locus point in the discourse and practice of nationalist politics. Comparing *kabaddi* with wrestling and cricket in India, Alter details the processes by which the rules of this sport have been steadily standardized at the same time as its meaning and significance have been harnessed to competing projects for shaping Indian nationalism. Actively promoted by political authorities as being especially indicative of Indian national character, *kabaddi* has, ironically, been rendered increasingly 'Indian' by bureaucratic efforts to ensure that it conforms to Western models of sport. Celebrated in terms of its wholesome, health-giving, good-character-building and pan-Indian nature, *kabaddi* has, nonetheless, been styled as a sport that India can export to the world. Alter's delineation of the development of *kabaddi* serves to demonstrate how internationalism in sport can be incorporated as a vital component of nationalism.

Moore's chapter investigates the politics of culture in Western Australian soccer. Although often proclaimed as 'the world game', soccer is here a marginal sport that is denied the label of 'football' by the more popular game of Australian Rules Football. Traditionally recognized as an 'ethnic' (non-Anglo-Australian) sport that is played and appreciated primarily by 'new Australians', the organization and control of the game reflects the determination of different groups of European immigrants to retain and mark their ethnicities through participation in and support of 'our game'. Moore's chapter focuses upon the vigorous political contestation that has ensued in the wake of state authorities' campaign to refashion and 'de-ethnicize' soccer in order to render it consistent with new state policies and definitions of 'multiculturalism'. Moore's account underscores the distinct limitations of a state's power to wrest control of a sport away from the people and cultural purposes and processes that sustain it.

The third section of the volume considers the organization and cultural meanings of sport for child and youth athletes as well as for their parents. Dyck's chapter on the construction of sport and childhood in Canada is the first of three chapters that look into one of the less developed sub-fields of sport studies: the relationship between children and sport. Dyck's examination of organized community sport activities for children and youth in Canada focuses upon the factors that for many parents make sport not only an attractive means of augmenting family child-rearing stratagems but also of constructing identities for themselves and their children. What are elucidated here are subtle and not-so-subtle disjunctures between the ideological justifications for measures taken on behalf of children, including the claim that participation in sport enhances children's 'self-esteem' and chances for future life success, and actual, commonplace experiences generated by children's sport. Dyck argues that, notwithstanding lingering dissatisfaction with general and particular aspects of children's sports, parents tend to remain responsive to the ministrations of sport bureaucracies because they fall victim to processes of secular theodicy.

Lithman's chapter on children's elite sport in Sweden reflects upon how participants in this field, including child athletes, parents and sport leaders, engage in joint acts of creating cultural meaning. These activities, Lithman maintains, can be comprehended only by locating children's sport within broader social and cultural contexts. Employing a cultural analytic perspective, the author explains how the athlete's body serves as a boundary and a sign, paving the way for the emergence of what he terms a 'one-dimensional' view of the person. The seriousness with which children's elite sport is constructed by adults and contested by young athletes underscores, in Lithman's view, 'the capacity of sport to provide a comprehensive, miniaturized and manifest image of human beings, of society, and of basic existential questions.' There is little evidence, argues Lithman, of elite-level children's sport contributing in any substantial way to a sense of belonging that transcends individuality. In his view, the extent to which sport activities foster 'communitas', if at all, is highly debatable.

Weiss's chapter explores the social world of American women gymnasts, portraying the fundamentally different modes of coming of age experienced by adolescent elite athletes and their contemporaries. Through the presentation of stylized case histories of 'Jane Gymnast' and 'Suzy Student', the author itemizes the larger and smaller social and cultural differences that separate the 'gym world' from other experiences of adolescence. The extensive international travel undertaken from an early age by top-level gymnasts, the intense but ambivalent relationships that they share with team members and coaches, and the competitive success and acclaim that they may achieve is largely hidden from or irrelevant to their peers at home. Moreover, Weiss notes that by the time a competitive gymnast's sport career is reaching its conclusion, other high school students are commencing adult lives for which they have prepared themselves quite differently than have elite gymnasts. Weiss's chapter raises significant questions concerning the efficacy of sport as an appropriate medium for the 'socialization' of children and youth.

In the final part of the volume sport is analysed as a complex form of cultural performance that is capable of being articulated in a number of directions. Springwood's chapter recounts a Japanese freelance essayist's unusual but persevering efforts to construct in his country a replica of the baseball diamond featured in the 1989 Hollywood film *Field of Dreams*. The translocation of this quintessentially American representation of 'America's game' from the cornfields of Iowa to a rice paddy outside of Hiroshima reflects not only the popularity of baseball in Japan but also a Japanese fascination with the elements and processes of American culture. Domestic tourist travel to this site and the staging of games between the visiting 'Iowa Ghost Players' and the locally constituted 'Corns' team reveals, in Springwood's view, a complicated political economic relationship and cultural transformation of the signs, symbols and experiences offered by American sport and film. But in constructing a Japanese version of America as 'white, spacious, bucolic' and nostalgically utopian, the essayist and his compatriots may, Springwood suggests, be practising a distinctive form of 'othering' that takes America as its object.

Finally, Sydnor's chapter interrogates the intricate relations between sport, celebrity and liminality. Grounding her analysis in an ethnography of a specific and highly celebrated tourist site, the Michael Jordan monument in Chicago, Sydnor reports the varied 'readings' of it gathered from visitors and written sources. She then turns to the interconnections between classic anthropological themes and postmodern theorizing of the dynamics of contemporary life. Fantasy, Sydnor notes, is an essential and powerful element of the search for self identity in everyday existence. Clearly, the capacity of sport to produce objects for global contemplation and consumption marks it as a field that warrants the attention of contemporary social theorists as well as anthropologists of sport. The liminal spaces of sport and celebrity are not, Sydnor concludes, temporary spaces but ever-present conditions that script life at the end of the twentieth century. The exploration of these spaces proposes a new and provocative way of viewing sport by anthropologists.

Notes

1. The debate initiated by MacAloon was subsequently joined by Nixon (1991) and other sport sociologists.
2. I am indebted to Philip Moore for reminding me of this important point.

References

Alter, Joseph S. (1992), The Wrestler's Body: Identity and Ideology in North India, Berkeley: University of California Press.

Archetti, E.P. (1997), 'The Moralities of Argentinian Football', in S. Howell (ed.), The Ethnography of Moralities, London/New York: Routledge, pp. 98-123.

Armstrong, Gary (1998), Football Hooligans: Knowing the Score, Oxford/New York: Berg.

Armstrong, Gary and Richard Giulianotti (eds), (1997), Entering the Field: New Perspectives on World Football, Oxford/New York: Berg.

Blanchard, Kendall (1995), The Anthropology of Sport: An Introduction (revised edition), Westport, Connecticut and London: Bergin & Garvey.

Brownell, Susan (1995), Training the Body for China: Sports in the Moral Order of the People's Republic, Chicago: University of Chicago Press.

— (1996), 'Representing Gender in the Chinese Nation: Chinese Sportswomen and Beijing's Bid for the 2000 Olympics', Identities: Global Studies in Culture and Identity, 2(3): 223-47.

Dyck, Noel (2000), 'Home Field Advantage? Exploring the Social Construction of Children's Sports', in Vered Amit (ed.), Constructing the 'Field': Ethnographic Fieldwork at the Turn of the Century, London/New York: Routledge, pp. 32-53.

Klein, Alan M. (1991), *Sugarball: The American Game, the Dominican Dream*, New Haven/London: Yale University Press.

— (1993), *Little Big Men: Bodybuilding Subculture and Gender Construction*, Albany: State University of New York Press.

— (1997), *Baseball on the Border: A Tale of Two Laredos*, Princeton, New Jersey: Princeton University Press.

MacAloon, John J. (1984), 'Olympic Games and the Theory of Spectacle in Modern Societies' in John J. MacAloon (ed.), *Rite, Drama, Festival, Spectacle: Rehearsals Toward a Theory of Cultural Performance*, Philadelphia: Institute for the Study of Human Issues, pp. 241-80.

— (1987) 'An Observer's View of Sport Sociology', *Sociology of Sport Journal*, (4): 103-15.

MacClancy, Jeremy (ed.), (1996), *Sport, Identity and Ethnicity*, Oxford: Berg.

Nixon, H.L. (1991), 'Sport Sociology That Matters: Imperatives and Challenges for the 1990s', *Sociology of Sport Journal*, 8(3): 281-94.

Part I

Theoretical Frames and Methodological Issues

1

Games, Bodies, Celebrations and Boundaries: Anthropological Perspectives on Sport[1]

Noel Dyck

Introduction

Imagine, if you will, a field of inquiry that comprises a wide range of recurring, complexly patterned activities, relationships, beliefs and purposes that revolve around competitive performances that combine physical, social and cultural elements. The forms of these activities are reported to vary across space and time, featuring continuity, discontinuity, particularity and dispersion. The competitions situated at the centre of this field enjoin larger and smaller levels of embodied participation, but regularly attract audiences ranging in size from a few onlookers to thousands and even millions of spectators who, though they may observe the proceedings either from close up or from a considerable distance, nonetheless watch, ponder, interpret, debate and celebrate what they witness and experience in a myriad of ways before, during and after these events. Consider also the manner in which contemplation of and commentary upon the form, meaning and significance of such activities may reach far beyond the venue of performance to larger issues of power, identity, gender, economy, polity, morality, colonialism, nationalism and globalization. Note that these practices and their diverse attendant relations, understandings and outcomes are capable of generating notions of recognized similarity and difference, even as they variously inspire fantasy, pleasure, despair, and, sometimes, more-or-less well-remunerated livelihoods for some of the featured performers.

A field of inquiry encompassing these and other elements in rich profusion would, one might imagine, render it a matter of compelling interest to anthropologists. The ethnographic opportunities presented and analytic questions raised by such commonly encountered phenomena would seem to mark them as promising candidates for sustained anthropological enthusiasm and attention. The merest possibility that a field such as this might not spark substantial anthropological interest would demand explanation.

Moving from the imaginary to the actual, much, if not all of anthropology's conventional stance toward the study of sports has exhibited a puzzling reluctance towards engagement, notwithstanding the many inviting attributes of this field. In fact, games and sports of all manner from around the world have been intermittently reported by ethnographic fieldworkers since the founding of anthropology as an academic discipline in the nineteenth century. Moreover, individual anthropologists have in different places and times conducted more-or-less detailed studies of indigenous games and forms of play, as well as large-scale sporting events such as the modern Olympic Games. Nevertheless, the deeper import of sport as a realm of social and cultural practice deserving of systematic and extended anthropological inquiry has not, until recently, begun to be realized. The work of anthropologists who examine sport has, instead, more often been appreciated within the growing interdisciplinary field of sport scholarship than within anthropology. This arrangement has tended to mute the distinctive contributions that anthropologists might make to the study of sport as well as the rich insights that a fuller and more critical appreciation of sport might furnish to anthropology.

Anthropology's ambivalence toward the study of sport is neither accidental nor irrevocable. Nor is it unique, for sociologists concerned with sport have frequently bemoaned the absence of encouragement for such work within their discipline. Bourdieu (1990: 156) for one, typifies the sociology of sport, a field about which he has written, as an area of study disdained by sociologists and despised by sports people. Dunning accounts for the prevailing sociological neglect of sport in terms of its notional placement

> on the negatively valued side of the complex of overlapping dichotomies which are conventionally perceived, such as those between 'work' and 'leisure,' 'mind' and 'body,' 'seriousness' and 'pleasure,' 'economic' and 'non-economic' phenomena. That is, in terms of the pervasive Western tendency towards reductionist and dualistic thinking, sport is perceived to be a trivial, pleasure-oriented leisure activity which engages the body rather than the mind and is of no economic value. (1986:4)

Anthropology, traditionally defined as the science of the non-modern and 'primitive', implicitly excluded the study of sports and competitive games because they were perceived, correctly, as central features of modernity (Archetti 1998b). But much has changed in social and cultural anthropology in the past two decades including, not least, a cumulative redefinition of the scope and objectives of the discipline. Ethnological essentialism has gradually given way to more historicized, postcolonial and processual perspectives that are receptive to the conceptual concerns prompted by many facets of contemporary sports. What is more, the practice of anthropology has increasingly been expanded to include 'here' as well as 'there', 'us' as well as 'them', thereby finally embracing the long mooted, but infrequently realized comparative potential of the discipline.

The recent appearance of a small but growing corpus of first-rate anthropological writing on sports points the way toward new and exciting possibilities in this field. Clearly, it is a propitious time for anthropology to be 'getting into the game', in both senses of the term.

This chapter examines the prospects for further serious, sustained and productive anthropological engagement with the study of sports. It begins by noting existing anthropological work on games and sports and the place that anthropologists have thus far established for themselves within the larger interdisciplinary field of sport studies. Included here is an assessment of some of the distinctive contributions that anthropological inquiry can make to the study of sports. The chapter then considers four aspects of sports – identified here in terms of 'games, bodies, celebrations and boundaries' – that speak directly and in intriguing ways to broader anthropological concerns.

Anthropology and the Study of Sports

Among early anthropological references to games and athletic contests were those recorded by ethnologists who sought to document the traditional ways of life of aboriginal peoples in the Americas. In the same year that he launched his investigation of the Ghost Dance religion,[2] James Mooney (1890) also published an article in the *American Anthropologist* on the Cherokee ball game. This was followed by Culin's (1907) encyclopaedic report of the morphology and religious significance of the games of North American Indians. While interest in the traditional games and athletic contests of the Americas (Nabokov 1987; Oxendine 1988; Scarborough and Wilcox 1991; Veenum 1994) as well as aboriginal participation in non-indigenous sports (Blanchard 1981) has continued to the present, elsewhere works examining non-Western games and non-Westerners' participation in sport as important matters in their own right were long the exception within anthropology. Ethnological accounts of indigenous games and athletic contests tended, for the most part, to be brief and incidental to concerns with other cultural issues (Blanchard 1995: 2).

Subsequent anthropological studies of the use of witchcraft in Pueblo baseball (Fox 1961), magic in professional baseball (Gmelch 1972), ritual in American football (Arens 1975), and the politics of Trobriand cricket (Leach 1976) did address sports practices, albeit in ways that sometimes tended to underscore the discipline's reputation for exoticism. Frankenberg's (1957) ethnography of religion, politics and football in a north Wales community employed an approach pioneered by the Manchester School in its studies of African tribal societies but did not prompt many anthropologists to turn their attention to the study of sports.[3] During the 1970s and 1980s the meetings and publications of The Anthropological Association for the Study of Play (TAASP)[4] brought a number of anthropologists into regular contact with students of play, games and sports from a range of disciplines, thereby acquainting them with both the advantages and challenges entailed in interdisciplinary work. Considerable attention was devoted by members of TAASP to defining the distinguishing characteristics of sports, a matter to which we will return below.

Beginning with MacAloon's (1981) book on the origins of the modern Olympic Games, anthropological treatments of sport have become increasingly sophisticated and better known within the field of sport studies. During the 1990s a growing number of ethnographically based accounts of diverse facets of a wide range of sports played in a variety of settings have established the basis for a solidly founded anthropology of sport. These include Brownell's (1995) study of sports in the Peoples' Republic of China, Alter's (1992) ethnography of wrestling, identity and ideology in North India, Klein's (1991, 1997) accounts of baseball and national identities in the Dominican Republic and along the border of the US and Mexico, Archetti's (1996, 1997a, 1997b, 1998a) analyses of the moralities of Argentinian football,[5] Armstrong's (1998) analysis of 'hooliganism' in British football, Giulianotti and Armstrong's (1997) volume of essays on the anthropology of football around the world, Klein's (1993) and Bolin's (1992, 1997) studies of bodybuilding and Appadurai's (1995) portrait of the vernacularization of cricket in India. In addition, Blanchard's (1995) introductory text on the anthropology of sport and MacClancy's (1996) volume on sports, identity and ethnicity have, respectively, examined general issues pertaining to this emerging field and presented additional ethnographic case studies of sports and related activities.

These and other anthropological writings reflect their authors' inextricable engagement with the broader field of sport studies. The works of sociologists, historians and geographers of sports, along with those of academics situated in cultural studies, gender studies, kinesiology and other programmes, are regularly cited by anthropologists of sport. The respectful but occasionally awkward disciplinary self-consciousness that tinged earlier discussions between anthropologists and non-anthropologists about whether sports could be legitimately and usefully treated as instances of ritual behaviour[6] has been superseded by pragmatic anthropological responses to this question (see MacAloon 1984; Brownell 1995; Sciama 1996) that have served to move the debate along to more substantive issues within the field. Moreover, the circumspect politeness that initially characterized interdisciplinary exchanges have on occasion given way to frank and sharply expressed differences of perspective between anthropologists and other students of sport,[7] differences that spring from some distinctive aspects of anthropological methodology, ontology and purpose.

Ethnography stands as the hallmark of social and cultural anthropology. More than merely a preferred research method, ethnographic inquiry comprises a set of investigative and intellectual practices that shape the anthropological endeavour in fundamental ways. While participant-observation research is by no means unique to anthropology, the ways in which it is conducted by anthropological fieldworkers requires further comment. The intensive personal immersion in given social settings undertaken by anthropological fieldworkers is designed to yield experience and insights that lie beyond the reach of other research approaches. What is sought is critical and comprehensive experience of a social setting, the acquisition of which employs all of an anthropologist's resources and capacities: intellectual, physical, emotional, positional and intuitive (Okely 1992). The development of face-to-face relations with a variety of subjects over an extended period of time renders fieldwork not a solitary but a decidedly social experience that is mediated and constituted through the fieldworker's relationships with others. In short, the researcher and his/her field relations intentionally serve as the primary means for eliciting findings and insights (Amit 2000).

In no other form of scholarly inquiry are 'relations of intimacy and familiarity between researcher and research subject envisioned as a fundamental medium of investigation rather than as an extraneous byproduct or even an impediment' (Amit 2000: 2). Although anthropologists regularly combine participant observation with other research methods, their presence in field situations affords them a vantagepoint imbued with significant analytical advantages. They encounter people in the field as rounded individuals with experiences, involvements and stories that reach beyond the limited purview of any research project (Amit 2000: 2). This makes it difficult for anthropological fieldworkers to view the people they work with as one-dimensional research subjects. Fieldwork obliges anthropologists to take account of intersubjective experience, language differences, meaning and social variability. The access to activities and lived experiences provided by ethnographic field research makes this a powerful and flexible but, nonetheless, demanding method of inquiry. The critical empathy that an ethnographer strives to achieve depends upon his/her ability to resolve the tensions that inevitably crop up between the personal and professional aspects of fieldwork. Prerequisites for good ethnography include a continuing reflexivity on the part of the fieldworker concerning the manner in which his/her involvement in the field may have shaped the findings as well as a careful balancing of the ethical dilemmas that may arise from using one's presence as an instrument of inquiry.

In contrast to the universalizing assumptions and objectives of the methodologies favoured by most sociologists of sport,[8] ethnographic inquiries are intentionally sited in particular places and times. Ethnographically based analyses must, in consequence, take account of the specificity and historicity of fieldwork findings. Complex and varying lives and events cannot be readily subsumed by simple categories, but they can be documented and analysed in ways that facilitate comparison across culture, space and time. Accordingly, ethnographic writing not only documents the particular but also strives to identify the processes by which similarities and differences in relationships, meanings and activities are generated. This analytical approach requires that careful attention be paid to identifying ethnographic settings and findings in terms of the immediate and larger geographical, cultural, social, historical, political and economic contexts within which they are located. In practical terms, ethnographic analysis involves moving from the particular to the general and back and forth again. Ongoing comparisons between 'there' and 'here', 'them' and 'us', and 'then' and 'now' furnish a mode of investigative and analytic triangulation without which ethnography would remain simply a narrowly focused and time-consuming means of description.

This disciplinary distinctiveness is exemplified by anthropological responses to the manner in which certain sociologists and historians of sport have contested in proprietorial fashion the meaning and application of the category of 'sport' itself. Use of the term 'sport' to refer cross-culturally to non-Western games and contests[9] or historically to embrace premodern athletic contests has been more-or-less stridently rejected by these sociologically inclined scholars.[10] They argue that the definitive features of modernism entirely separate 'modern' sports, created in industrialized societies during the nineteenth and twentieth centuries, from all purported counterparts.

One of the most influential of these formulations, Allen Guttmann's *From Ritual to Record: The Nature of Modern Sports* (1978), presents a schema that splits the category of 'play' into 'spontaneous play' and 'organized play', the latter being labelled as the realm of 'games'. The category of 'games' is thereafter divided into 'noncompetitive games' and 'competitive games', the second of which is seen as being synonymous with 'contests'. Finally, Guttmann distinguishes between 'intellectual contests' and 'physical contests' and identifies the latter as constituting 'sports'. Guttmann further specifies characteristics that distinguish modern sports from those of previous eras: (1) the fundamentally secular nature of modern sports ('We do not run in order that the earth be more fertile. We till the earth, or work in our factories and offices, so that we can have time to play' (Guttmann 1978: 26)); (2) the provision of equality of opportunity to compete and the creation of equal conditions of competition, both of which are vital to the establishment of the 'achievement' principle; (3) the specialization of roles in modern sport activities, which logically leads to professionalization; (4) the rationalization of modern sports through the adoption of standardized rules; (5) the bureaucratic organization of sports to decide and enforce rules and manage competitions; (6) the quantification of competition results to establish national and international standards of achievement; and (7) the concept of the 'record', which was a logical outcome of the quantification of sports. In Guttmann's view, 'primitive' sports may sometimes have been secular but shared none of the other six characteristics, while Greek, Roman and Medieval European sports shared some but not all of these essential properties of modern sports. Thus, concludes Guttmann, 'Once the gods have vanished from Mount Olympus or from Dante's paradise, we can no longer run to appease them or to save our souls, but we can set a new record. It is a uniquely modern form of immortality' (Guttmann 1978: 55).

Unlike Guttmann's typological characterization of modern sport, Blanchard (1995: 9) offers a broader and less historically and culturally constrained definition of sport as 'a gamelike activity having rules, a competitive element, and requiring some form of physical exertion.' The use of the term 'sport' in both wider and narrower senses has been remarked upon by Elias (1986: 129-32) who cautions against the possibility that a minimization of the differences and a maximization of the similarities between modern sports and the game-contests of antiquity may render a distorted representation of the relationships between them.

Nevertheless, what is included and what is excluded from various categorizations of 'sport'[11] may, as Sutton-Smith (1995: xii) suggests, tell us as much or more about the purposes of those engaged in such definitional exercises than about the phenomena they purport to explain:

> Those who interpret sports are in general those who are professionally a part of sports. All of these people with their personal investment wish to show you that the discussion of sports is important for understanding the modern world of women versus men, of corporations versus workers, of tradition versus modernism, of freedom versus compulsion. And all of their views are thoroughly grounded in the modern twentieth-century consciousness that thinks that children's play and adult sport are very different; that sports but not play have a great deal to do with power and violence; that play by contrast has to do with imagination rather than ritual; and that play, leisure, and recreation, but not sports, have in common the voluntary commitment of the participant. For good or bad all of these are twentieth-century values which permeate all attempts to "scientifically" define the character of sport.

Assuming that sport scholars are capable of recognizing the existence of differing academic and popular definitions of sport, how we choose to define 'sport' may be less significant than what we can learn from examining the processes by which one or another definition is championed in any given place and time and the uses to which particular definitions are put.[12]

The category of 'sport', as MacAloon has noted, emerged historically and has varied over time (1987: 106). To insist upon reducing all of the fascinating variation that this has entailed in order to shore up a general analytic definition of sport would be to risk losing the object 'in the act of trying to be "sociological" about it.' Paraphrasing Levi-Strauss, MacAloon cogently suggests that in the field of sport studies 'the general patterns we seek lie neither in similarities nor differences, but in the *similarities among the differences*' (McAloon 1987: 112). By the same token, recognition of salient disciplinary differences that shape how a field of common interest may be envisioned and approached analytically is an equally important matter, for the contributions that anthropologists are positioned to make to sport studies derive from distinctive aspects of anthropological thought and practice.

How the Game Is Played

The word 'sport' can, according to the *Oxford English Dictionary*, be used variously to denote amusement, fun or a lack of seriousness, a person who plays fairly and who is willing to take risks, or any game or pastime (or such activities and pastimes collectively), but arguably, it is now employed most commonly to refer to athletic activities engaged in for some combination of amusement, recreation, physical exercise or competitive achievement. At the centre of this usage of 'sport' resides a bewilderingly wide range of more-or-less elaborately organized games and athletic competitions. Formal and informal sport activities featuring individual competitions, team games or some combination of the two are relatively easy to locate, wherever one may be. Indeed, those who might prefer to avoid contact with sport in whatever form may be severely taxed in their efforts to do so. Yet notwithstanding the ubiquity of sport activities, these are by no means simple or transparent phenomena. The games and modes of athletic competition subsumed by either narrower or broader definitions of 'sport' are large in number, diverse in nature and more-or-less complex in organization and performance. These considerations need not perturb those who seek merely one or another form of satisfaction through active participation or a spectator's interest in sport. They do, however, make the work of comparatively inclined sport scholars infinitely more challenging.

The social designation of a keen and knowledgeable 'sports person' is characteristically linked to personal involvement with a particular sport or set of sports. Accordingly, an individual's experience and understanding of one or even several sports is likely to be limited spatially, temporally and, as we shall consider below, in a number of other respects. Sport expertise, whether gleaned as a participant or as a fan, is generally concerned with certain aspects of particular performances of selected games or competitions drawn from the combined sum of extant sport activities. The inclination of sports persons to configure their notions of 'sport' to match their own experience and knowledge of preferred games and competitive forms is entirely understandable. But this is not a viable option for anthropologists of sport who endeavour to study given sports and sport practices and relationships within a comparative perspective.

In light of the sheer volume, diversity and complexity of sport activities in the contemporary world, anthropologists of sport can usefully engage in serial and cumulative ethnographic inquiry that respects and records the particularity and subtlety of situated games and sport forms while searching for analytically significant differences and similarities within this vast and dispersed field of human endeavour. Games and athletic competitions, be they 'premodern', 'modern' or 'postmodern' in origin and/or local, regional or global in practice, offer an obvious starting point. But what should an ethnographic account of any given game or set of sport forms include?

The rules of a game or competition, whether standardized or varied, written or unwritten, are obvious but not unproblematic matters for inclusion. Consulting a rule book, if one exists, provides one version of a game or sport, albeit usually in the form of a set of required elements and prohibited practices and behaviours. But even in a sport played within a single city, varying sets of regulations may be adopted by different leagues and levels of competition. For example, within organized community soccer leagues for children in Canada the numbers of competitors on each team, the rules of substitution, the duration of games and a variety of other regulations are varied to fit what is seen as being most suitable for children at different age-graded levels of participation. Referees who officiate soccer games in different leagues and in different age divisions frequently consult with the coaches of the opposing teams before the commencement of a match to establish which rules pertain to this particular division. Formal sport rules, whatever the scope of their jurisdiction, may be intermittently or even frequently revised. What is more, notwithstanding the formal rules established for a particular sport or division of competition within a sport, a set of unwritten conventions and agreements may be applied or appealed to by officials, coaches or players.

Nor is such variation in the rules of a game limited to children's sport. Within the highest level of professional ice hockey, the National Hockey League, it is widely though unofficially acknowledged that the rigour with which rule infractions are likely to be penalized during the first two periods of a hockey match should be and regularly is relaxed during the final period of the game lest the outcome of the match suffer the ignominious fate of being 'decided by penalties'. Similarly, first-year players or 'rookies' in the National Basketball Association may initially chafe at an unwritten rule that dictates that officials' penalty decisions tend to favour 'veteran' players who are said to have already 'paid their dues'. The existence of formal, standardized rules for a game or sport does not ensure that the play that ensues will necessarily be or uniformly be seen to be regulated by impartial, constant and unproblematic rules. Although rules are a constituent element of games and sports and invest these activities with relatively predictable form and a required illusion of certainty, the manner in which sport rules are negotiated, invoked, enforced, manipulated, evaded and altered renders them intensely social matters that analysts can scarcely afford to take for granted.

The activities that comprise games and athletic competitions may be governed in certain respects by rules and officials, but the actual forms of play and athletic performance that figure so prominently in these events are not entirely or, in the case of some sports, even substantially prescribed by official codes or regulations. Bourdieu observes that a sport, at a given moment, is rather like a musical work: it is both the musical score (the rules of the game, etc.), and also the various competing interpretations (and a whole set of sedimented interpretations from the past); and each new interpreter is confronted by this, more unconsciously than consciously, when he proposes 'his' interpretation. (1990:163)

Further attention will be given to the implications of the non-verbal dimension and embodied nature of sport in the following section, but for the moment suffice it to say that ethnographic accounts of games and sports ignore at their peril the complex and evolving styles of play that for many participants and fans are the central attraction of these activities.

A comprehensive account of any sport or game will also list and eluci-date the identifiable roles performed at sporting events or in conjunction with their staging. In addition to players, athletes or competitors, a given event – depending upon the nature of the game or sport and where and by whom it is being played – may feature larger or smaller combinations of associated sport roles, including those of referees, judges, umpires and their assistants; individual or team coaches, managers and trainers; club, league or sport federation representatives, administrators and event organizers; financial sponsors and sport business personnel; announcers, analysts and media journalists; and, not least, spectators, fans, and viewers of televised sport events. The selection, assemblage and enactment of these and other roles within and around a particular match, sport per-formance or circuit of competitive events differs from one sport form to another and between competitive levels within a given sport. The struc-tural complexity of any given game or sport event will, therefore, reflect whether it is a children's game, a sport league for children organized by adults, a formal or informal adult recreational sport event, a nationally or internationally organized elite level of amateur competition or a profes-sional sport.

While it may be logistically convenient to limit one's examination of a given game or sport to one or another level of organization and competi-tion, to do so uncritically would be to overlook salient interconnections between them. For instance, ice hockey is not only one of Canada's proudest contributions to the world of sport but also a national passion. Within Canada and across parts of the US hockey is played by boys of all ages (as well as a growing number of girls) both in organized leagues and in impromptu games contested not in ice rinks but on the street, which, depending upon the season and the surface of the playing area, may involve the wearing of winter boots, running shoes or in-line roller skates. Community organized youth hockey is divided into recreational or 'house' leagues and tiered competitive leagues, which lead proficient 17-21-year-old players into either semi-professional major junior leagues in Canada or to athletic scholarships at a substantial number of American universi-ties. Beyond this lies the prospect of professional careers in Europe, Japan, or minor leagues in North America and ultimately the National Hockey League (NHL). But in addition to youth, college and professional hockey there are vast numbers of adult recreational leagues in which men can continue to play the game more-or-less frequently and intensively into middle age.

The playing styles, skill levels of competitors, spectator popularity, organizational complexity and financial underpinning of each of these manifestations of hockey differ from one another. Yet to identify top-level, professional hockey as the definitive form of the sport would be to classify all other organized and unorganized levels of hockey participation as incomplete and derivative versions of the 'genuine' sport. The capacity of professional hockey to captivate the attention and shape the playing styles and fantasies of youth players has long been recognized, even by children who in the midst of more-or-less enthusiastically contested 'street' hockey games often provide detailed, personalized and voluble 'play by play' accounts of their own performances, which mimic the game descriptions of sport commentators who appear on radio and television broadcasts of professional matches. The pastiche of 'street' hockey also regularly incorporates voluntarily negotiated but strictly honoured practices of individual handicapping[13] on the part of older, larger or better players that serve to balance out competitive disparities between unequally sized or skilled players. To do otherwise would be to make the game something other than 'fun' for the members of one of the teams and, thereby, to risk its chances of continuing. The rhetoric and pursuit of 'fun' is not, however, limited to children's hockey games. Professional players and teams in the NHL that are struggling to regain their competitive form are often advised by coaches not to 'think too much about the game' but instead to 'just go out there and have fun' as the best means for regaining competitive form and 'breaking out of a slump'. Markedly superior professional hockey teams on occasion also undemonstratively take care not to unduly 'run up the score' against hapless opponents.

The point is that games, sports and athletic competitions can, if one wishes to view them thus, be readily distinguished from one another in many ways including their composition, purposes and structural complexity. Even a common sport form can be performed or played in a variety of ways and by a range of competitors. Nevertheless, these ostensibly differing modes of a game or athletic performance may also be interpenetrated by overlapping cultural understandings and practices that experientially link these various forms of sport for their participants and enthusiasts. Accordingly, ethnographic accounts and analyses of games and sports need to pay attention to the broader sporting and social contexts within which particular games or sporting events take place. This is no small task, for it involves looking beyond focal figures and features of sport to examine less emphasized participants and activities that, nonetheless, may be integral parts of given games and sporting events. The understanding sought by anthropologists of the overall social and cultural construction of games and sports may well have to reach beyond and beneath what it is that players, officials, event organizers, or fans need to know in order to fulfil their given roles satisfactorily.

However onerous the demands this assignment places upon ethnographers of sport, it also affords them countless opportunities to make original and significant contributions to our understanding of sport. What types of resources are required to stage different types of games and athletic competitions not only on one occasion or for a season but over a period of years? Which people tend to play which roles in given sport activities, and how does their participation in these activities relate to or influence other aspects of their lives? What, in specific terms, does involvement in particular games and sports offer to different types of participants? What parallels can be drawn between the orchestration of large-scale sporting events and other types of social events? How can the development or discontinuation, geographic dispersion or containment of particular games or athletic competitions be explained? How do governments at the municipal, provincial and national level intervene in the organization, funding and direction of sport, and to what ends? These and other questions arise when anthropologists accord games and sport forms and events the status of social phenomena that merit serious and extended investigation. That so many people in so many places invest such substantial amounts of time, material resources and passion in these activities makes a poignant case for their inclusion in the ethnographic agenda.

Performing Bodies

What athletes exhibit in games and other competitive events and what spectators watch and celebrate are embodied sport techniques that unite the private realm of everyday body practices with the public world of shared performances (MacAloon 1984). Sport provides a major venue for displaying the body in public. The capacity of games and athletic competitions, viewed as performed sets of body techniques, to combine simultaneously the mundane and the dramatic affords them a versatility that is socially significant and analytically interesting (Brownell 1995: 28-9). Like other performance genres such as dance,[14] sport comprises a form of body practice in which meanings are generated but whose representations remain open to negotiation and contestation (MacClancy 1996a: 4). Since athletic performances are primarily non-verbal, their description and analysis remain elusive matters for scholars. There are, as Bourdieu (1990: 166) notes in a discussion of the problems posed by the teaching of body practice,

> heaps of things that we understand only with our bodies, outside conscious awareness, without being able to put our understanding into words . . . [S]porting practices are practices in which understanding is bodily. Very often, all you can do is say: 'Look, do what I'm doing.'

Ethnographic inquiry and comparative approaches have, nonetheless, furnished anthropologists with investigative and conceptual tools readily calibrated for recognizing and exploring the bodily dynamics and attractions of games and sports. Alter's (1992) ethnography of wrestling in India, Klein's (1993) investigation of bodybuilding[15] in the US and Brownell's (1995) study of what is involved in 'training the body for China', to cite but three examples, have made substantial contributions to sport studies as well as to anthropological writing about the body.

The disciplinary regimes to which athletes submit or surrender their bodies for longer and shorter periods of their lives differ in stringency and structure. The track and field athletes with whom Brownell trained and competed during the course of her fieldwork in China were subjected by their coaches to levels of bodily (and political) surveillance and control that differ in some important respects from the conditions experienced by their counterparts in the US. In contrast to athletes who are coached by club, team or individual trainers, competitive bodybuilders take responsibility for designing personal training programmes, albeit in gyms where the training regimes of other bodybuilders can be readily observed, discussed, copied and modified. So too are bodybuilders' decisions about whether or not to incorporate the use of steroids into their programmes made individually but with an awareness of the high probability that these may be employed advantageously by their competitors (Klein 1995; Bolin 1997).

Training programmes, whatever their general and/or specific objectives (improved health and well-being, appropriate child 'socialization', enhanced athletic performance, co-ordinated team play or, in the case of bodybuilding, a reconstructed body in itself) represent an amalgam of social purposes and culturally mediated understandings of the body. While the exaggerated musculature sought by male body builders connotes power, domination and virility (Klein 1993: 4) the physical bodies of female competitors challenge and transform conventional notions of femininity (Bolin 1997: 184). The competitive performances of wrestlers in Turkey are assessed not only in terms of the strength exhibited, but also the intelligence and honour displayed during matches (Stokes 1996). Lower-class boxers in the US steadfastly commit themselves to years of gruelling and physically painful discipline, frequently 'in the face of disillusionment and sometimes outright failure', as a means of 'asserting their moral superiority over those who opt for – or give in to – the shady trades of the informal economy' (Wacquant 1995a: 518). In doing so, these boxers use and experience their bodies in training and competition as a form of bodily and social capital (Wacquant 1995b). The rapid development of organized athletic competitions for 'senior' or 'masters' (age 55 years and over) athletes across North America seems to reflect less of a desire for healthy exercise than strategic use of body training and direct involvement in sport as vehicles for distancing participants from prevailing negative stereotypes associated with age and ageism.[16]

The unintended products of training and competition are no less socially and culturally mediated than those that they are designed to

Figure 1 Anticipating the pitch in youth baseball [Sam Beitel]

achieve. The likelihood that most athletes, from children to 'seniors' to professional competitors, will at some point encounter physical pain and injuries of greater or lesser seriousness and duration through participation in sport underscores the bodily nature of athletic activities. But distinguishing between the physiological foundations of pain and injury and the manner in which these are culturally interpreted and experienced by athletes can be a difficult matter. Whether pain is hidden, downplayed and ignored or, as in the case of male Inuit hockey players in the Canadian Arctic, overemphasized and proudly paraded (Collings and Condon 1996) reflects complex and varying constructions of gender, ethnicity and sport. In this way, as in others, the embodied experience of sport is necessarily ambiguous.

The often-overlooked distinction between forms of play and athletes' (and spectators') physical, emotional and cultural experience of the embodied actions that occur within these events is rebalanced in several anthropological accounts of team games. Klein's (1991) study of baseball in the Dominican Republic delineates the multifaceted training of young players who hope eventually to pursue playing careers in American professional leagues and offers an evocative portrayal of the carnivalesque atmosphere of Dominican baseball games. Archetti's (1996, 1997a, 1997b, 1998a) serial examination of preferred playing styles in Argentinian football not only underlines the discerning scrutiny that fans devote to the skilled movements and tactics demonstrated on a football field, but also shows how embodied, collective memories of particular plays ('the perfect pass') can be contemplated and celebrated for years to come. Similarly, Leite Lopes (1997) traces the origins and development of the style of play now associated globally with Brazilian football to the use of a distinctive body language by working-class and Black athletes who were originally not allowed to play league football in that country. By garnering international success for Brazil on the playing field, this locally developed style of play has contributed to reversing elite-generated racist stereotypes previously internalized by Brazilian society as a whole. Preferred styles of play, even within the same sport, frequently vary from one setting to another. Armstrong's (1998) account of muscle and masculinity in English football identifies the processes by which culturally mediated physical action on the field can fuel emotions of ecstasy and aggression, communion and conflict both in the stands and on streets beyond the football ground. Writing about a different sport on another continent, Appadurai (1995) explicates the ways in which cricket in India links gender, fantasy and nationalism through bodily excitement and the sensual pleasure that rests at the core of the male viewing experience.

A disciplinary commitment to ethnographic research ensures that anthropologists of sport will, in the course of their investigations into various aspects of games and athletic competitions, be hard pressed to ignore the complexity and diversity of body practices and cultures that are fundamental to this field. By attending, documenting and analysing training sessions, game events and athletic competitions, sometimes as active participants but always as attentive observers, anthropologists are well placed to make insightful contributions to sport scholarship as well as to the emerging field of anthropological studies of the body. Existing anthropological publications on various aspects of the bodily nature and dimensions of sport have, to say the least, been impressive, but equally exciting possibilities lie ahead. Consider, for instance, the role of the referee in a temporally continuous game such as soccer. The 'flow' of a soccer game reflects, among other things, the manner in which the referee communicates to players what he or she will and will not countenance in the way of play. Experienced and respected referees quickly and definitively establish the boundaries between 'hard but fair' and 'unacceptable' tackles. The ultimate compliment that can be paid to a referee is that he or she was barely noticeable during the match. While referees of this calibre may contrive to make inconspicuous their judicious control of matches that 'flow', an informed anthropological appraisal of football needs to recognize that all referees not only interpret and enforce rules of competition but also assist, with greater or lesser ability, in choreographing the experienced and observed movements that constitute games. Referees, along with coaches and, in some respects, spectators, are active co-participants with athletes in styling sport as embodied practice.

Celebrating Sports

No less important than the embodied nature of sport is its celebratory capacity, a faculty embedded in sport's constitution as a metalanguage. Games and athletic competitions tend to stand separate, temporally and experientially, from ordinary aspects of life because they comprise what their participants know as forms of 'play'.[17] 'Play', according to Bateson (1973: 152ff.) is fundamentally a communicative act, and in his famous example of monkeys engaging in play by pretending to fight, he observes that they share an implicit message: this is not serious, this is play. What makes such messages possible, in Csikszentmihalyi's view, 'is that play ultimately is a state of subjective experience' that can exist only 'when there is awareness of alternatives' (1981: 19). While distinguishing between 'playfulness' and 'seriousness' depends, of course, upon the context within which these are mooted and contrasted, nonetheless, the implicit and explicit communication of which is which and of which is preferred (and by whom) remain matters of primary concern both to participants and analysts. In the case of athletic games and competitions, as Blanchard (1995: 121) notes

> [s]port takes the act of 'playing at' one step further. Two boxers pounding away at each other's heads in a formal bout, like the monkeys, are communicating that message of fighting but not-fighting, the paradox of play. However, the boxing match is more than just play. It goes one step beyond the paradox by saying, 'this is not simply play; this is play with a purpose, a "playing for" as opposed to a "playing at".'

What is marked and celebrated by athletes, spectators and sports enthusiasts are varying forms of 'play with a purpose' that they choose to valorize in contrast to the 'alternatives' offered by everyday life.

The celebratory and communicative powers of sport can be manifested and exploited for a range of purposes. The attractions for athletes and other performers of taking part in games and competitions may reach well beyond the simple pleasures of camaraderie and playing 'for the fun of it' to embrace the studied pursuit of social recognition, fame and material rewards. The organizers and sponsors of sporting events associate themselves with socially valued pastimes, thereby situating themselves more-or-less advantageously to bask in any reflected honour that may issue from venues of competition. Yet through their control of these events they may also acquire tangible social, ideological, political and economic resources that can be employed both inside and outside the sporting realm. The influence that organizers and sponsors may exercise over the management of the meaning of games and sports is not the least of these rewards. For instance, Pierre de Coubertin envisioned and created the modern Olympic Games, including athletic competitions and associated cultural events, as a means for establishing a universal language with which a new conception of the human being could be propagated (MacAloon 1981). Similarly, the Chinese government's fostering of its athletes' involvement in international athletics competitions has been encased in an elaborate ceremonial framework that symbolically serves to link athletic success to the state (Brownell 1995). Multinational entertainment corporations that are purchasing professional sport teams and inventing new forms of 'sport entertainment' in order to integrate the manufacturing and global marketing of images and icons of sport are as attuned to the celebratory allure of sport as any politician.

Given the prominence and theatricality[18] of these manifestations of sport, it might seem appropriate to designate spectators and fans – however voluble, animated or 'televisible' their behaviour at these events may be – simply as observers or consumers of sport entertainment. To conclude further that what attracts fans to pay admission fees or to spend hours watching and/or listening to broadcasts of sport can be gleaned through careful analyses of media coverage of sport would be logically consistent with this approach and methodologically convenient. In fact, fans do attend games as observers and many also consume staggering amounts of sport media coverage. But although textual analyses of media depictions of sport may be useful for certain purposes, it cannot be assumed that these adequately or unproblematically comprehend the full scope of fans' attraction to, understanding of and involvement in games and athletic competitions.

Anthropological approaches to sport accord spectators and fans the status of essential participants in games and athletic competitions. As dramatic events in which alternative purposes to quotidian existence are selected and celebrated,[19] the role of the audience is vital, whether its members are immediately present, 'watching' from a distance or simply 'imagined' by the participants (for example 'street' hockey). Yet in addition to watching sport, spectators and fans talk about what they see, and, in so doing, contribute directly and significantly to the communicative construction and valorization of sport. In this field, as Archetti (1998b) has noted, saying is doing.[20] To demonstrate an extensive and discerning knowledge of particular games and sports that covers not only their general rules and structures but also the characteristics of their leading practitioners, record-setting performances, memorable matches and cherished myths is to wield a cultural resource that can be put to effective social use. A mastery of the particular genres and forms of speech favoured by fans of a sport testifies to one's previous social engagement with others of like mind and similar enthusiasm.[21] A willingness and ability to 'talk' a sport provides an instrument for initiating and sustaining social interaction with other supporters regardless of discrepancies of class, ethnicity, citizenship, age and even gender that might otherwise serve as barriers to conversation.

Discourse about sport serves as a medium for contemplating and elaborating notions of 'celebrity' (Sydnor, this volume), 'memory' (Stokes 1996) and 'nostalgia' (Springwood, this volume). It can also be used for exploring existential choices and matters that lead beyond the field of play. Archetti's (1997a) nuanced analysis of a story related to him by a Buenos Aires football fan (who had been told the story by his father) reveals the manner in which a scheme of preferences concerning styles of play can be anchored within a set of moral options that are highlighted with each retelling of the tale. Briefly, the story revolves around the interaction during a football game in the 1920s between two teammates who exemplified not only different playing styles but different moral stances towards the game: Lalin, a skilled and artistic 'juggler' of the ball, and Seoane, a very effective 'killer' or scorer of goals. Lalin delighted in dribbling the ball as though it was an orange until it softened and one could 'see the juice':

> Lalin was postponing the moment when winners and losers are divided and joy and disappointment are experienced. Seoane did not like it. In the [half-time] break, Seoane insisted on getting the ball: 'Lalin, if you can give me the ball, just one cross-ball, and that is what we need, I give you my guarantee, one cross-ball, one goal.' At the beginning of the second half, my father said, doubting for a moment, 'I think it was in the second minute, Lalin sent a cross-ball, a perfect cross-ball, and Seoane, like the goal-machine he was, volleyed it into the goal. Goal, what a nice score,' my father added. 'Seoane, very happy, ran to embrace and to thank Lalin and said: "You see, if we play like this we will win, we will always win." Lalin answered laconically: "Yes, I am sure, we can always win, but if we play in this way I do not enjoy the game."' (Archetti 1997a: 104)

This story, which Archetti encountered on a number of occasions during fieldwork, is part of a historical narrative of Argentinean football that mixes oral sources with written accounts. Elsewhere, Archetti (1998b) argues that football in Latin America engendered new modes of discourse that made possible the thinking of modernist 'national' projects.

The global commodification of professional sport features, among other things, 'packaged' interpretations of the meaning and significance of activities that may be seen on television or read about in newspapers. This development has expanded some fans' discussions of sport to include appraisals of proffered media and corporate interpretations of certain games and competitions. Dedicated followers of elite-level and professional sports that commercially warrant such media coverage may extend their claims of expertise by registering disagreement with media accounts and formulating alternative interpretations of games and sporting events into counter-discourses that are shared in countless private conversations and, occasionally, expressed in independently produced 'fanzines'[22] or on 'sports talk' radio programs that invite fans to phone in and express their opinions 'on air'. But these instances of media-inspired sport discourse pertain to only a fairly narrow spectrum of sport activities, participation and talk. A more sophisticated and comprehensive appreciation of the celebratory and imaginative[23] powers provided by sport requires extensive ethnographic inquiry into the ways in which a broad range of games and athletic competitions are discursively constructed and socially employed by their enthusiasts.

Identifying Boundaries

Certain notable attributes of sport may, ironically, have contributed to the manner in which it has, for the most part, been analytically bounded, trivialized and consigned to the margins of social science interest. The capacity of sport to absorb the attention of players and fans so utterly and intensively, the carnal pleasures of play that may visibly be shared by spectators as well as athletes, the excitement that is formulaically stoked up by the unscripted outcomes of games and athletic contests, the degree to which fate and chance may enter into distinguishing winners from losers, the ostensibly irrational faith and loyalty that some fans invest in particular teams and athletes – these and other properties of sport have been implicitly interpreted as legitimating the systematic segregation of sport from central social, cultural and political concerns. Once safely enclosed in the impermeable conceptual containers offered by such notions as 'false consciousness' or 'sub-cultures',[24] sporting phenomena and relationships can be safely ignored or, alternately, put to selective use as suits the taste and purpose of the analyst. Accordingly, football, baseball, cricket or any other game can be categorically styled as an 'opiate of the masses', a means of 'killing time' in a 'world without meaning', or as a potential launching site for 'rituals of rebellion' directed toward larger and less tractable structures of control. What is more, each of these treatments of sport can be accomplished without having to do much more than flip through a few newspapers or watch a bit of television.

In contrast, ethnographic inquiry into the activities, relationships and meanings of sport require substantial investments of time and invariably oblige practitioners to note and grapple with complex phenomena that, upon closer examination, inexorably lead the ethnographer away from 'simple' ethnographic fields to complicated contexts and challenging but intriguing analytical issues. Nonetheless, having met the demands of taking games and athletic competitions seriously and having subjected them to sustained ethnographic inquiry, anthropologists of sport are now in a position to demonstrate that what we are studying speaks not only to interests shared by others active in the field of sport studies but also to matters of fundamental interest within anthropology. One of these issues, which anthropologists of sport have been studying most productively, concerns the ways in which sport serves variously to observe, reinforce, redefine, invent and transgress 'boundaries' of all manner.

The concept of 'boundary' has been central to anthropological thinking from the outset of the discipline, albeit for different reasons at different times (Cohen 1994: 62-7). Barth's (1969) seminal linking of
'boundaries' to the social organization of cultural difference notes that
while marked ethnic boundaries have a most definite 'appearance', they
typically separate quite indefinite, shifting and even overlapping 'substance'. In other words, the nature of substantive differences between self-
or externally defined ethnic groups may be less certain than the processes by which 'differentiation' is insisted upon and accomplished. This
places analytic priority upon the definitional activities that proclaim certain selected distinctions to be diacritical boundary markers at any given
moment. While the nature of actual differences between (and within)
groups can vary over time, still the insistence upon identifying and acti-
vating differences between groups can continue. Boundaries may be dis-
regarded for many practical, everyday purposes without jeopardizing the
claim that 'important' differences 'really' exist and need to be respected.
In consequence, the politics of identity can be seen to revolve around the
definitional processes by which boundaries are noted, maintained,
relaxed or shifted over time. To draw attention to the boundaries that are
said to separate 'us' from 'them' is to proclaim a programme for managing
social relations behind as well as across boundaries.

'Boundary work' in sport, as in other areas of social life, pertains to the
processes by which differences and similarities are declared, made culturally significant and fashioned into identities for the groups or 'imagined
communities' thus constructed. Moreover, since consciousness and production of boundaries occurs both at the level of collectivities and individuals, this raises the question 'of what the individual is conscious when
she or he invokes a boundary as a means or source of social identity'
(Cohen 1994: 65). In their efforts to explicate the complex dynamics of
sport, it is precisely this set of problems that anthropologists of sport have
been addressing.

Ethnographic accounts of games and athletic contests offer rich evidence of the myriad ways in which persons, both as individuals and as
members of groups, utilize involvement in sport to organize comprehen-
sible lives out of the increasingly fragmented and contradictory elements
of contemporary existence. Sport participation may be marshalled to fashion one or another rendering of gender, age, class, ethnicity, multiculturalism, nationality and the place of individuals and collectivities in the
larger world. For example, the essays presented in two recent volumes on
the anthropology of sport (MacClancy 1996; Armstrong and Giulianotti
1997) cumulatively explore each of these arenas of boundary maintenance and identity formation in thought-provoking analyses of sport activities and settings from around the world. What emerges from these and
other ethnographic accounts of sport is an appreciation of the multivo-
cality of sport as a vehicle for not only organizing leisure time but also
responding to larger concerns. Thus, Giulianotti and Armstrong (1997:

6ff.) note the manner in which football clubs in Britain are made to serve by their supporters as repositories of intertwined gender, class, national, political and regional identities.

The striking instrumentality with which sport can be mobilized to promote recognition of similarity and/or difference, to foster unity or to spark conflict may be manifestly apparent, but anthropologists are also peering beneath these surfaces to discover more nuanced and flexible stratagems and purposes for which sport may be enlisted. The British imperial project in Africa and India was promulgated in part through exhibition and subsequent propagation of games of 'muscular Christianity'. Football in southern and central Africa was originally introduced by British colonial authorities as a means for controlling social disorder among youths in locations that were experiencing rapid and large-scale urban migration, but over time the game was transformed into a powerful and important arena for forging African identities (Stuart 1996). Similarly, cricket, the quintessentially English game, was gradually stripped of its hegemonic connotations and locally reinvented as a means by which Indian males are enabled to enjoy the embodied excitement of 'Indianness' without the divisive scars of Indian nationalism (Appadurai 1995: 46). The cultural and structural ambivalence that may accompany the taking up of a colonial power's games is also illustrated in Klein's (1991) account of baseball in the Dominican Republic. Yet beyond the realm of hegemony and resistance lie usages of sport for less partisan purposes. Richards' (1997) report of the resort to football as a means of social rehabilitation in war-torn Sierra Leone underlines the frequently overlooked capacity of sport to invoke civility and contain contestation within agreed upon rules of play.[25] Bromberger's (1994: 173) specification of the capacity of football to link the universal to the particular and to reconcile the prominent values of the modern world (competition and achievement) with 'basic truths' (that goods and riches are finite in quantity, that happiness for some must mean unhappiness for others) identifies sport as a medium through which the realities of globalization can be acknowledged without having entirely to surrender situated lives and preferences.

These are, as MacClancy (1996a: 17) observes, scarcely 'marginal' or 'unserious' activities but key aspects of the constitution of contemporary societies.

Concluding Remarks

The prospects for continuing and fruitful anthropological engagement with the study of games, sports and cultures are, I conclude, highly promising. Several of the distinctive ontological, methodological and theoretical contributions that anthropologists are well equipped to make to the rapidly growing field of sport studies have been identified and examined in this chapter. What anthropologists have already accomplished through the practice of ethnographic inquiry, comparison, contextualization and the analytical linking of decidedly diverse activities and purposes to processes of more general concern is readily evident in a small but impressive and even exciting corpus of anthropological publications on games and sport. In seeking to elucidate similarities amongst the countless differences manifested in the organization, performance and salience of various games, sports and forms of athletic competition, anthropologists have begun to make their mark in the interdisciplinary field of sport studies.

No less important is the service that anthropologists of games and sports have done and will continue to do for their own discipline by bringing the study of complexly constructed, subtly nuanced, passionately pursued and intellectually fascinating sets of activities, relationships, beliefs and purposes from the margins into the mainstream of anthropological concern. Anthropology has much to gain by belatedly turning its attention to the ways in which games and sports are played and the manner in which athletic competitions of many kinds revolve around bodily performance, cultural celebration and the observation, creation or transcendence of social and cultural boundaries.

Notes

1. I wish to thank Vered Amit for her critical and constructive reading of an earlier draft of this chapter.
2. This project produced a classic anthropological study of a millenarian movement and a remarkable account of the tragic events that occurred at Wounded Knee in 1890 (Mooney 1896).
3. Similarly, Azoy's (1982) study of *buzkashi*, a traditional Afghan equestrian contest that has been transformed into a regulated, if highly localized sport, remains a nicely analysed ethnographic account that is not cited by students of sport and power as frequently as it deserves to be.
4. See Blanchard (1995: 21ff.) for a discussion of the TAASP and its successor body, the Association for the Study of Play (TASP). Some of the published proceedings of the TAASP include: Stevens (1977), Schwartzman (1980), Cheska (1981), Loy (1982), Sutton-Smith and Kelly-Byrne (1984), Blanchard (1986) and Mergen (1986). These published proceedings were succeeded by the journal *Play and Culture*.
5. Outside the US, Canada and Australia, the term 'football' refers to what North Americans identify as the game of 'soccer'.
6. See, for instance, Duthie (1980), Goodger (1986), Gluckman and Gluckman (1977), and Harris (1982).
7. See, for example, MacAloon's (1987) critical observations on the development of sport sociology, Nixon's (1991) assessment of this critique and MacAloon's (1992) subsequent critique of the use of cultural hegemony theory in sports studies. See also Dunning, Murphy and Waddington's (1991) critique of anthropological analyses of football hooliganism and Armstrong's (1998) trenchant rebuttal of sociological explanations of football hooliganism.

8. Gruneau (1999) represents an important exception to this sociological tendency.
9. Blanchard (1995), among others, takes this approach.
10. Kidd (1996: 12-14), for example, provides a relatively blunt statement of this position, while Elias (1986: 129-32) offers a more reflexive argument in support of it.
11. There is a substantial literature that has attended to defining and distinguishing the nature of sport, play and games in a variety of ways. In addition to the works cited above, see Bale (1989), Blanchard (1986), Callois (1961), Duthie (1980), Elias (1986), Elias and Dunning (1986), Luschen (1981), Meier (1986), Salter (1980) and Stevens (1980; 1992).
12. A similar point has been made by MacAloon (1987: 112).
13. Such handicapping in 'street' hockey may, for example, prohibit a superior player from shooting directly on goal unless the puck or ball has been passed at least twice between team members immediately prior to the shot.
14. Wulff's (1998) ethnography of the world of ballet dancers provides an intriguing account of a field which parallels sport in many ways but which differs from it in some important respects.
15. Klein (1993: 44) addresses the matter of whether bodybuilding should be considered a sport by reformulating the question. 'The real question may be whether or not to stick with conventional definitions of sport. As suspect as its past may be, bodybuilding has evolved into a unique activity that combines a variety of cultural forms into something that purists have difficulty categorizing. Bodybuilding can offer us an alternative to traditional athletic events by fusing physical development through training with artistic expression, eroticism, and spectacle.'
16. I am indebted to John Gives for bringing this aspect of 'senior' sports to my attention.
17. See Blanchard (1995) for a useful overview of the voluminous literature that has resulted from the attempt to define the nature of 'play'. As Blanchard notes, 'play' has yet to be assigned a generally agreed-upon meaning by either anthropologists or other social scientists.
18. The seminal work of Victor Turner (1967, 1969, 1974, 1987) on ritual, social drama, liminality, communitas, metaphors and performance has influenced the analytic approaches of a number of anthropologists of sport.
19. Giulianotti and Armstrong characterize British football matches in terms of their dramatic activity, noting that 'the match' traditionally was and still is a 'liminal zone in which much male behaviour and opinion is enlivened by ridicule, rejoicing and indignation' (1997: 8-9). See also Bromberger (1994), De Biasi and Lanfranchi (1997), Hognestad (1997) and Hughson (1997) for analyses of the dramatic capacities of football.

20. MacAloon also aptly reminds us that what participants have to say in ordinary speech about sporting events and institutions 'is not some superficial or bewildering thicket of illusions to be smashed through to real realities underneath. Ordinary discourse, the more ordinary the better, is not only patterned, it contains essential clues to social reality. Indeed it plays no small role in constituting that reality, and in that sense discourse is what is . . . Who says what to whom in which contexts about an institution such as sport is a matter of carefully studying the social positioning of the speakers and their groups' (1987: 108-9).

21. Giulianotti and Armstrong (1997: 7) suggest that an essential part of becoming a football fan is learning to speak in 'football tongues'.

22. See Giulianotti (1997) for an account of the production of 'fanzines' by football fans in Scotland.

23. Appadurai's analysis of Indian cricket (1995) for instance, takes to heart his own earlier invocation to anthropologists to heed the power of imagination and fantasy in the fabrication of social lives and to afford 'a new alertness to the fact that ordinary lives today are increasingly powered not by the givenness of things but by the possibilities that the media (either directly or indirectly) suggest are available' (1991: 197).

24. Hognestad (1997: 196) offers a pertinent critique of the notion of 'sub-cultures' of sport.

25. The civilizing properties of sport have been given extended attention by the 'figurationalist' school of sport sociology; see, for instance, Elias and Dunning (1986).

References

Alter, Joseph S. (1992), *The Wrestler's Body: Identity and Ideology in North India*, Berkeley: University of California Press.

Amit, Vered (2000), 'Introduction: Constructing the Field', in Vered Amit (ed.) *Constructing the Field: Ethnography in the Contemporary World*, London/New York: Routledge, pp.1-18.

Appadurai, Arjun (1991), 'Global Ethnoscapes: Notes and Queries for a Transnational Anthropology', in Richard G. Fox (ed.), *Recapturing Anthropology: Working in the Present*, Santa Fe, New Mexico: School of American Research Press, pp.191-210.

— (1995), 'Playing With Modernity: The Decolonization of Indian cricket', in Carol A. Breckenridge (ed.), *Consuming Modernity: Public Culture in a South Asian World*, Minneapolis/London: University of Minnesota Press, pp. 23-48.

Archetti, E.P. (1996), 'Playing Styles and Masculine Virtues in Argentine Football', in M. Melhuus and K.A. Stølen (eds), *Machos, Mistresses, Madonnas: Contesting the Power of Latin American Gendered Imagery*, London: Verso, pp.34-55.

— (1997a), 'The Moralities of Argentinian Football', in S. Howell (ed.), *The Ethnography of Moralities*, London/New York: Routledge, pp. 98-123.

— (1997b), '"And Give Joy to my Heart": Ideology and Emotions in the Argentinian Cult of Maradona', in Gary Armstrong and Richard Giulianotti (eds), *Entering the Field: New Perspectives on World Football*, Oxford/New York: Berg, pp.31-51.

— (1998a), 'The Potero and the Pibe: Territory and Belonging in the Mythical Account of Argentinian Football', in Nadia Lovell (ed.), *Locality and Belonging*, London/New York: Routledge, pp.189-210.

— (1998b), 'The Meanings of Sport in Anthropology: A View from Latin America', *European Review of Latin American and Caribbean Studies*, 65: 91-103.

Arens, William (1975), 'The Great American Football Ritual', *Natural History*, 84: 72-81.

Armstrong, Gary (1998), *Football Hooligans: Knowing the Score*, Oxford/New York: Berg.

Armstrong, Gary and Richard Giulianotti (eds) (1997), *Entering the Field: New Perspectives on World Football*, Oxford/New York: Berg.

Azoy, G. Whitney (1982), *Buzkashi: Game and Power in Afghanistan*, Philadelphia: University of Pennsylvania Press.

Bale, John (1989), *Sports Geography*, London: E. & F.N. Spon.

Barth, Fredrik (1969), 'Introduction', in Fredrik Barth (ed.), *Ethnic Groups and Boundaries: The Social Organization of Cultural Difference*, London: George Allen & Unwin, pp. 9-38.

Bateson, Gregory (1973), 'A Theory of Play and Fantasy', in G. Bateson, *Steps to an Ecology of Mind: Collected Essays in Anthropology, Psychiatry, Evolution and Epistemology*, St. Albans, UK: Paladin, pp. 150-67.

Blanchard, Kendall (1981), *The Mississippi Choctaws at Play: The Serious Side of Leisure*, Urbana: University of Illinois Press.

— (1995), *The Anthropology of Sport: An Introduction* (revised edition), Westport, Connecticut and London: Bergin & Garvey

Blanchard, Kendall (ed.) (1986), *The Many Faces of Play. The Association for the Anthropological Study of Play*, Vol. 9, Champaign, Illinois: Human Kinetics Publishers.

Bolin, Anne (1992), 'Vandalized Vanity: Feminine Physiques Betrayed and Portrayed', in F.E. Mascia-Lees and P. Sharpe (eds), *Tattoo, Torture, and Adornment*, Albany, New York: State University of New York Press, pp. 79-99.

— (1997) 'Flex Appeal, Food, and Fat: Competitive Bodybuilding, Gender, and Diet', in Pamela L. Moore (ed.), *Building Bodies*, New Brunswick: Rutger's University Press, pp. 184-208.

Bourdieu, Pierre (1990), 'Programme for a Sociology of Sport', in P. Bourdieu, *In Other Words: Essays Towards a Reflexive Sociology*, Stanford: Stanford University Press, pp. 156-67.

Bromberger, Christian (1994), 'Foreign Footballers, Cultural Dreams and Community Identity in Some North-western Mediterranean Cities', in John Bale and Joseph Maguire (eds), *The Global Sports Arena: Athletic Talent Migration in an Interdependent World*, London: Frank Cass, pp.171-82.

Brownell, Susan (1995), *Training the Body for China: Sports in the Moral Order of the People's Republic*, Chicago: University of Chicago Press.

Caillois, Roger (1961), *Man, Play and Games*, New York: Free Press of Glencoe.

Cheska, Alyce T. (ed.), (1981), *Play as Content: 1979 proceedings of the Association for the Anthropological Study of Play*, West Point: Leisure Press.

Cohen, Anthony P. (1994), 'Boundaries of Consciousness, Consciousness of Boundaries: Critical Questions for Anthropology', in Hans Vermeulen and Cora Govers (eds), *The Anthropology of Ethnicity: Beyond 'Ethnic Groups and Boundaries'*, pp. 59-79.

Collings, Peter and Richard G. Condon (1996), 'Blood on the Ice: Status, Self-Esteem, and Ritual Injury Among Inuit Hockey Players', *Human Organization*, 55(3): 253-62.

Csikszentmihalyi, Mihaly (1981), 'Some Paradoxes in the Definition of Play', A.T. Cheska (ed.), *Play as Context: 1979 Proceedings of the Association for the Anthropological Study of Play*, West Point, New York: Leisure Press, pp. 14-26.

Culin, Stewart (1907), *Games of the North American Indians*, Volume 2: Games of Skill, Lincoln/London: University of Nebraska Press, reprinted 1992.

De Biasi, Rocco and Pierre Lanfranchi (1997), 'The Importance of Difference: Football Identities in Italy', in Gary Armstrong and Richard Giulianotti (eds), *Entering the Field: New Perspectives on World Football*, Oxford/New York: Berg, pp. 87-104.

Dunning, E., P. Murphy, and I. Waddington (1991), 'Anthropological Versus Sociological Approaches to the Study of Soccer Hooliganism: Some Critical Notes', *Sociological Review*, 39(3): 459-78.

Dunning, Eric (1986), 'Preface', in Norbert Elias and Eric Dunning, *Quest for Excitement: Sport and Leisure in the Civilising Process*, Oxford: Basil Blackwell, pp. 1-18.

Duthie, J.H. (1980), 'Athletics: The Ritual of a Technological Society?', in Helen B. Schwartzman (ed.), *Play and Culture*, West Point, New York: Leisure Press, pp. 91-8.

Elias, Norbert (1986), 'The Genesis of Sport as a Sociological Problem', in Norbert Elias and Eric Dunning, *Quest for Excitement: Sport and Leisure in the Civilising Process*, Oxford: Basil Blackwell, pp. 126-49.

Elias, Norbert and Eric Dunning (1986), *Quest for Excitement: Sport and Leisure in the Civilising Process*, Oxford: Basil Blackwell.

Fox, Robin (1961), 'Pueblo Baseball: A New Use for Old Witchcraft', *Journal of American Folklore*, 74: 9-16.

Frankenberg, Ronald (1957), *Village on the Border: A Social Study of Religion,*

Politics and Football in a North Wales Community, London: Cohen and West.

Giulianotti, Richard (1997), 'Enlightening the North: Aberdeen Fanzines and Local Football Identity', in Gary Armstrong and Richard Giulianotti (eds), *Entering the Field: New Perspectives on World Football*, Oxford/New York: Berg, pp. 211-37.

Giulianotti, Richard and Gary Armstrong (1997), 'Introduction: Reclaiming the Game – An Introduction of the Anthropology of Football', in Gary Armstrong and Richard Giulianotti (eds), *Entering the Field: New Perspectives on World Football*, Oxford/New York: Berg, pp. 1-29.

Gluckman, Max and Mary Gluckman (1977), 'On Drama, and Games, and Athletic Contests', in Sally F. Moore and Barbara Meyeroff (eds), *Secular Ritual*, Assen/Amsterdam: Van Gorcum, pp. 227-43.

Gmelch, George (1972), 'Magic in Professional Baseball' in Gregory P. Stone (ed.), *Games, Sports and Power*, New Brunswick, New Jersey: Dutton, pp. 128-37.

Goodger, J. (1986), 'Ritual Solidarity and Sport', *Acta Sociologica*, 29(3): 219-24.

Gruneau, Richard (1999), 'A Postscript, 15 Years Later', in *Class, Sports and Social Development*, (revised edition), Champaign, IL: Human Kinetics Press.

Guttmann, Allen (1978), F*rom Ritual to Record: The Nature of Modern Sports*, New York: Columbia University Press.

Harris, Janet C. (1982), 'Sport and Ritual: A Macroscopic Comparison of Form', in John W. Loy (ed.), *The Paradoxes of Play*, West Point, New York: Leisure Press, pp. 205-14.

Hognestad, Hans Kristian (1997), 'The Jambo Experience: An Anthropological Study of Hearts Fans', in Gary Armstrong and Richard Giulianotti (eds), *Entering the Field: New Perspectives on World Football*, Oxford/New York: Berg, pp. 193-210.

Hughson, John (1997), 'The Bad Blue Boys and the 'Magical Recovery' of John Clarke', in Gary Armstrong and Richard Giulianotti (eds), *Entering the Field: New Perspectives on World Football*, Oxford/New York: Berg, pp. 239-59.

Kidd, Bruce (1996), *The Struggle for Canadian Sport*, Toronto/Buffalo/London: University of Toronto Press.

Klein, Alan M. (1991), *Sugarball: The American Game, the Dominican Dream*, New Haven/London: Yale University Press.

— (1993), *Little Big Men: Bodybuilding Subculture and Gender Construction*, Albany: State University of New York Press.

— (1995), 'Life's Too Short to Die Small: Steroid Use Among Male Bodybuilders', in Donald Sabo and David Frederick Gordon (eds), *Men's Health and Illness: Gender, Power, and the Body*, Thousand Oaks, CA: Sage Publications, pp. 105-20.

— (1997), *Baseball on the Border: A Tale of Two Laredos*, Princeton, New

Jersey: Princeton University Press.

Leach, Jerry W. (1976), *Structure and Message in Trobriand Cricket*, Unpublished paper written to accompany the movie *Trobriand Cricket*, Berkeley, CA: University of California Extension Center.

Leite Lopes, Jose Sergio (1997), 'Successes and Contradictions in "Multiracial" Brazilian Football', in Gary Armstrong and Richard Giulianotti (eds), *Entering the Field: New Perspectives on World Football*, Oxford/New York: Berg, pp. 53-86.

Loy, John W. (ed.) (1982), *The Paradoxes of Play. West Point*, New York: Leisure Press.

Luschen, Gunther (1981), 'The Interdependence of Sport and Culture', in J.W. Loy, Jr., G.S. Kenyon, and B.D. MacPherson (eds), *Sport, Culture and Society: A Reader on the Sociology of Sport* (second and revised edition), Philadelphia: Lea & Febiger, pp. 287-95.

MacAloon, John J. (1981), *This Great Symbol: Pierre de Coubertin and the Origins of the Modern Olympic Games*, Chicago/London: University of Chicago Press.

— (1984), 'Olympic Games and the Theory of Spectacle in Modern Societies', in John J. MacAloon (ed.), *Rite, Drama, Festival, Spectacle: Rehearsals Toward a Theory of Cultural Performance*, Philadelphia: Institute for the Study of Human Issues, pp. 241-80.

— (1987), 'An Observer's View of Sport Sociology', *Sociology of Sport Journal* (4): 103-15.

— (1992), 'The Ethnographic Imperative in Comparative Olympic Research', *Sociology of Sport Journal*, 9(2): 104-30.

MacClancy, Jeremy (1996a), 'Sport, Identity and Ethnicity', in J. MacClancy (ed.), *Sport, Identity and Ethnicity*,. Oxford: Berg, pp. 1-20.

MacClancy, Jeremy (ed.) (1996), *Sport, Identity and Ethnicity*, Oxford: Berg.

Meier, Klaus V. (1986), 'Play and Paradigmatic Integration', in K. Blanchard (ed.), *The Many Faces of Play*, The Association for the Anthropological Study of Play, Vol. 9. Champaign, Illinois: Human Kinetics Publishers, pp. 268-88.

Mergen, Bernard (ed.), (1986), *Cultural Dimensions of Play, Games and Sport*, The Association for the Anthropological Study of Play, Vol. 10, Champaign, IL: Human Kinetics Publishers.

Mooney, James (1890), 'The Cherokee Ball Game', *American Anthropologist*, 3: 105-32.

— (1896), *The Ghost Dance Religion and the Sioux Outbreak of 1890*, Part 2, Fourteenth Annual Report of the Bureau of Ethnology to the Secretary of the Smithsonian Institution, 1892-93, Washington: Government Printing Office.

Nabokov, Peter (1987), *Indian Running: Native American History and Tradition* (second edition), Santa Fe: Ancient City Press.

Nixon, H.L. (1991), 'Sport Sociology That Matters: Imperatives and Challenges for the 1990s', *Sociology of Sport Journal*, 8(3): 281-94.

Okely, Judith (1992), 'Anthropology and Autobiography: Participatory

Experience and Embodied Knowledge', in J. Okely and H. Callaway (eds), *Anthropology and Autobiography*, ASA Monographs 29, London/New York: Routledge, pp. 1-28.

Oxendine, Joseph B. (1988), *American Indian Sports Heritage*, Champaign, IL: Human Kinetics Books.

Richards, Paul (1997), 'Soccer and Violence in War-Torn Africa: Soccer and Rehabilitation in Sierra Leone', in Gary Armstrong and Richard Giulianotti (eds), *Entering the Field: New Perspectives on World Football*, Oxford/New York: Berg, pp. 141-57.

Salter, Michael A. (1980), 'Play in Ritual: An Ethnohistorical Overview of Native North America', in Helen B. Schwartzman (ed.), *Play and Culture*, West Point, New York: Leisure Press, pp. 70-82.

Scarborough, Vernon L. and David R. Wilcox (eds) (1991), *The Mesoamerican Ballgame*, Tucson: University of Arizona Press.

Schwartzman, Helen B. (ed.) (1980), *Play and Culture: 1978 Proceedings of the Association for the Anthropological Study of Play*, West Point, New York: Leisure Press.

Sciama, Lidia D. (1996), 'The Venice Regatta: From Ritual to Sport', in J. MacClancy (ed.), *Sport, Identity and Ethnicity*, Oxford: Berg, pp. 137-65.

Stevens, Phillips, Jr. (1980), 'Play and Work: A False Dichotomy?' in Helen B. Schwartzman (ed.), *Play and Culture*, West Point, New York: Leisure Press, pp. 316-23.

— (1992), 'On Depth in Play, Culture and Ethnographic Description', *Play and Culture*, 5(3): 252-7.

Stevens, Phillips Jr. (ed.) (1977), *Studies in the Anthropology of Play*, West Point, New York: Leisure Press.

Stokes, Martin (1996), '"Strong as a Turk": Power, Performance and Representation in Turkish Wrestling', in J. MacClancy (ed.), *Sport, Identity and Ethnicity*, Oxford: Berg, pp. 21-41.

Stuart, Ossie (1996), 'Players, Workers, Protestors: Social Change and Soccer in Colonial Zimbabwe', in J. MacClancy (ed.), *Sport, Identity and Ethnicity*, Oxford: Berg, pp. 167-80.

Sutton-Smith, Brian (1995), 'Foreword', in Kendall Blanchard, *The Anthropology of Play: An Introduction* (revised edition), Westport, Connecticut/London: Bergin and Garvey, pp. xi-xiii.

Sutton-Smith, Brian, and Diana Kelly-Byrne (eds) (1984), *The Masks of Play*, New York: Leisure Press.

Turner, Victor W. (1967), *The Forest of Symbols*, Ithaca: Cornell University Press.

— (1969), *The Ritual Process: Structure and Anti-Structure*, London: Routledge & Kegan Paul.

— (1974), *Dramas, Fields and Metaphors: Symbolic Action in Human Society*, Ithaca, New York: Cornell University Press.

— (1987), *The Anthropology of Performance*, New York: PAJ Publications.

Wacquant, Loïc J.D. (1995a), 'The Pugilistic Point of View: How Boxers Think and Feel About Their Trade', *Theory and Society*, 24(4): 489-535.

— (1995b), 'Pugs at Work: Bodily Capital and Labour Among Professional Boxers', *Body and Society*, 1(1): 65-93.

Wulff, Helena (1998), *Ballet Across Borders: Career and Culture in the World of Dancers*, Oxford/New York: Berg.

2

Why Should an Anthropologist Study Sports in China?

Susan Brownell

Why should an anthropologist study sports in China? This question raises two key issues: Why should an anthropologist study sports? And what can the study of sports contribute to an anthropological understanding of China? The nature of my research in China has led me to an interest in a particular subcategory of the anthropology of sports, that is, the anthropology of the Olympic movement. It is my contention that a focus on the Olympic movement offers the most fertile ground for the development of an anthropology of sport that lies on the cutting edge of current developments both inside and outside the discipline. This chapter, then, will address the question of why an anthropologist should study Olympic sports, with examples from my research in China to illustrate the points. It begins by summarizing the limitations of the anthropology of sport before the emergence of the interdisciplinary developments in postcolonial studies, practice theory, the interest in the body, feminism and transnational theory. It then traces the usefulness of each of these developments for the study of sport, with a focus on how I have used them in my research on sports in China.

Anthropology and Sports

Sports, loosely defined, are found everywhere in the world in which anthropologists work: in 1945 George Peter Murdock listed 'athletic sports' as a human universal (1945: 124). Anthropologists, and particularly folklorists, have paid attention to sports, play and games throughout the history of the discipline. However, these treatments of sports were typically peripheral to the issues regarded as more central to the discipline, such as kinship, ritual, the evolution of the state and so on.

Despite the publication of Kendall Blanchard's and Alyce Cheska's *The Anthropology of Sport* in 1985, the anthropology of sport has never become an established subfield. There is no professional journal on the anthropology of sport, nor is there an international organization of scholars; there is not even an association of that title under the American Anthropological Association, which includes everything from the Society for the Anthropology of Consciousness to the Society for the Anthropology of Work. Attempts to go beyond the simple cataloguing of folk sports by theorizing sports and games have been rare, although the few that do exist have been influential. These have included attempts to develop cross-cultural classifications of sports, play and games (Roberts, Arth and Bush 1959); or to apply Freudian theory to the symbolism and practices of various sports from the Palio of Siena to US football to cock-fighting (Dundes 1975, 1978, 1985, 1994, a folklorist). One theoretical debate that was highly anthropological originated not with an anthropologist, but with a historian. Alan Guttmann's *From Ritual to Record* (1978) utilized modernization theory to trace the historical development of sports from the ancient Greeks to modern Olympic sports, suggesting that this development was characterized by a shift from the 'traditional' to the 'modern'. This model had a great influence among sport historians and resulted in a follow-up conference and book a decade later (Carter and Krüger 1990). However, although it could have served as a model for other anthropological interpretations, it does not appear to have inspired anthropologists to take up the question.

Victor Turner was one of the few major theorists of the 1970s and 1980s whose theories were capable of illuminating sports issues, and he mentioned sports and leisure activities briefly in his later works on 'liminoid genres'. By this he meant activities that, due to their separation from the structural world of work, contain the potential for creativity and social change (Turner 1982, 1988). One of his students, John MacAloon, applied Turnerian ideas specifically to sports in his essay on 'Olympic Games and the theory of spectacle in modern societies' in *Rite, Drama, Festival, Spectacle: Rehearsals Toward a Theory of Cultural Performance* (MacAloon 1984). This chapter, which discusses the importance of the concentric 'frames' of game, ritual, festival and spectacle in the Olympic Games, has influenced scholars of the Olympic Games, but again has had limited attraction to anthropologists outside this circle.

One of the more intriguing pieces in this puzzle is Clifford Geertz's 'Deep play: notes on the Balinese cockfight' (1973), one of the most widely read anthropological essays of our time. Although cockfights are rather distant from the ideal kind of sport, the concept of 'deep play' which is used to read the cockfight as a text about Balinese culture could easily apply to sports involving human competitors as well. One might have thought that this article would give rise to a number of similar interpretations of other sports, but it did not. Why not? Probably this parallels the general response to Geertz's work. Geertz's vagueness about his interpretive 'methods' and his dazzling writing style make him impossible to imitate.

Many of the best anthropologists of sport, therefore, have had no choice but to turn to their colleagues in sociology and other disciplines for intellectual exchange. Alan Klein was one of the first anthropologists to write about a sport – baseball – in the context of issues of nationalism and resistance to US cultural imperialism. *Sugarball: The American Game, The Dominican Dream* (1991) is remarkable, among other things, for its application of Gramscian theory of hegemony and resistance – a move that would probably have not taken place before the postmodern turn in sports studies in the late 1980s. His varied research on sports continued with *Little Big Men* (1993), which discussed gender in bodybuilding, and *Baseball on the Border* (1997), which developed a theory of nationalism based on research on a team that represented both Mexico and the US. All of these works are theoretically framed, but again this has failed to give them much of a purchase in the discipline of anthropology, although Klein is influential among sports scholars. An anthropologist by training, Klein, after years of neglect in his own discipline, found intellectual comrades in the North American Society for Sport Sociology (NASSS). His involvement in NASSS culminated in his election as president for 1998 to 1999. He is not alone. Many anthropologists have had no choice but to look outside their own discipline to interdisciplinary networks with sociologists, physical educators and historians for intellectual exchange. Intellectually, this is not necessarily a bad thing. However, the problem is that the reality of academic politics means disciplines still form the strongest power bases. Without a solid foothold in individual disciplines, sports studies have been marginalized.

The state of sports studies in the interdisciplinary field of Sinology is also relevant to this chapter. Book-length academic works on sport in China are almost non existent, being limited to a political science work (Kolatch 1972) and a recent history (Fan 1997). A smattering of articles and chapters in books fills out the picture. There are works in progress, such as a dissertation on republican-era physical education by Andrew Morris.

More generally, scholarship on sports in East Asia is lacking. In a 1998 survey of the 217 members of the ConsumAsian network, a Hong-Kong based network focused on research on consumerism and popular culture, members were asked to check relevant categories on a list. The survey found that subjects like advertising, media, film, travel and leisure were well represented, 'and the only real area of disinclination so far appears to be *sports*' (Skov and Moeran 1998: 3). Only seven readers listed sports as an interest, with theatre/performance (16) and events/expositions (20) being the next closest categories. While interesting dissertation work is being written up or has just been completed by anthropologists (Laura Ginsberg on fitness clubs in Japan; Kenji Tierney on Sumo in Japan) very little has appeared in print. Among established anthropologists, William Kelly has published small pieces of a larger work in progress on baseball in Japan. There is also work in progress in other disciplines, including a book on baseball in the Meiji period by Allen Guttmann.

It seems curious that sport studies have remained so peripheral in the discipline of anthropology, which for much of this century was already a 'science of leftovers' compared to sociology, but failed to even take up the leftover category of sports to the degree that sociologists did. It is my contention that the marginality of sports was largely due to their inadequate theorization. And this, in turn, was a product of the state of the discipline as a whole.

There are, of course, other reasons as well. One of them appears to be a residual elitist bias in notions of culture utilized by American anthropologists. Despite the opposition within the discipline to the humanist conception of 'high culture' attributable to the influence of Franz Boas since the early 1900s (Stocking 1968: 195-233) sports have not received as much attention from anthropologists as the analogues of European 'high culture' such as painting, sculpture, dance, music and theatre. However, this is not my main point here.

I believe that a central obstacle to the development of sport studies in anthropology was a confusion about what could be said about sports that was of general importance to the discipline. To a large extent, anthropology is a theory-driven discipline. If practices are peripheral to, or cannot be explained by, the dominant theories of the day, they tend to be forgotten. In general, this was the state of sports studies, except for the few attempts mentioned above.

Fortunately, we have now entered an exciting period in which the theories that have become important in the discipline of anthropology are capable of embracing sport practices. The new approaches include postcolonial studies, practice theory, feminism and transnational theory. In addition there is the huge and still growing literature on 'the body' which crosscuts different approaches. Thus, the conditions have been set for sports studies to be pulled into the larger fold of the discipline, where they can make important contributions. However, this process has been slow. These theories have already been around for several decades and became popular approaches in some circles of anthropology as early as the mid 1980s, but have yet to generate many studies of sports.

In what follows, I will give my own (necessarily idiosyncratic) view of what the emergence of these theories means for the anthropology of sport, and explain why I feel the moment is now ripe for significant developments in sport studies. I will illustrate my argument with examples from my work on sports in China.

Postcolonial Studies and Sports

To my mind, the great and largely unexplored territory awaiting anthropologists is that occupied by the relationship between sports and colonialism. In carrying out this task, an essential component is a critical evaluation of the Olympic movement in its colonial and postcolonial context. Without a full understanding of the origins of the modern Olympic movement as a Western-European-dominated, ideological movement with aspirations to universalism, it is impossible to fully appreciate the significance of either the current dominance of Olympic sports worldwide, or the demise of indigenous sports that often goes along with it.

As has been much discussed, until recent decades anthropologists tended to study societies as if the twentieth century did not exist. Colonial governments were often nearly invisible in ethnographic accounts; affairs of the nation state ignored, transnational flows of culture wished away. Modern Olympic sports, of course, were left to the sociologists along with much of the rest of the twentieth century. It was not until the discipline turned its attention to issues such as postcolonialism, transnationalism and the world system of nation states, that the theoretical importance of sports could become visible. It is now apparent that the 'modern' sports that comprise the Olympic Games are products of a specific history involving the rise of physical education along with modern nationalism in Europe, the spread of this idea to other parts of the world, and the use of sports as 'civilizing' disciplines in colonial regimes (particularly the British empire) and missionary regimes (particularly the YMCA).

John MacAloon's biography of Pierre de Coubertin, founder of the modern Olympic movement, clearly reveals the origins of the Olympic movement in the political strategizing of a French aristocrat whose concept of 'internationalism' echoed early anthropological ideas at the turn of the century. MacAloon also develops a detailed argument for the relationship between the Olympics, popular ethnography and academic ethnology (1981: 44-7, 134-6, 217-21, 236-41, 262-9, ff.). MacAloon's work is the foundational starting point for anyone interested in developing a critical approach to the history of the Olympic movement.

Much of the significance of folk or indigenous sports, as it turns out, lies in their implication in these processes, a point that anthropologists almost completely missed until recently. Folk sports die out due to neglect in formal physical education programs that emphasize 'modern' sports for nation building (for example Tutsi highjumping – Bale and Sang 1996: 59-64); or they are 'sportized' and promoted internationally in strategies to legitimate national cultures in the international arena (for example Chinese martial arts – Brownell 1995a: 51-6); or they fiercely defend their 'traditional' authenticity against the threat of the loss of local identities before the force of Westernization (for example wrestling in India – Alter 1992). One might have thought that such issues would attract the attention of anthropologists early on, but they did not.

Unfortunately, the important early works of one of the key critics of the Olympic movement, Henning Eichberg, have never been translated into English (Eichberg 1973, 1977, 1978, 1986). Thus, while his ideas have been influential in European sports circles, he is practically unknown in North America. In *Der Weg des Sports in die Industrielle Zivilisation [Sport on its Way into Industrial Civilization]* (1973) a book motivated by the debates about the huge budget overrun of the 1972 Munich Olympics, Eichberg outlined the similar features of modern sports and industrial society. He then used this as a starting point for a critique of modern 'achievement society', claims of Olympic universalism and nationalism in sports. In opposition, he formulated a Green, or ecological, position on sports

(Eichberg 1979: 171-5). Eichberg's work has been influential in European sports studies, and among Anglophone sports scholars with European connections (most prominently, Allen Guttmann) but was certainly unknown in American anthropology. The situation might change somewhat with the publication of a collection of his essays in English (Eichberg 1998a).

If the critiques of Olympism were better understood by anthropologists, perhaps more of them would see the potential for significant research (both theoretical and empirical) in this area. However, most anthropologists are probably as bedazzled by the Olympic dream as the popular audience, and this misrecognition (in the Bourdieuian sense) prevents them from seeing the practical implications. The general audience is not aware that the International Olympic Committee (IOC) promotes an official ideology, known as Olympism, with the goal of disseminating it worldwide for the betterment of humankind. The spread of this ideal is called the Olympic movement. As Eichberg put it

> The International Olympic Committee (IOC), as an oligarchic, self-co-opting organization with worldwide monopolistic tendencies, lacks democratic structure, legitimation and control from below. Although a *social* problem from the very beginning, this was not regarded as a special *political* problem as long as the IOC members were, elected or not, a mirror of the nations and cultures represented in the Olympic Games. Since the decolonisation of Africa and Asia, however, and since the rise of non-European sports movements, this has changed, and the Olympic structure now demonstrates a remarkable national-cultural inequality. (1998c:100)

The People's Republic of China, of course, was a victim of this inequality, which resulted in its exclusion from the Olympic Games from 1956 until the Winter Games of 1980 and the Summer Games of 1984, due to the IOC's refusal to seriously negotiate the resolution of the Taiwan question (this refusal was made with a good degree of hypocrisy by claiming that sports and politics are separate). Since its return to the IOC and international sports federations, China has also been an active leader in redressing this imbalance because of the prominence of the IOC member in China, He Zhenliang, who has risen to the position of Vice President. Through systematic sports diplomacy, China has employed a number of strategies to strengthen the position of it and other Third World nations in the IOC.

MacAloon has developed the notion of sports as an 'empty form' as a framework to describe how contemporary international sports have been emptied of their original colonialist content and then refilled with diverse local cultural meanings (1994: 20). He argues that this emptying process has three aspects (1995: 3-4). First, histories of sports are appropriated by rival groups and reinvented. Second, sports are naturalized when their foreign – frequently imperial and colonial – origins are forgotten or neutralized. Third, sports forms of different origins are mixed, as when East Asian martial arts are popularized in the West.

This process is well illustrated by Arjun Appadurai's (1991, 1995) exploration of the ways in which cricket was emptied of its British colonial legacy and assigned new nationalist meanings. This is a model that awaits application to other sports in other places. Appadurai is another of the few prominent anthropologists who have written about sports (it may be relevant, however, that he is not strictly an anthropologist by training, but received his Ph.D. from the innovative and interdisciplinary Committee on Social Thought at the University of Chicago, which also produced John MacAloon).

This process has been taking place in China since the turn of the century. When sports were introduced into China by Western missionary schools and YMCAs they were taught along with rules of fair play and sportsmanship which were used to justify sport as a means of character training in schools in England. However, the English concept of 'fair play' does not seem to have had a significant equivalent in the Chinese language (Fei 1985: 186) and it was not easily understood by Chinese students. National Director of the YMCA Eugene Barnett recalled

> More difficult to inculcate than the skills and rules were the meaning and the requirements of team play and sportsmanship, whether in victory or defeat . . . It was not uncommon in the early days for the losing team and its schoolmates to seek retrieval of their lost face by launching bodily assaults on the winning team and its supporters! (1990: 89)

Because they were backed by governments then more powerful than the Chinese, people like Barnett were in a position to dictate the cultural meanings attached to sport, and to try to change local meanings, such as the symbolism of 'face', that offended their sensibilities. Over time, as Chinese took control of their sports, they began the process of emptying them of this morality and replacing them with meanings derived from their own culture.

Instead of fair play, there is a notion that permeates Chinese sports discourse in the same way that fair play and sportsmanship permeate Western sports discourse. This is the notion of 'face', which dominates the popular discourse on sports. People who are overly concerned with promoting their own reputations are said to 'love face'. In everyday speech, people often attribute the desire of state leaders to win medals at the Olympics to the fact that medals reflect well on the face of China, which in turn gives face to state leaders. Like the love of 'fair play', which was sometimes portrayed as a national characteristic of the English, Chinese people often mentioned that 'Chinese people love face', as if it were a part of the national character. This is because the notion of prestige, face, shapes the behaviour of individuals, influences relationships between groups and even pervades China's actions as a nation. This is an example of the way in which distinctly Chinese meanings have been added to the moral content of international sports in China.

As MacAloon noted, the construction of sports history plays an important role in the local appropriation of international sports. When Western
sports were introduced at the turn of the century, the word *tiyu* was introduced to label them. In the early part of the century, they were called 'new
physical culture' (*xin tiyu*) or 'foreign physical culture' (*yang* or *xiyang
tiyu*). Reformers and revolutionaries emphasized their newness and foreignness in their attempt to break with the traditions of the imperial past.
Modern sports were conceived in opposition to the martial arts, which
were hailed by traditionalists as essentially Chinese, and attacked by
reformers as outmoded and feudal. In the 1920s, a decade after the founding of the Republic of China (1912) the indigenous martial arts were
'sportized' when they were turned into a competitive sport following the
Western model and promoted as the 'national arts'. After the founding of
the People's Republic of China in 1949, the colonial origins of Olympic
sports were neutralized by suggesting that the Communist Party-state per-
fected the flawed sports system introduced by the imperialists. In the
1980s the history of sports was subtly rewritten. What had formerly been
'new' or 'foreign physical culture' was now labelled 'modern physical culture' (*jindai tiyu*). This version of history acknowledged that the phrase
'physical culture' had first appeared in the 'modern' period of Western
contact at the end of the nineteenth century. However, it emphasized the
continuities between modern and historical sports rather than the revolutionary break with the past.

Many of the new histories targeted a foreign audience (for example
Beijing Review 1986; New World Press 1986; People's Sports Publishing
House 1986). These histories expressed a desire to demonstrate that
China had a long and illustrious sports history to contribute to the inter-
national sportsworld, a history every bit as valid as the Western one. The
State Sports Commission set an official agenda to promote the spread of
martial arts worldwide and their inclusion in the Olympic Games.

In addition, China's ancient game of kick ball was described in ways that
implied it was the ancestor of modern soccer. The New World Press leaves
the question of the link between kick ball and modern soccer ambiguous
when it states, 'Modern football was practically unknown in China until
the end of the last century. However, the game in its ancient form can be
traced back to time immemorial' (1986: 80).

In sum, from their inception in the late nineteenth century to the late
1990s, sports in China were emptied of their muscular Christian morality
of fair play, citizenship and democracy and this was replaced with Chinese
discourses about national prestige and international competition. As predicted by MacAloon's notion of sport as an empty form, sport histories
were rewritten, the colonial origins of sport were naturalized, and the
indigenous sports were 'sportized' in the Western model. While the physical structure of modern sports is fixed by international rules, there is quite
a bit of room for variability in the cultural beliefs that accompany them.
This appropriation of meaning was inseparable from China's changing

position in the global political economy and is, more generally, one of the important expressions of postcolonialism.

Practice Theory, the Body, and Sports

A second theoretical development that has the effect of de-marginalizing sports studies is practice theory. Marcel Mauss, in 1939, was the first to propose the notion of 'techniques of the body', 'the ways in which from society to society [people] know how to use their bodies' (1979: 97). Pierre Bourdieu further developed this point with his notion of 'habitus', which refers to the system of predispositions, a habitual way of being, that becomes inculcated in the body through the practice of everyday life. Bourdieu acknowledges the theoretical importance of sports for his model. '[S]port is, with dance, one of the areas where the problem of the relations between theory and practice, and also between language and body, is posed with maximum acuteness' (1988: 80).

In my own work, I have chosen to draw on Bourdieu's notion of habitus while framing my discussions within the concept of body culture. I define body culture as the entire repertoire of things that people do to and with their bodies, and the elements of culture that shape their doing. Body culture can include daily practices of health, hygiene, fitness, beauty, dress and decoration; postures, gestures, manners, ways of speaking and eating; ritual, dance, sports and other kinds of bodily performance. It includes the methods for training these practices into the body, the way the body is publicly displayed and the meanings that are expressed in that display. Body culture is embodied culture (see Brownell 1995a: 8-21). This concept is drawn from the work of Henning Eichberg, who uses the notion of *Körperkultur* to look at the body primarily as cultural, emphasizing the multiple roles of the body in social process and historical change (Eichberg 1998: 11-27). This concept is undergirded by a political agenda that has the goal of recuperating the body/self from the fragmenting effects of professionalized, competitive sports that characterized the use of *Körperkultur* in the East German sports regime before the fall of the Berlin Wall. The concept of body culture is valuable to sports anthropologists because it reconstitutes the field of practices from which sport was historically singled out, and it encourages us to look at the relationship between sports and other kinds of body techniques. From this perspective, sports are no longer a separate, peripheral topic of study, but are linked with everyday practices such as table manners or bodily decorum (to name only two of the infinite possibilities) as well as with other kinds of bodily performance such as ritual, theatre and so on. As Eichberg puts it, 'Body culture as the new paradigm places sport in the context of *culture*' (1998: 118). This, then, has the effect of placing sport firmly within the dominant paradigm of cultural anthropology.

The concept of body culture is useful in understanding the nature of the changes in everyday life that have occurred in China since the era of reform began in 1978. I roughly characterize this as a shift from 'communism' to 'consumerism'. The body culture that was promoted by the Party after 1949, which reached extremes during the Cultural Revolution, was highly militarized. By that, I mean that military discipline was the ideal, the paradigm, which shaped body techniques in most other realms of life. The military paradigm was characterized by an ideology of strengthening the body in order to strengthen the nation for war. Its practices were characterized by highly rigid body movements performed in unison by large numbers of people, reminiscent of military marching displays. These techniques were normalizing and homogenizing in that they were the same for everyone, and did not vary by age, sex, ethnicity and so on. Mass calisthenics were the most widespread example. For many Westerners, television images of thousands of green-clad androgynous Chinese performing them in unison became one of the enduring images of the Cultural Revolution. Marching displays and mass calisthenics were also the performance genre used in opening and closing ceremonies of sports meets at every level, from the local elementary school to the National Sports Games. A core national team of choreographers had choreographed every mass calisthenics show in the National Games opening ceremonies from 1959 onwards. This genre was not questioned until the 1987 National Games when the choreographers began debating, for the first time, whether this militarized body technique reflected China in the era of reform. They experimented in small ways with a more 'artistic' type of performance that emphasized ethnic minority dances, costumes and singing (see Brownell 1995a: 115-19 for more detail).

Sports were also dominated by the military paradigm. In 1985-6, I represented Beijing University in track and field competitions during a year of language study. This was a continuation of my long-time daily routine as a student athlete in the US where I had competed in the 1984 Olympic Trials while working toward my Ph.D. I was selected to represent Beijing City in the 1986 National College Games, and I participated in a 2½ month training camp with my teammates before the Games. We had a 6:30 roll call every day followed by marching practice three times a week. Our performance was a technically difficult one. As students of the capital city, Beijing, we would lead the rest of the nation into the stadium during the Parade of Athletes in the nationally televised opening ceremonies. We would march down the 100 m straightway, cradling flowers in our right arms. As we approached the reviewing area where the high officials sat around Li Peng, the highest official present, we would begin goose-stepping, shouting slogans and unfurling banners. This performance would display our team spirit and bodily discipline to all of China. The banners were unfurled to spell out the corresponding slogans as we shouted them:

Figure 2 Parade of athletes, Beijing City College Track Meet 1988
[Susan Brownel]

- Train the body! (This was shouted out by our march leader, followed by a response by the rest of us. Our responses were:)
- Study diligently!
- Bravely scale the peaks!
- Carry out the Four Modernizations!
- Defend the nation!

In our practice sessions, the column of women behind me was bent over by laughter at my marching form. How was I managing to put the same arm and leg forward simultaneously? They asked me, hadn't I ever learned to goose-step? I told them, no, and asked where they had learned it. They had all learned in school from the time they were small. The importance of the opening ceremonies in school sports meets is an example of the 'micro-physics of power' that Foucault makes symptomatic of the modern state. These are the occasions on which the techniques of military discipline are imparted to all Chinese children.

In addition to the rigid schedules for eating, training and sleeping, sports-team rules were especially draconian with respect to gender and sexuality. The provincial, municipal and national teams administered by the State Sports Commission forbade athletes to have romantic relationships with members of the opposite sex, and sex segregation was strictly enforced in the dormitories. Violation of these rules could result in expulsion from the team. Until the late 1980s, athletes were allowed to be engaged only after the ages of around 24 (for women) and 26 (for men) and were not permitted to marry while still competing. This contrasted with the minimum legal ages for marriage of 20 (for women) and 22 (for men) for the general populace. In an influential article that criticized the sports system, 'Superpower Dream', Zhao Yu commented that 'not a few leaders and coaches of professional sports teams stand guard against love as if they were standing guard against a flood' (Zhao 1988).

The dress code on sports teams forbade women to wear long hair hanging loose over their shoulders. Until very recently, sportswomen were required to wear their hair short or tied back in public, including in competitions. If tied back, the ponytail or pigtails should be low on the head because a high ponytail was considered too provocative. The popular press frequently reported approvingly that several famous male coaches required their female athletes to cut their hair, and forbade them to wear face cream, make-up or high heels.

At the same time, these were the women whose bodies were presented as the feminine ideal. Because of strict anti-pornography rules, bikini calendars and revealing clothing were taboo. However, calendars and magazine covers depicting Chinese gymnasts in leotards, Western women in tennis or golf outfits and Western women bodybuilders were common and permitted in the early days of reform.

With the growth of consumerism, body culture has changed rapidly in China. This reflected in the changes in the opening ceremonies of the 1990 Asian Games in Beijing, when the new China was represented to the outside world through aerobic dancing, opera, ballet, folk dancing, martial arts and a much scaled-down mass calisthenics (see Brownell 1996). In the media, female athletes are no longer the main body images. They vie with actresses, pop singers and models from China, Hong Kong, Taiwan, the West and elsewhere.

Ironically, in the 1990s many, perhaps most, of China's runway models were former athletes who had been chosen to do sports because of their height. Their experience of the transformation from sportswoman to runway model captures in microcosm the larger transformation of body culture in society at large. When sportswomen represented the Chinese nation in the 1980s, the meanings of their performances were anchored in Cold War national oppositions, an ideology of self-sacrifice and a suppression of sexuality. But when the Chinese government began to promote fashion models with the goal of sending out representatives onto international runways, their performances were anchored in the logic of the global fashion market, the symbols of cosmopolitan elitism and the aesthetics of sexuality.

Since its establishment, the Ministry of Health has collected measurements such as height, weight and chest circumference in order to quantify the state of health of the population. In the culture of the sporting body, age, height, body shape and 'quality' (*suzhi*) were measured as indices of military strength or the general standard of living. By contrast with this practice, the measurements of runway models were tracked for purposes of comparison with the prevailing standards for runway models, with the goal of cultivating Chinese models who could compete with Europeans and Americans for modelling jobs. For example, the fourth Chinese Supermodel contest in 1995 was organized to promote Chinese models in the international fashion world. Youth and height were the most desperately sought traits in the contest, with the maximum age set at 23 and the minimum height at 5 ft. 9 in. The models in the fourth Chinese Supermodel contest averaged 19.5 years old and 5 ft. 11 in. height; this contest was regarded as successful in these respects, because the models were younger and taller than in previous years.

The young sportswomen who became runway models found themselves adjusting to a new and different body culture that in many ways directly conflicted with the old. Fashion industry insiders criticized the sports background because they noted that sports teach a completely different way of carrying the body from runway modelling, and they said it accounted for the lack of grace, musicality, femininity and 'aesthetic awareness' in the movements of Chinese models.

The young women who had made this career shift experienced it as a kind of personal transformation. For example, a former basketball player decided to take a modelling class in the early 1990s after she graduated from the Beijing University of Sports and her boyfriend broke up with her. She told me

> On the sports team when I was younger, we were forbidden to dress up. Long hair over the shoulders was forbidden. We always wore our hair in a ponytail or pigtails. All the Chinese athletes did . . . I didn't even have the idea of make-up in my brain until I took the modeling class . . . I had short hair like yours and an athlete's demeanor . . . the way I moved and carried myself, and my hunched back . . . I learned to have confidence in my appearance, to improve my posture, and to carry myself like I'm somebody.

There is much more that can be said on this topic. However, let this suffice to make the point that practice theory and a theory of body culture provide a lens on the transformations of everyday life that have taken place under the rapid social changes in China. Because these theories link sports with the entire repertoire of techniques of the body, they show the relationship between sports and the larger forces that structure the practices of everyday life – not just the lives of athletes.

Feminism, Nationalism and Sports

One of the most useful contributions of feminist theory to an understanding of sports in China has been to draw attention to the relationship between gender and state nationalist projects. In the China field, several influential feminist scholars have utilized the works of Michel Foucault to illuminate this relationship. In sports studies, J.A. Mangan's numerous authored and edited books on sports, colonialism and gender contributed a quantity of good social history toward a rethinking of the implication of gender in British colonialism (Mangan 1981, 1986, 1987; Mangan and

Baker 1987). Mangan's training in social anthropology, sociology and social history positioned him well to accomplish this task.

The story of sports, gender and nationalism in China, however, has an unusual twist. In China, *female* athletes have had greater successes than male, hence they have been the heroes in the resurgence of Chinese nationalism. In particular, the victory of the Chinese women's volleyball team in the 1981 World Cup is identified by many Chinese as the pivotal point in their rediscovery of national pride after the devastation of the Cultural Revolution (1966-76). Since the 1980s, the women have, on the whole, had more success in international sports than the men. This has been true in basketball, soccer, track and field, swimming, judo, weightlifting, softball/baseball and so on. Only in gymnastics, diving, table tennis and badminton have Chinese men achieved successes comparable with the women. The superiority of Chinese sportswomen has been a constant topic of debate – both conversational and published – for more than a decade now. It has been expressed in the aphorism, 'the yin waxes and the yang wanes' (*yin sheng yang shuai*).

The nationalist representations of sportswomen continued some of the themes of Chinese nationalism over the last century that have been discussed by feminist scholars in China and abroad. They have argued that modern nationalism in China has been characterized by the use of female bodily suffering and self-sacrifice as a signifier of a male nationalism which saw itself as wounded by and impotent against Western and Japanese imperialism (Barlow 1994; Duara 1995; Liu 1994; Meng 1993). The subject-position in this nationalism is male; females must suffer because males are impotent to right the injustices done to *males* through their women. Thus, female suffering is above all a sign of male impotence – and *this* is ultimately the source of greatest popular concern.

Women's superior results internationally have generally been explained as follows: First, women's sports worldwide got a later start than men's and they tend to get less government and economic support than men's sports; hence the level of competition is lower, and therefore women's gold medals are easier to attain than men's for a country that invests in women's sports. Second, the Chinese government has given relatively equal support to men's and women's sports since the establishment of the sports school system in 1955, and this gives Chinese women a relative advantage over women from other countries. It also proves the superiority of women's position under socialism. Third, Chinese women are more obedient than Chinese men, and sportswomen train harder than sportsmen. This last point is the one that is most often emphasized: Chinese women are better able than men to 'eat bitterness and endure hard labour' (*chi ku nai lao*).

This statement begs for a feminist analysis. If one unpacks it, it turns out that people almost universally acknowledge that women's social status is lower than men's, particularly peasant women, and that their hard lives prepare them for sports. In addition, sports offer a path of mobility that may be denied in other realms. This symbolism has further significance if we consider the ways in which female athletes are utilized by the Party as a signifier for Chinese nationalism: these women who symbolized national unity and progress were clearly subordinated to a (masculine) Party state. This was reiterated in the official speeches and pronouncements, which usually attempted to link their success to the guidance of the Party. The main connotation of this formula is that woman obeys the guidance of man just as the nation or the people obey the guidance of the Party state. The much-praised 'obedience' of female athletes has greater political resonances (see Brownell 1999 for fuller discussion).

Again, there is much more that can be said on this topic. However, this brief summary has illustrated the point that sports have played a pivotal role in Chinese nationalism, and that this nationalism cannot be fully understood without an examination of its gendered nature.

Transnational Theory and Sports

Arjun Appadurai has been one of the most influential theorists of the transnational in the discipline of anthropology. This theory emphasizes the ever-increasing flow of information and people across national borders which will begin to make the nation state obsolete in the coming 'postnational' global order (Appadurai 1993: 419-20). Part of what drives this process is the growing number of cosmopolitan elites with little allegiance to the nation state (see Editors, *Public Culture* 1988: 3). The relatively free-floating mass media play a key role in the creation of cultures that transcend territorial boundaries.

Two China anthropologists, Mayfair Yang and Benjamin Lee, have argued that this process is occurring in mainland China. Yang (1996) finds that in recent years the increasingly transnational mass media (her essay concentrates on television) have contributed to the deterritorialization of Chinese nationalism and the linking of Chinese subjectivity with Taiwan, Hong Kong and the Chinese diaspora. This opens up the possibility of the emergence of a transnational public sphere that is no longer grounded in any one nation state. Benjamin Lee argued that a transnational Chinese public had already emerged in the aftermath of the 1989 student demonstrations. He stated that '[I]n some cases, the leading edge of change lies in the intersections and interstices of processes beyond the nation-state that have their own global infrastructure' (1993: 174).

At first glance, television would appear to be the most quintessential mass medium, and telecasts of international sporting events would appear to be the most remarkable example of its power. The Olympic opening ceremonies probably attract the single largest global television audience, with over one billion people around the world watching the same event (Larson and Park 1993: 6). The abstract assertions of transnational theory have been rigorously researched in two pathbreaking studies on Olympic television. Larson and Park's (1993) book on television in the

1988 Seoul Olympics, and a collaborative international project that collected information from 30 nations worldwide on the 1992 Barcelona Olympics (Moragas Spa, Rivenburgh and Larson 1995) show that the picture is by no means this simple. As suggested by Lee's statement above, international sports television does have its own global infrastructure, and it does tend to be at the leading edge of technological advances in television. However, it is somewhat less clear that sports telecasting is at the leading edge of the emergence of a transnational public sphere, because its technological infrastructure as well as its content tend to reinforce distinctions between nations at the same time that it creates new interconnections between them. Inspired by the work of Moragas Spa and Rivenburgh, I researched sports telecasting in China (see Brownell 1995b, 1999). I found that in China, these telecasts, because of their global and regional linkages, do tend to move out from under domination by the Party state, but the people who use this technology in China do not tend to be committed, cosmopolitan boundary crossers. From the 1978 Football World Cup in Argentina until the 1996 Atlanta Olympics, China Central Television primarily relied on the coverage of major sporting events provided for members of the Asia-Pacific Broadcasting Union by the Hong-Kong based Television Broadcasts Ltd (TVB) (Read 1993: 508). Founded by the wealthy entrepreneur Sir Run Run Shaw in 1967, TVB was large and successful, and could offer superior personnel and technology in making international sports coverage available to other Asian stations. The size of the ABU dwarfs all other regional broadcasting unions in the world: with member nations from China to New Zealand, Japan to Iran, the ABU covers two-fifths of the world's circumference and nearly two-thirds of its population (over two billion persons). Sports television has led China's other realms of television as many kinds of new technology such as satellite linkages and simultaneous transmissions were first used for major sporting events. Until around 1994, change was very slow in Chinese sports television. It was difficult for CCTV to develop international links because it lacked the financial resources, its personnel spoke little English and lacked international experience, and the people who were sent abroad tended to be senior journalists and officials set in their ways. After 1994, advertising revenues and innovative arrangements with advertising companies that produce sport shows for television increased to the point that these revenues allowed for more independence from the state and more freedom to innovate. In 1996, CCTV was finally able to purchase limited individual broadcasting rights to the Atlanta Olympics. Nevertheless, although it was dependent until this time on regional connections with the ABU and the owners of satellites, the content of the broadcast certainly reinforced national boundaries rather than transcending them. In part, this was because the mainland Chinese controlling this technology were not the cosmopolitan elites envisioned by transnational theory, but rather were people with relatively little international experience, at least initially. My interviews with Song Shixiong, China's most famous sports commentator, and Ma Guoli, director of the Sports Bureau at CCTV, have revealed both of them to possess a great deal of national pride along with a good dose of anti-American sentiment. Song Shixiong's opening cere-monies commentary, to give just one example, contained a good amount of formulaic nationalist rhetoric.

In sum, the study of Olympic television in China has much to con-tribute to the development of transnational theory, which too often has been based on vague impressions rather than a real understanding of local, on-the-ground realities. This study shows that the global television infrastructure increasingly draws Chinese telecasters into relationships with other national and regional broadcasters, opening up the possibility of the emergence of a transnational public sphere that is somewhat autonomous from the Party state in mainland China. However, this is no simple process, and it is entirely possible that transnational linkages will serve to reinforce national boundaries in some ways while transcending them in others.

Whither the Anthropology of Sport?

This essay should make clear my preference for approaches to the anthropology of sport that continue to link sports with the biggest and most pressing problems of our day: the postcolonial legacy of Western cul-tural imperialism; the move from Cold War politics to global economies of consumerism; the emergence of new nationalisms and the growth of transnationalism; and the central location of the body and gender in all of these. Sport studies have an important contribution to make to these the-ories because sports are strongly implicated in all of these phenomena. Sports were important all along, but it has taken the emergence of new kinds of theory to make this importance materialize before our very eyes, which for too long were blinded by disciplinary blinkers.

References

Appadurai, Arjun (1991), 'Decolonizing the Production of Culture: Cricket in Contemporary India', in S. Kang, J. MacAloon and R. DaMatta (eds), *The Olympics and Cultural Exchange: The Papers of the First International Conference on the Olympics and East/West and South/North Cultural Exchange in the World System*, Seoul: Hanyang University Press, pp. 163-90.

Appadurai, Arjun (1993), 'Patriotism and Its Futures', *Public Culture*, 5(3): 411-29.

— (1995), 'Playing with Modernity: The Decolonization of Indian Cricket', in C. Breckenridge (ed.), *Consuming Modernity: Public Culture in a South Asian World*, Minneapolis, Minnesota: University of Minnesota Press, pp. 23-48.

Alter, Joseph S. (1992), *The Wrestler's Body: Identity and Ideology in North*

India, Berkeley: University of California Press.

Bale, John and Joe Sang (1996), *Kenyan Running: Movement Culture, Geography and Global Change*, London: Frank Cass.

Barlow, Tani E. (1994), 'Theorizing Woman: *Funü, Guojia, Jiating* [Chinese Woman, Chinese State, Chinese Family]', in Angela Zito and Tani E. Barlow (eds), *Body, Subject and Power in China*, Chicago: The University of Chicago Press, pp. 253-89.

Barnett, Eugene E. (1990), *My Life in China, 1910-1936*, East Lansing, Michigan: Asian Studies Center, Michigan State University.

Beijing Review (1986), 'Sports in China Has Ancient History', Beijing Review, 29(5): 32-22.

Bourdieu, Pierre (1988), 'A Program for the Comparative Sociology of Sport', in S. Kang, J MacAloon and R DaMatta (eds), *The Olympics and Cultural Exchange: The Papers of the First International Conference on the Olympics and East/West and South/North Cultural Exchange in the World System*, Seoul: Hanyang University Press, pp. 67-83.

Brownell, Susan (1995a), *Training the Body for China: Sports in the Moral Order of the People's Republic*, Chicago: The University of Chicago Press.

— (1995b), 'Cultural Variations in Olympic Telecasts: China and the 1992 Olympic Games and Ceremonies', *The Journal of International Communication*, (special issue on 'Olympian Communication) 2(1): 26-41.

— (1996), 'Representing Gender in the Chinese Nation: Chinese Sportswomen and Beijing's Bid for the 2000 Olympics', *Identities: Global Studies in Culture and Power*, 2(3): 223-47.

— (1999), 'Strong Women and Impotent Men: Sports, Gender, and Nationalism in Chinese Public Culture', in M. Yang (ed.), *Spaces of Their Own: Women's Public Sphere in Transnational China*, Minneapolis: University of Minnesota Press.

China Sports (1983), 'Confucius as Physical Culture Promoter', China Sports, 2 (February): 24-7.

Duara, Prasenjit (1995), 'Of Authenticity and Woman: Personal Narratives of Middle-class Women in Modern China', paper prepared for the conference on 'Becoming Chinese: Passages to Modernity and Beyond, 1900-1950', June 2-4, Berkeley.

Dundes, Alan (1978), 'Into the Endzone for a Touchdown: A Psychoanalytic Consideration of American Football', *Western Folklore*, 37: 75-88.

— (1985), 'The American Game of "Smear the Queer" and the Homosexual Component of Male Competitive Sport and Warfare', *Journal of Psychoanalytic Anthropology*, 8: 115-29.

— (ed.) (1994), *The Cockfight: a Casebook*, Madison, Wisconsin: University of Wisconsin Press.

— and Alessandra Falassi (1975), *La Terra in Piazza: An Interpretation of the Palio of Siena*, Berkeley: University of California Press.

Editors (1988), Editorial Statement in *Public Culture*, 1(1): 1-4.

Eichberg, Henning (1973), *Der Weg des Sports in die industrielle Zivilisation [Sport on its way into industrial civilization]*, Baden-Baden: Nomos. (English language summary pp. 165-72).

— (1977), 'Den einen Sport gibt es nicht – Das Beispiel West-Sumatra Zur Kritik des olympischen Universalismus' ['There is not just one sport – the example of West Sumatra as a critique of Olympic universalism'], in *Sport und Kulturwandel*. Stuttgart: Institut für Auslandsbeziehungen, pp. 72-8.

— (1978), *Leistung, Spannung, Geschwindigkeit [Achievement, Tension, Speed]*, Stuttgart: Klett-Cotta.

— (1979), 'Nachwort zur 2. Auflage' ['Afterword to second edition'], in *Der Weg des Sports in die industrielle Zivilisation [Sport on its way into industrial civilization]*, Baden-Baden: Nomos, pp. 165-75.

— (1986), *Die Veränderung des Sports ist gesellschaftlich [The Transformation of Sport is Social]*, Münster: Lito.

— (1998a), *Body Cultures: Essays on sport, space and identity*, London and New York: Routledge.

— (1998b), 'Body Culture as Paradigm: The Danish Sociology of Sport', in H. Eichberg, *Body Cultures: Essays on sport, space and identity*, London and New York: Routledge, pp. 111-27.

— (1998c), 'Olympic Sport: Neo-colonialism and Alternatives', in H. Eichberg, *Body Cultures: Essays on sport, space and identity*, London and New York: Routledge, pp. 100-10.

Fan Hong (1997), *Footbinding, Feminism and Freedom: The Liberation of Women's Bodies in Modern China*, London: Frank Cass.

Fei Xiaotong (1985), *Meiguorende xingge [The American Character] (1947)*, reprinted in *Meiguo yu Meiguoren [America and Americans]*, Beijing: Sanlian shudian, pp. 155-215.

Geertz, Clifford (1973), *The Interpretation of Cultures*, New York: Basic Books.

Guttmann, Allen (1978), *From Ritual to Record: The Nature of Modern Sports*, New York: Columbia University Press.

Klein, Alan M. (1997), *Baseball on the Border: A Tale of Two Laredos*, Princeton, New Jersey: Princeton University Press.

— (1993), *Little Big Men: Bodybuilding Subculture and Gender Construction*, Albany, New York: SUNY Press.

— (1991), *Sugarball: The American Game, the Dominican Dream*, New Haven, Connecticut: Yale University Press.

Kolatch, Jonathan (1972), *Sports, Politics, and Ideology in China*, Middle Village, New York: Jonathan David Publishers.

— (1992), *Is the Moon in China Just as Round? Sporting Life and Sundry Scenes*, Middle Village, NY: Jonathan David Publishers.

Larson, James F. and Heung-Soo Park (1993), *Global Television and the Politics of the Seoul Olympics*, Boulder, Colorado: Westview Press.

Lee, Benjamin (1993), 'Going Public', *Public Culture* 5(2): 165-78.

Liu, Lydia (1994), 'The Female Body and Nationalist Discourse:

Manchuria in Xiao Hong's *Field of Life and Death*', in Angela Zito and Tani E. Barlow (eds), *Body, Subject, and Power in China*, Chicago: The University of Chicago Press, pp. 157-77.

MacAloon, John J. (1995), 'Humanism as Political Necessity? Reflections on the Pathos of Anthropological Science in Pluricultural Contexts,' James Fernandez and Milton Singer (eds), *The Conditions of Reciprocal Understanding*, Chicago: The Center for International Studies, University of Chicago, pp. 206-35.

— (1994), 'Interval Training', in Susan L. Foster (ed.), *Choreographing History*, Bloomington, Indiana: Indiana University Press, pp. 32-53.

— (1984), 'Olympic Games and the Theory of Spectacle in Modern Societies', in John MacAloon (ed.), *Rite, Drama, Festival, Spectacle: Rehearsals Toward a Theory of Cultural Performance*, Philadelphia: Institute for the Study of Human Issues, pp. 241-80.

— (1981), *This Great Symbol: Pierre de Coubertin and the Origins of the Modern Olympic Games*, Chicago: University of Chicago Press.

Mangan, J.A. (1981), *Athleticism in the Victorian and Edwardian Public School: The Emergence and Consolidation of an Educational Ideology*, Cambridge: Cambridge University Press.

— (1986), *The Games Ethic and Imperialism*, Middlesex, England: Viking.

— (1987), *Pleasure, Profit and Proselytism: British Culture and Sport at Home and Abroad 1700-1914*, London: Cass.

— and William J. Baker (eds) (1987), *Sport in Africa: Essays in Social History*, New York: Holmes & Meier.

Mauss, Marcel (1979), 'Body Techniques', in *Sociology and Psychology: Essays* (1935), London: Routledge & Kegan Paul, pp. 97-105. Translator: Ben Brewster.

Meng Yue (1993), 'Female Images and National Myth', in T. E. Barlow (ed.), *Gender Politics in Modern China*, Durham: Duke University Press, pp. 118-36.

Moragas Spa, Miquel de, Nancy K. Rivenburgh, and James F. Larson (1995), *Television in the Olympics*, London: John Libbey.

Murdock, George Peter (1945), 'The Common Denominator of Cultures', in Ralph Linton (ed.), *The Science of Man in the World Crisis*, New York: Columbia University Press, pp. 123-42.

New World Press (1986), *Sports and Games in Ancient China*, Beijing: New World Press.

People's Sports Publishing House (1986), *Sports in Ancient China*, Beijing: People's Sports Publishing House.

Read, Richard (1993), 'Satisfying Two Thousand Million Spectators', in *Olympic Review*, Lausanne, Switzerland: International Olympic Committee, pp. 508-10.

Roberts, John M., Malcolm J. Arth, and Robert R. Bush (1959), 'Games in Culture', *American Anthropologist*, 61: 597-605.

Skov, Lise and Brian Moeran (1998), '"Members" Interests', *ConsumAsian Newsletter* 6 (September): 3-4.

Stocking, George (1968), *Race, Culture, and Evolution: Essays in the History of Anthropology*, New York: The Free Press.

Turner, Victor W. (1988), *The Anthropology of Performance*, New York: PAJ Publications.

— (1982), *From Ritual to Theatre: The Human Seriousness of Play*, New York: Performing Arts Journal Publications.

Yang, Mayfair Mei-hui (1996), 'Mass Media and Transnational Subjectivity in Shanghai: Notes on (Re)cosmopolitanism in a Chinese Metropolis', in Aihwa Ong and Donald Nonini (ed.), *On the Edges of Empire: Modernity and Identity in Chinese Transnationalism*, New York: Routledge, pp. 288-320.

Zhao Yu (1988), '*Qiangguo meng*' ['Superpower dream']. *Dangdai [Contemporary Times]*, February, pp. 163-98.

3

Society, Body and Style: An Archery Contest in an Amerindian Society

George Mentore

How does a society take persuasive hold of its individual members? Can it be shown, for example, that it does so on the occasion of an archery competition? In this paper I argue that applying the distinctive cultural techniques of ritual activity, a society can use the body of an athlete to display and implement its fundamental logic and moral philosophy for both participating competitors and spectators. The particular society under discussion is that of the Waiwai, a Cariban-speaking people who live in the forests of southern Guyana and northern Brazil. Here society and culture create and prescribe gendered roles and artifacts for the actions of participants in an indigenous archery contest. These actions, in turn, depict and reinforce the strong ideological beliefs that work to shape social relations. The exclusive role that Waiwai men play as hunters finds itself particularly set off against and complementary to women's exclusion from hunting in the central presence and use of the bow and arrow in ritual competition. The Waiwai call the archery competition in question *Tïwosom*, after the carved wooden animals used as targets by the archers. *Tïwosom* is one part of a much more elaborate ceremonial festival held once or twice a year called *Kesemanïtopo*. In this case, those community beliefs of concern that are depicted and administered by the ritual games converge around the ability of the hunter to kill, the nature of the relations between the hunter and his prey and the overall political emphasis on Waiwai masculinity. While it may indeed be a general purpose of all competition to decide winners and losers (Armstrong 1998; Bailey 1969; Scarry 1987), in the sport of archery among the Waiwai of South America, to compete serves principally to place the hunter as athlete at the centre of the social gaze. In this ritual position, masculinity not only displays and makes claims about the predatory character of its athletic prowess but also reinforces its legitimacy to be at the centre of the social gaze. It is, therefore, not just a question of how society takes hold of its members or whether it can, in fact, show us it does so through an instance of athletic competition, but rather that it does so in ways which make the exercise of power appear immanently appropriate and seemingly unimpeachable.

Some general but brief remarks on society, the body and obedience will first be offered in an attempt to be anthropologically convincing about the above argument. This will lead to the opinion that there exists a relation between the ways in which society takes hold of its individuals and the effect of the social persons it produces and, provocatively, that sport, as a dramatic form of emphasizing the body, functions to assist in producing a local style of social personhood. Because the ambience of Western capitalist societies is more familiar to us, it can serve as a comparison here, and makes a coherent point of departure for a discussion on the Waiwai and their ritual competition of archery. The comprehensive argument should be that, when looking at the games of different societies, from centralized states and capitalist economies to acephalous societies and barter economies, however different they are – from the Olympics to *kesemani̇topo* – the actual elements producing the differences remain, in terms of anthropology, much the same.

The Style of Obedience and Playing the Game

Society constantly seeks to retrieve through the individual human body the substances for its own existence. There is no society without the individual, yet because the individual needs social roles and moral terrains for its meaningful existence and agency, there is no individual without the potential existence of society. The individual body acquires its agency and moral values by being made into a social person. Using the specific techniques of culture, society takes hold of the body and provides it with the categorical features of personhood. To constitute and perpetuate itself, society forcefully persuades the body to give itself up to the social. It makes sons and daughters, fathers and mothers, clansmen and citizens; it turns girls into wives, boys into husbands, civilians into warriors, athletes into heroes but, most emphatically, it ensures its own existence by securing the individual as social being.

To make the person and to substantiate itself society continues into the body of the individual. It has first to wait patiently for the individual to arrive and then extend itself into its somatic form. Long after the mortal body has come and gone, however, society remains in occupation as the social categories influencing other individual bodies. Within a single social biography, it can produce many categories of the person, allowing the individual to switch roles and moral terrains. At one moment a daughter, at the next a wife and yet another a mother, the individual can be mutable and capable of being multiple persons. This requires knowledge of the correct parts to play and perception of the moral attributes governing social roles. It also necessitates a certain attributable history to the categories of the person and a regular display of collective values as social power. In these ways both personhood and society can and do objectify themselves in, on, and through the individual.

Objectification allows the categories of personhood and the values of society to be shared and, in so doing, provides confidence in the kinds of behaviour and beliefs expected from others in society. Objectifying, which can be said to become culture, certainly serves both individual and society. In this capacity it helps in organizing the world of the individual, making it possible for the individual to interact with the world in meaningful ways. At the same time, it provides the means by which one society can achieve its distinctiveness, thus allowing that society to distinguish itself from others. Because not all societies take hold of their individual members in the same way, not all effects of cultural objectification will be the same. The different styles in which societies appropriate the body of the individual can be said to be the cultural means by which they distinguish themselves one from the other.

Hence the style in which modern capitalist societies seize their individuals – as 'natural' autonomous entities ideally possessing 'equal' rights one with the other – can be identified as the cultural means by which they distinguish themselves as being, for example, politically democratic. In such cases the ideology of democracy tends to turn back upon its formative economic structure to assist it in shaping individuals to be, for example, independent and equal consumers of commodity goods. In these instances, individuals receive the legitimacy to desire access not only to political polity but also to economic goods. In taking hold of members in ways which objectify them as autonomous individuals, Western capitalist societies allow their states and markets to engage individuals principally as persons understood to be citizens and consumers respectively. Yet, at the level of belief, the cause of the desire for polities and commodities is placed not in political and economic forces, but rather in the human individual as the source of self-conscious being. Perhaps, because of this location of desire, what modern state societies judge as being most uncertain about their own existence is the depth of commitment by their individual citizens.

Modern state societies build community membership from the body of the individual and assume for each individual the capacity of a motivated conscious self of which they can never be fully certain. They constantly seek the reassurances of commitment from their citizens and, to this end, the disciplined body of the individual plays its crucial part in helping to deliver its own awareness into the safekeeping of the state. In obediently responding, for example, to government and market forces, the disciplined body presents the possibility of corroborating the effect of the state's claim over the individual. In addition, the disciplined body can confirm with its docility the individual's sense of meaningful existence in the known value system of the state. Regular obedience to culture makes the world real for the individual. Dramatizing this necessary character of relations between the individual and state thus becomes a means of satisfying social desires. I would like to argue (as others have done) that in our modern Western world of belief in the autonomous individual and the democratic state, competitive sports repeatedly re-enact the dramatic obedience of the athletic body to spectators and, in doing so, function to present and satisfy certain social desires for the individual and the state (Bourdieu 1990; Faure 1996; Hargreaves 1986).

For the obedient bodies of individual citizens living in modern Western states there arguably appears a sense in which, when seeing two teams competing upon the field of play, such concepts as equity and fraternity become objectified and subliminally desirable. Two teams with an equal number of players, two goals or baskets with the same dimensions, matched halves to be defended and attacked, and equivalent time to determine the length of play, are all forms of balances that help to convey the perception in competitive sport that a natural equity of sorts exists in the world and that obedient bodies merely mimic this by organizing their playful confrontations in its image. In addition, by helping to maintain the rules, safety and proper 'spirit' of competition in the drama of sporting events, referees, linesmen and officials reiterate the idea that the 'brotherhood' of team play is a desirable ideal. Hence equity and fraternity appear like the 'natural order of things'. In fact citizens and states perceive and even find reassuring that winners and losers (in other words, an inevitable hierarchy) essentially come about because of a natural fraternal justice. What tests this perception and brings about the appearance of its certainty is, in fact, the playing of the game.[1]

What has been called the godlike role which athletes perform in the game – by making winning and losing actual – opens up the possibility of perceiving and finally understanding that which is just (Barthes 1981: 25). Athletes, as winners and losers, turn the forces of the unpredictable and the asocial into the consistent and the social. In this regard they act like gods seeking to subordinate the forces existing beyond ordinary human will. These forces, like their representatives, behave like natural justice; they determine winners and losers. They are tested and confirmed by the game being played. Playing the game provides the possibility of perceiving and confirming that a natural fraternal justice exists; one to which citizens and states may indeed have access and to which they may be subject, but which ultimately exists beyond their immediate and direct control.

With each game played citizens share in moments of collective moral order. In doing so, however, they make available to the state the single most important property for its own legitimacy, that is, the apparent objectified commitment of citizens (or, as some would say, 'public consensus').[2] This is because both sport and the state feed into and depend upon the same style of governance and, hence, demand the same rational response from their participants. Obedience to the natural order of things becomes palatable when the responsibilities for obeying reside in the external forces of the inevitable. Obeying the governing authorities of sport or state quite literally translates as obeying nature itself. To use what already appears to be an in-place fact (citizens and states following 'natural law') can be construed as highly efficient and rational. Sport has the unobtrusive ability to convey the apparent fact that public commitment and obedience to the state appear in unison with each other as well as with nature. Hardly surprising, therefore, that for the modern state, sport has developed into a dominant style of expressing the nation-ness of committed and obedient citizens.

Sport captures and presents the qualities of individuality while at the same time demonstrating how such individuality, when disciplined by rational order, can become aesthetically pleasing and desirable as fraternal communality. Distinctive sports with athletes who attain substantive esteem and renown draw individuals together not just at local levels but at the level of national consciousness. National sports become the vehicles for collective consciousness because they can appropriate and redistribute the simultaneity of human sentiments (Anderson 1992). Sharable emotions and revealed values objectify individuals as persons who can possess nation-ness.[3] Fans, yes, but look how smoothly such fanaticism turns into national pride and patrimony when 'blessed' by the game.[4] I would argue that it is the repetition of playing the game which performs the bulk of this basic socializing work for sports.

With all its qualities of repetitive ritual drama, sport is the fixing and framing of form against the indeterminacies that can work against the possibility of imagining the community (Anderson 1992; Turner 1988). From the repeated appearances of similar sanctioned athletic equipment, the reiterated normative and pragmatic movements of the athlete, to the reenacted procedures of how, when and where the game should begin, pause and end, the ritual performance of sports culturally dramatizes a bodily obedience made into the social substance of community. Particularly in its mimicry of obedience, sporting performance determines the capacity of the individual to possess community. In the Western world, for example, to find a modern state without a national sport or a citizen without a nationality would indeed be extremely difficult. Every time the game commences and every time the athlete repeats the disciplined actions that define or give form to the game, shared sentiments and knowledge make the individual perceive social community. To be part of the proceedings, to support one competitor or team rather than another, even to anticipate the actions of the athlete or the sequence of the game can all be turned to the cause of making the individual into a person with community. Such aspects of human behaviour seemingly accomplish their socializing work well when formed by the repetition of sport's ritual performances. I would now like to argue they do so just as well in the Waiwai archery competition of *Tïwosom* as in the sporting performances of Western societies.

Tïwosom: An Amerindian Archery Competition

The Waiwai currently (1998) occupy five separate and autonomous villages on the Essequibo River and the New River in Guyana, and on the Rio Mapuera, the Rio Anawa and the Rio Jatapo in Brazil. Mortar Village (*Akomïtu-pono*) on the upper Essequibo River is the largest Waiwai village in Guyana with a population of 230 people.[5] Howler Monkey Rock Village

(*Shepurïtopon*) on the Rio Mapuera is, with a population of 1,147, the largest of all Waiwai villages.[6] Every year during the short rainy-season around December or January, each village prepares for the ceremonial festival of *Kesemanïtopo*.

The festival always begins with an announcement of its forthcoming proceedings and a formal request from the village leader (*Kayaritomo*) for 'seekers of animals' (*Woto-yeposo*). In the formal request for hunters to go out into the forest to kill animals, the festival, in its commencement, is not much different from other more routine community activities.

The daily routine of a Waiwai village often revolves around some form of communal activity. Farming, building canoes, constructing and repairing houses and much more keep a village in regular if not constant collective action. To entice and repay the labour for such work, communal meals (*honari*) have to be provided. Initiated by the village leader but actually administered by specific work leaders (*Antomanye-komo*) collective work and communal meals always begin with leadership's formal request for hunted meat.

It is the young unmarried men (*Karipamsham-komo*) who usually comprise the greater proportion of hunters in the group, but the older active married men (*Porintomo-komo*) also participate. The village leader's authority to request and contract the activities of these hunters stems overtly and immediately from the persuasive eloquence of his voice (that is, in Waiwai parlance, from his ability to speak publicly without fear, shame or reluctance). More substantively, but less obvious and immediate, his authority to initiate and direct communal activities derives from the influences of his kinship and marriage relations to village members. Indeed he is village leader because he can be found at the centre of a core group of consanguineous and affinal kinsmen who constitute the interrelated relations of the village. He is, in this sense, understood to be more prominently associated with the village than any other of its members. The authority of his request for hunters does not, therefore, depend solely upon his public and formal entreaty, but rather on the combination of his persuasive voice and his informal influence over immediate kinsmen. Both effects create an obedience that ultimately benefits the village community. The labour of hunters in the provision of meat for village activities and, perhaps more importantly, the village leader's political capacity to govern depend upon the particular stylistic hold Waiwai society has on the compliant bodies of its village members.

Where the festival of *Kesemanïtopo* probably most cogently departs from the ordinary village activities is in its sustained sequential efforts at collective enjoyment. On the day they return to the village, the hunters, with great pomp and ceremony, dance around the plaza carrying their packs of freshly killed meat on their backs, while whistling and blowing their bark horns. They ceremoniously present their backpacks of meat to the village leader, after which, every returning hunter receives a bowl of palm drink from the women of the village. The festivities can now begin in earnest.

Figure 3 Preparing for the archery contest [George Mentore]

Each day various games and activities take place, from dancing to the music of the bone flute and tortoise resonator, to chasing and pretending to kill different forest creatures whose image and behaviour the villagers mimic very convincingly. The festival itself may last from three to five days or as long as the food and drink will last. It often ends simply with the exhausted participants remaining in their hammocks and later returning to the regular routine of daily life. It is within the festivities, after the 'seekers of animals' have returned from their hunt, that the actual competition of *Tïwosom* takes place. The archery contest is usually held on the day after the hunters have returned.

The 'seekers of animals' usually spend about two to three days hunting from their canoes along the rivers and/or in the high forests of the mountains. While they have been out in the forests, other men who have remained in the village (*Etïnomshapu-komo*) have made the arrows and targets to be used in the competition. Each man has fashioned the finest arrow he can possibly produce. There is a good deal of friendly rivalry as to who can make the best arrow. These arrows are given to the returning hunters to use in the archery competition. One man has been commissioned to carve from softwood the life-size figures of a toucan (*yakwe*) and a maam (*potwo*). When completed, these figures are placed as targets around the axle of the central pole up inside the large conical roof of the meeting house. If a village does not have such an edifice, a scaffold is specially built for the competition and the carved birds perched up on its frame. The targets are usually about 23 m from the ground, and the archers shoot upwards as they would when in the forest hunting birds and monkeys.

Every male member of the village takes part in the contest (there is a rumour, however, that the larger Waiwai village in Brazil also allows women to take part). They all line up one behind the other with each contestant taking a single shot at his target, seeking to lodge his arrow in either one of the carved and painted birds. A fair amount of jovial banter takes place between the contestants and the spectators, particularly between the archer taking aim and the female spectators. For example, as he is about to shoot, an archer will loudly boast *Onpoyiero opichi oyasi* (this is why my wife took me as her husband). Everyone smiles, but if he misses, tremendous laughter will burst forth from all those present. The laughter in this context may well be embarrassing for the archer who misses, but it also helps to deflect the greater shame incurred from his inability to hit the target. When all the contestants have fired off their arrows, a work leader brings down the birds festooned with arrows. From these arrows only, he will choose the most attractive and present it to the village leader. The rest he will distribute to all the attending archers who hit their target. No contestant ever receives the arrow he has shot. In this and other aspects, the distribution of arrows copies the sharing of meat by work leaders at communal meals, where careful attention is paid to the custom that no hunter should eat the meat from his own kill.

The best hunters, 'renown killers of animals' (*Woto-wapari-komo*) and/or 'renown killers of fish' (*Otï-wapari-komo*) will often take the opportunity of the festival hunt to demonstrate further their esteemed talents. Their high regard derives from the privileged location of hunting in the regular routine of village life. The Waiwai can quite correctly be referred to as slash-and-burn agriculturalists, but it is also the case that hunting takes pride of place at the centre of their economic and cultural life. Manioc is indeed the staple root crop and the basic source of bread and many beverages, but hunted meat completes the ideal daily meal. From such evidence, it could be argued that *Tiwosom* celebrates, or more correctly dramatizes, the contribution hunters make to village life. This is perhaps no better illustrated than by the prominent presence of the bow and arrow in both the regular round of hunting activities and the ritual competition of *Tiwosom*.

Feminine Bow, Masculine Arrow: Establishing and Maintaining Complimentary Oppositions

The long bow (krapa) has remained, even now long after the introduction of shotguns into Waiwai culture, the quintessential instrument of labour and the primary symbol of masculine identity. When a man dies his bow must be burnt or buried with him. Every man knows which trees produce the best wood for bows, and can, with varying degrees of skill, make his own bow and arrows. As soon as a boy is old enough to grasp the connection between gender and activity he can be seen carrying a bow and a couple of blunt-tipped arrows, and, at every opportunity, playfully taking aim and shooting at the various domestic targets in and around the village plaza. So deep and strong are the cultural connections between masculinity and the bow that their meanings have become intricately interwoven at many different levels of Waiwai material and intellectual life.

A Waiwai bow – a simple yet remarkably efficient weapon – consists of a single stave of wood tapered at each end where the knotted bow-string (*krapa yawyechi*) is attached.[7] The cross-section (classified as 'elliptical concave high stacked' following Heath and Chiara 1977: 167) reveals the 'back-of-the-bow' (*krapa tïmkakim*). The bow-string's terminal knot (*krapa yawyechi tipuri*) a semi-detachable loop, goes over the top nock or 'nose-of-the-bow' (*krapa ewnari*) and sits on the shoulders or more correctly the 'head-of-the-bow' (*krapa itepuri*). The permanent middle knot sits on the bottom nock or 'buttocks-of-the-bow' (*krapa mapiri*). It is only removed when the bow string breaks and has to be remade. For this purpose, particularly in emergencies, the length of another bow string continues on from the middle knot and wraps around the lower end of the stave to about half way up the bow. The Waiwai call the bow-string wrap *krapa katami*. The word *katami*, the same used for referring to the back apron traditionally worn only by adult women, declares the feminine body of the bow.

Indeed, a bow remains 'naked' until adorned with the 'clothes' of its ornamentation. In Waiwai ideas (as in other Amerindian conceptual schemes) decorating a human body, animal, or object, produces cultural and social meanings that go beyond the mere aesthetic, providing perceptible and hence distributive realities to intangible concepts (Seeger 1975; Turner 1980). Significantly, a bow remains bare and, in fact, unusable until dressed with its bow string. The bow string wrap, the bow's 'back apron', marks a gendered functionality. Like the decorative aprons on women's backs, the wrap begins at the centre of the bow (*krapa yasïtopo*) – the thickest and most powerful section of its stave. This connotes the compressing of an energy at the centre, emphasized by a two-inch cotton bind interlaced above the bow string wrap. Here red and yellow breast feathers of the macaw hang in tied tassels. The only other place where decorative feathers can be found is at the terminal knot of a bow's top nock. The feathers seek to enhance the significance of the energy source located at the centre and along the back. Their vibrant colours, suggestive of heat

73

and strength, convey and confirm the Waiwai knowledge that such forces possess supernatural as well as natural energies.

This, in fact, is why the word particle *yasï* in *krapa [yasï]topo* refers to the centre of the bow. *Yasï* is the same particle used in the first syllable of *yaskomo*, the Waiwai word for shaman. Corresponding to the way the source of shamanic power finds a temporary shelter at the centre of a shaman's body – and indeed the way women's backs gain their strength to carry routinely their heavy back packs of firewood and manioc tubers – in the same way the intrinsic mystical and material power of the bow can be found in its back and at its centre. From inside the shaman's body, the heat and strength of his mystical energy gives birth to his powerful words sent like arrows to kill or to heal. Correspondingly, to support her pregnancy, a similar vibrant vigour converges in the back and at the centre of a woman's body. Indeed, in Waiwai ideas, it is the very same mystical force originating at the centre of the world that permeates and finds a presence in the bodies of the bow, the shaman and the woman. In this regard, feminizing the bow (and arguably even the shaman) amounts to making the claim that the power of the bow derives from mystical and material qualities beyond its immediate form. Thus the bow's feminine and mystical features subtly interchange and carry over into each other to provide the bow itself with its distinctive quality of centralized energy. To make authoritative and competent statements about their manhood Waiwai men must set themselves in proper relations with their bow, their women and their shamans. The following representations can hence be found in the archery competition of *Tïwosom*: the spectacle of each archer taking aim at his target, the overtly stated connections between hunting, meat and marriage, and the whimsicality of an arrows flight. It is these same elements which recur in owning a bow, having a wife and existing on good terms with the certainty of shamanic forces (all highly desirable conditions for Waiwai hunters). And in each, a man must align himself to the emanating forces of the centre.

It has long been recognized that for Amerindian societies of lowland South America strong oppositions, particularly between male and female, must first be established and maintained in order to be finally brought together in mutual interdependence (Lévi-Strauss 1972; Crocker 1985; Hugh-Jones 1979). In such societies, it is considered part of the social dynamics of human existence to know and understand the limits of elements believed to be in complimentary opposition to each other. It may seem to us like high irony that an artifact used to objectify and bring full meaning to Amerindian masculinity should be given a distinctive feminine feature. In our world, for example, where much of sport has in the past been restricted mainly to men, the feminizing of athletic equipment can often be interpreted as a form of endearment or familiarity conducive to making the relation between athlete and his essential instrument of play more intimate. Such feminizing, it could be argued, betrays a desire to subordinate sporting equipment, that is, to bring the instruments of play under greater control and to bend them to the will of the athlete. For us, suggestively, a tell-tale correlation apparently exists between politics, work and play. Yet, for native South Americans, and certainly for the Waiwai, the logic carried over from politics and production to play is not so much that of domination but rather that of accommodation. To be politically and economically productive, oppositional forces must be brought together in mutual cooperation; here it is not a question of defeating the opposition, but of bringing opposing differences into effect by coupling them together in mutual interaction.

Feminizing the bow, for the Waiwai, would not be a case of seeking greater intimacy with the bow in order to subordinate its energies to a more efficient masculine will, but rather of bringing the essential requirement of feminine opposition into action to make masculinity actual and effective. To be a Waiwai man, in other words, means to be a hunter with a bow – that is, to be in proper relations with feminine forces that do not just enhance masculinity but actually bring masculinity into socially productive reality. By considering some of the physical and symbolic features of the bow, its feminizing contribution to masculinity may be best interpreted in the ritual of *Tïwosom* as a dominant stylistic hold on the individual bodies of men.

If it can be reasonably determined that the bow contains certain features of femininity, then by the very form of complimentary opposition, it can be deduced that the arrow (*waywu*) holds certain aspects of Waiwai masculinity. To do so comprehensively, however, would involve moving through the appropriated symbols of Waiwai manhood to meet the metaphor of 'men are like birds'. This is a complicated analogy to interpret, yet it has a place in many different aspects of Waiwai material and intellectual life. From body adornment and house thatching to the defining characteristics of the layered celestial realm, men and birds operate as dynamic tropes. Particularly with arrows and their principal motion of flight, men and birds sustain strong associations. Here the somatic reference allows the wings of birds and the arms of men to combine specifically at the fletching of an arrow. In Waiwai, the word *yaporï* means both arm and wing: hence calling the fletching of an arrow *waywu yaporï* (arm/wing-of-the-arrow) assists in carrying all the symbolic load of men and birds to the arrow.

The body or shaft of an arrow (*waywu*) has a butt end (*waywu mapiri*), a head (*waywu putiri*), a fore shaft (*waywu takpo*) and a fore end (*waywu-ponumchi*).8 The butt end usually has about an inch of cotton and/or fibre binding, which holds in place an inserted grooved hardwood plug serving as the arrow's nock (*waywu mayewnari*). The binding also has an additional coating of black adhesive latex (*maani*). Above the fletching, held between the overlapped spliced ends of the main feathers' quill, are red and/or yellow tufts of parrot feathers (*waywu mawyuru*). Some arrow makers add coloured tufts of feathers below the main fletching. They apply these ornamental feathers so as to 'dress' the arrow and, in so doing, to be able to identify the arrow with its maker. For the main functional feathers of the fletching (*waywu yapori*) the Waiwai always use the black primary flight feathers of the powis (*powishi*).[9] On and along the fletching bind, some arrow makers paint their special individual designs, once again allowing any arrow to be identified with its particular maker.

Waiwai arrow heads come in many different sizes, shapes and materials, with the type of head used being primarily dependent upon the kind of animal hunted. The most versatile arrow head they call *tiyashkem*. It is a long pointed rod of hardwood with barbs carved either on both sides or on one side only. It has a long tang that is inserted and bound at the fore end of the arrow shaft. So well balanced is this arrow that if an archer misses his target, when shooting upwards into the tree tops, the weighted arrow head will turn the arrow back down to land near the archer. The Waiwai use *tiyashkem* principally to shoot large birds. However, because it is the most frequent arrow made and most frequent carried by the hunter, it can be used to shoot small monkeys and at times even larger game like deer and peccary. The proper arrow head for big game, however, is *rapu*. Traditionally carved from segments of strong thick bamboo (although today some can be found made from hammered and sharpened pieces of an old machete) *rapu* arrows have a broad-bladed lanceolate head, which hunters use at close range on animals like the tapir, peccary and capybara. When newly made, both *tiyashkem* and *rapu* arrow heads can be seen adorned with white cotton thread and red painted designs. There are many other arrow heads belonging to the arsenal of the hunter, but to mention them all would merely serve to make the technical ingenuity and craftsmanship of Waiwai arrow making that much more obvious. Yet, with all this diversity, there remains the particularly noticeable fact that the one type of arrow Waiwai men most identify with happens to be the *tiyashkem*: the only arrow used in the archery competition of *Tiwosom*. *Tiyashkem*, more so than any other arrow, becomes most closely associated with masculinity precisely because it carries death to birds.

Death provides the opportunity for an exchange to occur between the successful hunter and the spiritual custodian of the deceased animal. Technically speaking, it is the entry of the arrow into the animal's body that dislodges its vital essence (*ekati*) and initiates the process of death. Corporal life actually ceases when the vital essence of the animal can no longer return to the material form of its body. For proper death to take place, the animal's violently dislodged essence must be returned to its original celestial domain where the main source of all life's spiritual vitality resides. In *Tiwosom*, this process, which normally takes place in the wild and remote forest, is re-enacted in the familiar domesticity of the village. The site of the archery competition is a transferred ritual space, nevertheless it seeks to mimic a dimension that goes beyond the forest and the village. The targets of the carved and painted birds, placed in the three-tier canopy of the conical roof, signify not earthly but celestial beings.

Sky or heaven or its three-tier realm called *kapu* houses the main source of vitality that gives life to all living things. The Waiwai speak of *kapu* in avian terms. Its lower and first stratum, *Maratu-yena* (Marial Guan-people) has the characteristics of dull-coloured birds who keep mostly to the floor and lower levels of the forest.[10] The middle and second stratum, *Kwaro-yena* (Macaw-people) possess the characteristics of gregarious and bright-ly plumed birds who live in the upper reaches of the forest and fly above the forest canopy. The upper and third stratum, *Kurum-yena* (Vulture-people) possess the characteristics of high-soaring carrion and carnivorous birds. The predominant avian attributes of flight, talon and beak – which converge around ideas about missiles that rip and cut – belong to the cosmic birds of *kapu*, but they also become transferred to the hunter's principal weapon of death: the arrow. In this case, they become the features of the arrow used primarily for killing birds: the *tiyashkem*.

After *tiyashkem* has dislodged the vital essence of its victim, the bird's vitality must find its way to *kapu* and the custodial cosmic energy of *Kwarokiyim* (Great Spirit/Father of the Macaw). This can occur successfully only if the hunter has properly killed his prey and correctly distributed its meat, that is, not 'tortured' or 'sickened' or wastefully left its carcass to rot. To allow a hunted animal to suffer needlessly or to leave its carcass behind after its death is to maroon that animal's vital essence on the earthly stratum where it not only can do vengeful harm to humans, but can also avoid being properly received by its spiritual custodian. When the hunter carries out his obligations successfully to the dying bird, the meat of its body becomes a gift in exchange from *Kwarokiyim*. It is in this sense that the *tiyashkem* arrow presents an opportunity for an exchange to take place between the hunter and the spiritual custodian of the deceased bird. The ripping and cutting missile of *tiyashkem*, an instrument of death, becomes masculine because it is made and used by men and, in its making and use, it emulates the single most important force with which men identify: the Great Spirit of the Macaw. With its cosmic avian attributes, the Great Spirit empowers *tiyashkem* by offering the object of its custody to the hunter, thereby placing the hunter under an obligation to reciprocate. This occurs precisely because the hunter is the immediate beneficiary of the effect of the arrow's flight, that is, the meat of birds. In due course and through the hunter's relations with other village members, the meat changes into the social currency of masculine honour and esteem that, in Waiwai understanding, has to be reciprocated with subordinate behaviour toward the Great Spirit of the Macaw. In part, the ritual competition of *Tïwosom*, is exactly this: an objectified annually repeated statement of subordination to forces beyond Waiwai society.

Conclusion

Waiwai society, through the archery competition of *Tïwosom*, reaffirms its hold upon its individual members. By persuading its archers to take part, and requiring them to follow the rules of competition, society demands and receives a reassuring obedience. *Tiwosom* makes the archer use his bow and arrow in competitive display, publicly testing his skills in archery. This style of retrieving obedience succeeds in projecting to members some of the concepts critical to the opposition between men and women. The archer's equipment and actions, for example, assist in rationalizing and legitimizing not only the complimentary differences between men and women, but also those between husbands and wives, and, indirectly, those between hunting and farming. Men's instruments of labour (the bow and arrow) as well as the products of their labour (meat) and hence men themselves, become celebrated in and privileged by the competition. The repetitive actions of the archers in taking aim and shooting at the target of birds draws attention to the particular predatory relations men have as hunters with their prey. These relations have the capacity not only to provide men with the opportunity to fulfil their obligatory subordination to higher divine authorities, they also substantiate a seemingly inevitable hierarchy between humans and the divine. In the substantiation, the 'natural' ranking between humans and gods becomes translated into a 'natural' ranking between men and women. The overall ideological statement from the ritual archery competition of *Tiwosom* carries the principal message of a hunting man's reciprocal subordination to the great cosmic spirit of birds. At the same time, however, *Tiwosom* also makes the claim that men are, by their exchanges with the Great Spirit, closer than women to this eminence. The cultural drama of *Tiwosom* fixes and frames the form of bodily obedience into the social substance of Waiwai society, and it does so in a style that allows society to maintain unchallenged the exercise of its power.

Acknowledgements

This chapter is dedicated to my brother Lloyd Forbes Mentore 1954-98, a consummate sportsman. My thanks to Edith Turner and Terry Roopnaraine; this chapter could not have been written without you.

Notes

1. One has merely to enter at any page of *Beyond a Boundary* by C.L.R. James (1963) to find an eloquence on these topics eminently prepared.
2. We are all, for example, supposed to recognize the wrongdoing and certainly to disapprove of the boxer who bites off a piece of his opponent's ear in an internationally televised championship fight; we are all, in addition, supposed to recognize and condone the right of boxing's governing body to fine and to suspend the boxer for his action, which, after all, was not just against the rules and hence outlawed but was also immoral, bringing great 'shame' and 'dishonour' to the sport of boxing. In collectively responding with similar abhorrence to the outlawed immoral actions of the boxer we make claims to ourselves and to others that we recognize, know and abide by similar standards

of social life – the very same standards that allow us to imagine we live and belong to a national community of people who share the same values. Note, incidentally, how support for the governing body of sport can also be translated into support for the governing body of the state.

3. Think here of the tightening in the chest and the welling-up of tears at sight of the flag and sound of the anthem as our athlete stands on the winner's podium.

4. For surely the game could not and would not support an unjust and immoral nation? Think here, for example, of the ways in which Jesse Owens' heroic but unpredictable successes at the 'Nazi' Olympics have been interpreted as if they were an independent vindication for the injustices and evils of racism: a remarkably strange contradiction when one considers how the concepts of race themselves rely heavily on the independent variable of nature.

5. I have been working since 1971 with the community who now live at Akomïtu, but who, in 1986 under the leadership of Mawasha, had moved from their up-river village of Shepariymo (Big Dog Village). In June 1998 the population was 133 males and 97 females: three males and three females under the age of twelve months, 28 males and 19 females between one and five years of age, 29 males and 22 females between six and 14 years of age, 57 males and 42 females between 15 and 44 years of age, and 16 males and 11 females between 45 and 60 years of age.

6. In the language of the Hiskaryena (Red Deer People) with whom the Waiwai share the settlement, they also call the village *Mawtohorï*, meaning 'Howler Monkey Rock Village'.

7. The average length of a bow, ideally made from 'letter wood' or 'leopard wood' (*Brosimum aubletii*) is around 2.6 m, but many men have bows reaching 2.29 m. Bow-strings are made from a plant called *krewetu* specially grown in farms and manufactured into strong rope by twisting the fibres of its leaves together.

8. Arrows are made from a light straight arrow reed often grown in a single patch amongst a householder's regular farm crops. The minimum length of Waiwai arrows is 1.91 m, maximum length 2.03 m, and average length 1.97 m (as recorded by Heath and Chiara 1977: 143).

9. They cut a single feather in half, along its quill, and trim each half in the shape of a parallelogram. The halves of the feather are placed in a radial position along the length of the arrow shaft. They are attached using a variety of binding techniques, for example, a 'continuous open bind', an 'interval bind', a 'continuous close bind' or a combination of one or the other of these (following Heath and Chiara 1977: 159-60).

10. In Waiwai belief, the final resting place for all human '*ekatï* of the eye' is among the Guan-people – to be more precise, the eye-*ekatï* of the human dead actually take up residence in the narrow void between the strata of the earth and *Maratuyena*, but to all intents and purposes this void is thought to be part of *Maratuyena*.

References

Anderson, B. (1992), *Imagined Communities: Reflections on the Origin and Spread of Nationalism*, London: Verso.

Armstrong, G. (1998), *Football Hooligans: Knowing the Score.* Oxford: Berg.

Bailey, F.G. (1969), *Stratagems and Spoils: A Social Anthropology of Politics*, Oxford: Basil Blackwell.

Barthes, R. (1981), *Mythologies*, New York: Hill & Wang.

Bourdieu, P. (1990), *In Other Words: Essays Towards a Reflexive Sociology*, Stanford: Stanford University Press.

Crocker, J.C. (1985), *Vital Souls: Bororo Cosmology, Natural Symbolism, and Shamanism*, Tucson: University of Arizona Press.

Faure, Jean-Michel (1996), 'Forging a French Fighting Spirit: The Nation, Sport, Violence and War', in J.A. Mangan (ed.), *Tribal Identities: Nationalism, Europe, Sport*, London: Frank Cass.

Hargreaves, J. (1986), *Sport, Power, and Culture: A Social and Historical Analysis of Popular Sports in Britain*, Cambridge: Polity Press.

Heath E.G. and Vilma Chiara (1977), *Brazilian Indian Archery: A Preliminary Ethno-toxological Study of the Archery of the Brazilian Indians*, Manchester: Simon Archery Foundation.

Hugh-Jones, S. (1979), *The Palm and the Pleiades: Initiation and Cosmology in Northwest Amazonia*, Cambridge: Cambridge University Press.

James, C.L.R. (1963), *Beyond a Boundary*, London: Hutchinson.

Lévi-Strauss, C. (1972), *Structural Anthropology*, Harmondsworth: Penguin Books Ltd.

Scarry, E. (1987), *The Body in Pain: The Making and Unmaking of the World*, New York: Oxford University Press.

Seeger, A. (1975), 'The Meaning of Body Ornaments', *Ethnology* 14(3): 211-24.

Turner, T (1980), 'The Social Skin', in J. Cherfas and R. Lewin (eds), *Not Work Alone*, Beverly Hills: Sage Publications.

Turner, V. (1988), *The Anthropology of Performance*, New York: PAJ Publications.

Part II

Sport and the Politics of Identity

4
Kabaddi, A National Sport of India: The Internationalism of Nationalism and the Foreignness of Indianness

Joseph S. Alter

In view of the large number of players and the extent of its diffusion, kabaddi can be called India's national sport. There is no doubt, however, that since India has won a gold medal in Olympic hockey and because the radio is always broadcasting the 'wonders of cricket' that many people are mistaken in thinking that these two are India's most important sports. (Bhalla, 1979)

Introduction: Wrestling with Cricket and the Question of Indianness

It is now well accepted that sports are intimately linked to the complex politics of colonialism, decolonization and nationalism (see, for example Bale and Sang 1996; Bernett 1978; Blecking 1987, 1991; Brownell 1995; Jarvie 1991; Mangan 1986; MacAloon 1981; MacClancy 1996; Stuart 1996; Sugden and Bairner 1993). My own work in India has focused primarily on the way in which the culture and history of Indian wrestling provides a context within which concerns with fitness, health and strength articulate with various forms of nationalism (Alter 1992, 1993, 1994, 1995, n.d.). An integral feature of this articulation is the way in which wrestling is thought of as being Indian through and through and as providing a kind of radical solution to the problems associated with modernity. In the vision of many wrestlers, the various forms of self discipline associated with the sport provide the basic moral coordinates around which a new India is imagined and embodied.

In a very different way, cricket in India also articulates with nationalism. Although linked, through history and imagination, with the elite civility of England in general and the empire in particular, in modern India the game has been decolonized by way of a modern synthesis and transmutation of meaning on a global scale. As Arjun Appadurai points out, it is no longer the game it once was but has taken on a new transnational character variably manifest in the public culture of local events (1995; see also Cashman 1980; Diawara 1990; Nandy 1989; Stoddart 1988; Roberts 1985). Rules, protocols, aesthetics and style have been transformed into something that is no longer quintessentially English. What is most significant about this transformation is that what cricket has become stands in such marked contrast to the image of what it was. And, despite radical change, that image remains as an extremely powerful referent defining the scope and pattern of the game's various modern forms. Thus, cricket in India sheds light on nationalism because of the broader postcolonial irony it invokes, the structure of history it helps to define, and the hegemonic system of values it throws into question.

Because cricket has become extremely popular throughout India, but has only recently 'become Indian', and because wrestling is thought of as being Indian through and through but is only 'popular' in specific places and among a small though diverse segment of the population, one may conclude that there is a degree of ambiguity in the way in which these two sports instantiate the complex relationship between decolonization and nationalism. In the case of cricket, decolonization is a highly relative concept because, despite the significant changes analysed by Appadurai, the sport retains its basic non-Indian structure, is embedded in a non-Indian past and, despite its vernacularization, is linked to big business and the media. Although consumed by the masses – and transformed through the process of being consumed – there is a sense in which Indian cricket played on the national and international stage is an elite sport, at least on a relative scale.

Wrestling, on the other hand, bills itself as a sport of – but not exclusively for – the masses, and purports to be everything that is, or can be, good and virtuous in India. Wrestlers are very clear on how national ideals can be embodied and how these ideals will serve to rebuild a nation that has been sapped of its strength, first by colonialism and then by various forms of post-colonial Westernization. The sport itself has developed in opposition to so-called 'foreign' sports such as hockey, football and cricket. So even though many wrestlers aspire to international fame, the inherent 'traditionalism' manifest in earthen pits, indigenous exercises, copious diets of milk and *ghi* and long-duration bouts, means that Indian wrestlers do not do very well in world-class competition. For this and many other reasons, but certainly in part because of the sport's inherently rural and somewhat plebeian character, wrestling is simply not very popular on a national level where the pervading image of how modern India should be tends to be urban and middle class – even when imagined in rural terms – if not exactly urbane and cosmopolitan.

The ambiguities and contradictions in how cricket and wrestling factor into the politics of national transformation raise a number of questions.[1] One of the most interesting of these – in general, but here more specifically with regard to sport – is what counts as Indianness, and how does Indianness come to be articulated in national terms to local, regional, national and international audiences all at once? Another question has to do with the role of the state. Relatively speaking, the Indian government has had very little to do either with the promotion of cricket or the development of wrestling. Where, then, if anywhere, is the state's vested interest in sport, and how does the state's interest play into the question of Indianness?[2]

Unlike other institutions, sports are often highly charged symbolic events that are cast, on some level, as being simply for leisure and recreation. Therefore, the important question suggested by sport is how can something that is meant to be all fun and games take on much greater significance, and what does that significance tell us about the dynamics of society at large. To a large extent, therefore, the critical issue in an academic study of sport is what defines the most meaningful context for understanding how sports are imbued with social significance. In this regard, the works of Norbert Elias (1986), Eric Dunning (1986) and Henning Eichberg (1998) are particularly noteworthy. In the broadest sense the question these authors pose is 'why do sports take the form they do at particular points in time and in relation to the whole matrix of values and morals that contribute to the perceived sense of cultural ecumene at those times?' Whereas Elias and Dunning tend to focus on specific sports as they relate to the civilizing process, Eichberg frames his enquiry in terms of 'body culture', thus opening up the field of inquiry for a more synthetic, comparative analysis of different kinds of sport, physical training, recreation and dance as these forms of body culture interface with social forces in general and various forms of power in particular (see in particular 1998: 47-67, 111-27, 128-48). The value of such an inquiry is to identify significant configurations in the intersection of culture and history that help to elucidate large-scale transformations in society. In line with this, what follows is an essay on the contextual configuration of culture and history that made it possible for *kabaddi* to be made into one of India's national sports.[3] Thus, *kabaddi* is analysed in terms of how it has come to represent a certain kind of Indianness that is characteristically different from both the rather vague, transnational, elite Indianness of decolonized cricket and the concrete, unambiguous – but rather marginal – 'lumpen' Indianness of the Indian wrestler. What I will argue is that *kabaddi* is 'nationalistic' in terms of and through its progressive conformity to an international standard of sophistication and administration, and that the Indianness of *kabaddi* is not so much a function of its indigenous cultural form as of its foreignness.[4] Or, more accurately, *kabaddi* has become Indian by way of self-reflection that is a product of its formal conformity to a foreign model of modern sport wherein class and ethnicity are important historical, discursive facts but are relatively insignificant as social facts in the context of nationalism.

Kabaddi: Diction and Diversity, Mockery and the Masses

In its vernacular form, as I remember playing it, and as I have seen it played in villages, *kabaddi* is a vigorous game played by groups of children divided into two teams. It is played in an open area and the teams are separated by a line drawn in the dirt. In turn, each team sends one person –

Figure 4 Feinting and parrying in kabbadi [Noel Dyck]

now officially called a raider – across the centre line to try to tag out members of the opposition, now officially called anti-raiders. What gives the game its distinctive character is that when raiders try to tag anti-raiders out, they must do so in one breath. While letting their breath out slowly, they must cant a rhyming, repetitive phrase that contains the word *kabaddi*.[5] Before they run out of breath they must return across the centre line. To get someone out, all a raider must do is touch an anti-raider, but the objective of the anti-raiders' is to capture the raiders before they can return across the centre line to their own side. It is the capturing dimension of the game that makes it vigorous and dramatic, because a typical encounter entails a brief period of feints and parries and ends either with a mass of anti-raiders wrestling their opponent to the ground as the raider gasps for breath, or else with a dramatic escape where almost all of the anti-raiders are tagged out as the raider slips away.

The meaning of the term *kabaddi* is ambiguous, but it seems to be comprised of strongly aspirated consonants that require clear lip and tongue movement so that it is clearly apparent if the raider is breathing while the word is being spoken.[6] With somewhat more interpretive license, however, Laxmikant Pande provides the following etymology for the term

> The word is composed of two parts 'ka' and 'baddi.' Since 'ka' is the first letter of the alphabet we can take it to mean 'beginning' or 'start.' 'Baddi' is associated, by way of its derivation from the term barbarana [roar], with the idea of 'coming to life.' Thus we can say that the fundamental meaning of *kabaddi* is to begin living. It is a command to begin life, learn the art of living and loudly proclaim an answer to the question – how should life be lived? (1982: 61)

Kabaddi can be canted rapidly or very slowly, loudly or very softly to keep pace with changes in the raider's tactical strategy of attack, feint, or retreat. Part of the game's enjoyment is derived from a rhyming, repetitive cant where the raider engages in a kind of taunting, burlesque word play. One form of this is to bracket a concise, well-known phrase with the word *kabaddi* at the beginning and the end. Thus, adopting popular Hindu religious slogans, one might cant, 'kabaddi, Ram, Lakshman, Janki, kabaddi, kabaddi' or 'kabaddi, jai bolo Hanuman ki kabaddi, kabaddi' or simply using sounds, 'kabaddi, hu, tu, tu, kabaddi, kabaddi' (Pande 1982: 61).[7] Alternatively, using the term *kabaddi* as the basis for a rhyme, taunting couplets are often made up on the spot. In this regard common preface words such as 'chal' which means mockery, trickery or deception and 'sel' which means pike or spear, signify the way in which raiders try to thrust into the rank of anti-raiders and mock them while trying to trick them into coming close enough to get tagged out. The fact that 'chal' is used very often would also suggest that part of the fun is in inventing various 'devious' means by which one's opponents cannot easily tell if one has or has not 'broken' the cant by taking a breath. The following common ones appear to be in wide usage and, with some license taken in translation, give a sense of the overall tone:

Chal kabaddi lal lal	Trick *kabaddi* bright red
tere muche lal lal	your moustache is bright red
khel kabaddi Aslal	Play *kabaddi* Aslal
mar gaya Prakash Lal	Death has come to Prakash Lal
chal kabaddi tara	Trick *kabaddi* stars-a-twinkling
Sultan Beg mara	Sultan Beg is dead [and stinking].
sel kabaddi adda	Spike *kabaddi* half [a dram]
bap tera buddha	Your father is an old man
ma teri langri	Your mother is a cripple
pakar liya tangri	Grabbed your leg, [you're in a pickle]
sel kabaddi akara	Spike *kabaddi* now you're stuck
bul bul ko pakara	The bul bul bird [is out of luck] (has been caught)
chotte upar tir kaman	Little one on top, bow and arrow
khel kabaddi bara jawan	Play *kabbadi* big brawny fellow
chal kabaddi ane do	Trick *kabaddi* let them come
tabala bajane do	Let me play your little drum

Without trying to establish what form the sport might have taken at some 'prehistoric' point in time, the historical development of the sport is very clearly articulated. Part of this historical development has been the articulation of a 'prehistoric' past. Bhalla argues that the game must have evolved out of early man's encounter with dangerous wild animals, and the first consolidated attempts at collective self defence and heroic, individualized, against-all-odds, hunting (1976: 11-12). Gole points out that because the cant is reminiscent of military drill commands some believe that the game was developed to provide the basis for training in war tactics (Gole 1978a: 9; Rao 1971: 3). Others claim that it may be a derivative of wrestling (Pande 1982: 61) or, more specifically a game that evolved out of the exercise routine of wrestlers in training (Chauhan 1990: 7; Reddy 1974: 1). Most accounts tend to suggest that *kabaddi* must have been popular during the Vedic age and point out that the earliest reference is found in the writings of Tukaram who claimed that it was played by Lord Krishna as a young boy (Bhalla 1976: 11; Chauhan 1990: 7; de Mellow 1987: 3.1; Gole 1978a: 6).

All of the accounts I have read inevitably point out that *kabaddi* is a game that is played throughout all parts of India even though it is played in different ways and is known by different names (see, for example, Rao 1971: 1; Reddy 1974: 1). In fact, the variation in names and regional styles is almost always noted as a distinctive feature of the game's 'national' character. For example Chauhan, clearly using the past tense, writes:

> Emerging from the ancient period of history, *kabaddi* was known by many many different names and played in many many different places. In Mysore and Tamil Nadu it was called chedu-gudu, in Kerala vangkali, in Bengal hu-du-du, and in Panjab jabarjang. In North India proper it was called *kabaddi* and in Maharashtra hu-tu-tu.

Given the variety of names and variety of places where it was played, there were no standard rules or regulations. In all these various places it was played in accordance with rules that were established on the basis of local experience and tradition. The only thing that was uniform was the fact that whatever word was canted, that word had to be canted in a single breath. There was no boundary to the field, no time limit to the game and there were many different styles and techniques of play (1990: 7-8).

Gole, claiming that there were 'no written rules', is somewhat more specific in his delineation of local variations, pointing out that the Jats of Patiala district in the Punjab call it *sanchi pakki* and use 'kit, kit' or 'du, du' as the cant. In some districts of Gujarat it is known as *bhati, bhati* (Gole 1978a: 6) and in Andhra as *balchheppalam* (Reddy 1974: 1). Some notable examples in the range of different regional styles are often drawn from the Punjab where there was – and may well still be – a game called *amar kabaddi* that is played in a circle. As de Mellow notes, somewhat cryptically, '[i]n some regions it is played without a court, and is named *goongi* kabaddi. This *goongi* kabaddi is nothing but wrestling between two players'

(1987: 3.9). Other variations from the same area include a style where only one or two anti-raiders are allowed to capture a raider. When there is only one raider left, only one anti-raider is allowed to capture the raider during an attack (Gole 1978a: 8). Outside of the Punjab three basic forms of the sport have come to be recognized as 'standard' variants. The first is called *surjivani* where a player who is out gets reinstated once a player from the opposing team has been tagged out. When a whole team is tagged out, a *lona* worth two bonus points is awarded to the surviving team. In the *gamini* form of the game, no players are reinstated, and play ends when one team is tagged out. In *amar* kabaddi, a player who is tagged does not go out of the game. Instead a point is awarded to the raiding team and at the end of a fixed period of time, the team with the most points wins.

As will become clear, *kabaddi* has been turned into a civilized sport that has been designed by various nationalist groups and state bodies to conform with international standards for rules and regulations of play. Retrospectively, therefore, some sense of the vernacular form of the game's overall character can be had by reading between the lines – or, in a subalternist fashion, against the grain – of what have become the official rules of play. As de Mellow notes, 'throttling', 'stifling a cant by covering up the raider's mouth', using a 'scissors hold to immobilize a raider' and employing a 'direct kick' to tag a raider out or immobilize a raider, pulling hair and grabbing clothes, are all regarded as technical fouls. Therefore, it is safe to assume that these were – and perhaps still are in some circles – tactical strategies in how the game was played before it was subject to a civilizing process of formalization and standardization (1987: 3.8; YMCA, 1991: 309).

Almost all modern accounts also emphasize the rustic simplicity, youthful wholesomeness and recreational pleasure of the game's populist, vernacular form. Bhalla captures the tone of many when he remarks that,

> Kabaddi is played from Kashmire to Kanyakumari and from Bengal to Gujarat. Unlike Cricket and Hockey it is not just something played by a few members of elite society. Linked as it is to the very soil of the nation it is the most popular form of recreation for peasants and proletarian workers. (1976: 9)

Gole's account is similar:

> In the Punjab the game *kabaddi* was played by well built people and considered to be the game of the strong and healthy folk. Often the rich offered a bait of money that was tied up to a poll for the winning side. By and large this game was played by the common man in almost all parts of India. (1978a: 8)

Curiously, the history of modern *kabaddi* is directly at odds with this kind of populist image of 'traditional' *kabaddi*, even though the populist image is itself a product of modernity. In other words, the production of the kind of sentiments expressed by Bhalla are inextricably linked to the

institutionalization of *kabbadi* as a modern sport, even though the sentiments evoke a non-institutionalized, subaltern form of the game.

The International Language of Sport and the Status of a Vulgar Game

As it is reproduced in most books on the subject, the history of modern
kabaddi begins in Satara district of what is now the state of Maharashtra in
1915 when a group of middle-class enthusiasts began to organize competitions. Subsequently, in 1921, D. R. Paranjape, Yashwant Rao Pathak, S.C.
Vaidya and K. K. Bendre organized competitions in Pune and Satara.
Significantly, at this time only two forms of the sport – *surjivani* and *gamini* – were played. According to Pande there was an explicitly political and
nationalist motive behind Paranjape, Pathak, Vaidya and Bendre's effort.
At this time Gandhi had started the Swadeshi campaign, appealing to all
Indians to renounce Western clothes in particular and Western influences
in general in favour of indigenous clothes and indigenous forms of culture broadly defined. As Pande puts it, 'it was at this time that *kabaddi*
became a modern sport, on par with any Western sport that has ever been
played' (1982: 62).

From 1921 on, the official history of *kabbadi's* development shows how
the sport was formalized and institutionalized. In 1923 a group of three
men – Bhagwat, Poddhar and Hardikar – first tried to standardize the
rules of the game.[8] At the same time the first all-India *Kabaddi*
Competition was organized in Baroda by the Hind Vijay Gymkhana.[9]
Based on experience gained from this competition the rules were further
revised and published in 1928. In 1927 the Maharashtra Sharirik Shiksha
Mandal (MSSM) was established with the primary objective of developing
indigenous sports and games along with promoting various forms of physical education (cf. Rao 1971: 4-6). As Bhalla recounts

> In those days players of *kabaddi* would often get hurt and for this reason teams
> would often end up engaged in a free-for-all fight. Moreover, there continued
> to be a great deal of variation in how the game was played in different places.
> For this reason the Mandal formed a grand committee to review and re-evalu-
> ate the rules. Based on the advice of this committee the rules were revised and
> published in final form in 1934. However, these revised rules and regulations
> were not followed in most places (1979: 15).

Although many attempts were made at standardization, from the late
1920s onward through 1950, competitions held in different parts of the
country under the auspices of different organizations were played according to different rules. Although the MSSM rules provided one standard –
followed mostly in the area around Bombay and Pune – the situation was
complicated by the Young Men's Christian Association (YMCA) and the
efforts of Drs J.H. Gray, A.G. Noehren and Mr H.C. Buck in particular (see
Harsha 1982).[10]

Beginning in 1908, Dr J.H. Gray had made efforts to popularize 'scientific physical training' throughout Bengal under the auspices of the Calcutta YMCA.[11] It was not until 1920, however, that the idea of a school for physical education was realized in the establishment of India's first Training School for Indian Physical Directors in Madras, where Dr Noehren had been promoting gymnastics and sports for some time within the framework of the YMCA's existing structure. Mr H.C. Buck from the US was enlisted to be the director of the training school, which became known as The College of Physical Education.[12] Whereas Gray and Noehren had been instrumental in introducing gymnastics, basketball, table tennis, track and field, tennis and football on a large scale, and also devoted a great deal of time and energy in recruiting and training the first Indian Olympic team, Buck took a special interest in indigenous sports and games. Moreover, Buck was also concerned with promoting consciousness and conscientiousness about the need for standardized rules 'for the orderly conduct of play and for development of understanding and friendship' (David 1992: 177). Hence in 1928, Buck published his *Book of Rules* for both Western and indigenous games in order to 'introduce uniformity' and bring sports in India up to an Olympic standard. However, his goal was not fully achieved until mid-century.[13]

Starting in 1938, *kabaddi* competitions became a regular feature of the Indian Olympic Games – subsequently known as the National Games – that had been held every other year since 1924. When the games were held in Bombay in 1950 there was a meeting of the regional state representatives and it was decided that an All India Kabaddi Federation should be formed to regulate the sport. Subsequently a national *kabaddi* competition has been held every year under the auspices of this body now known as the Amateur Kabaddi Federation of India. In 1952, under the presidency of Mr Sadubhai Godbole, a grand committee was convened during the annual competition held that year in Madras to once again, and finally, standardize the rules of play. As Bhalla points out, the most important decision reached by this committee was 'that the word kabaddi would be the only legitimate "cant" allowed and that no other words could be spoken in conjunction with the word kabaddi' (1979: 16). Apparently this and other changes made the new rules of 1953 significantly different from both Buck's rules and the MSSM rules upon which Buck's rules had been partially based. Specifically, the dimensions of the field and two courts were changed and the 'lobby' rule was instituted (Gole 1978a: 4). Further amendments were made in 1956, 1960, 1966 and 1972.

Along with the '*kabaddi* only' ruling of 1953, another very significant event of the post-independence period was the establishment of a women's national competition in 1955 and the writing of separate rules for men, women and junior level competition (Pande 1982: 63). Obviously this has important implications for the gendered – and age-graded – articulation of nationalistic 'body culture'. With respect to gender, suffice it to say that the standardization of *kabaddi* – its civilization –

made it possible for a fairly violent masculine game to become ungendered while developing into a national sport.[14] More could be said on the subject, but the neutralization of gender as a criterion for nationalism is reflected in Chauhan's single list of winners of the Arjun Award, a medal and prize money given to individual athletes by the central government under the auspices of the Sports Authority of India. For the years 1972 through 1989 seven medals were given out in *kabaddi*, four to women and three to men. When listing the country's most well-known players from Uttar Pradesh, the names of Ms Sunita and Ms Suman Chaudhuri are given along with the names of four men by the name of Singh (1990: 38-9). Bhalla provides a list of men's and women's national championship winners from 1938 through 1979, showing that the women of Maharashtra have won every year from 1955 through 1979, except in 1975 when they were defeated by the women's team from West Bengal (1979: 119). The relatively ungendered nature of the official sport should not, however, be confused with an attitude of gender equality on the part of those who write the rules and write about the history of the sport. The fact that all pronouns in the literature I have read and quoted here are masculine, and the tacit assumption that all players wear *langots* or *janghia* undergarments, among other things, is clearly indicative of an implicit male bias at the very least. There is, however, very little overt masculinity expressed in discussions of skill and technical proficiency. In other words, writers often make an assumption that the typical player of *kabaddi* is male, but his masculinity is not celebrated as such. This is in very sharp contrast to the overtly masculinized body of the wrestler, the wrestler's conception of strength and skill as being the product of male physiology, and the pervasive fear of and antipathy toward women in general and female sexuality in particular that is expressed in the articulation of a wrestling way of life.

The age- and weight-graded aspect of official *kabaddi* competitions are also significant with respect to the question of nationalism and the development of a national sport. In its vernacular form, kabbadi is a game played by young children in general and adolescent boys in particular. Official matches, however, recognize three age grades and four weight classes: below 17 years, 17-21 years, and over 21; below 27 kg, below 34 kg, below 40 kg and below 50 kg (de Mellow 1987: 3.9). Thus the sport has not only been calibrated, but the calibration is, in part, a function of the sport being played by older men and women. Clearly, the senior and open level 'heavy weight' matches are the ones that are regarded as more important in the sense that the quality of play can be said to have fully matured and individual skill has fully developed. In the transformation of indigenous games into national sports, the 'ageing' of the players marks the enhanced seriousness of competition and what competition comes to stand for in terms of the state's interest in being taken seriously as a grown-up player on the stage of international relations.

The history of *kabaddi* is essentially a history of progressive standardization, formalization and structured administration with the driving force behind this history being the Olympic standard of uniform, uncontested, international rules of play. Thus, as cricket became decolonized, *kabaddi* was subject to the mechanics of a complex process of technical colonization in so far as what happened over the course of the 32-year period between 1921 and 1953 was a strategic elimination of the game's multiplex, vernacular forms and their replacement by a national standard that could be held up as pan-Indian and also – in theory at least – be easily exported to other countries. The reason why Bhalla suggests that the 1953 'kabaddi only' ruling is significant is that it made the verbal expression of regional differences impossible, and these verbal expressions of difference were, in all probability, all that remained of more complex variations in techniques, styles and rules that had been standardized much earlier in the interest of fair and equal competition. As Gole points out somewhat obliquely, '[i]n the coastal areas of Maharashtra "cants" were said that did not conform to the present definition of cant' (1978a: 7).

Indianization: Breathless Articulations of Culture

Parallel to the technical homogenization and nationalization of the sport, which was designed to make it more modern and give it more universal appeal, there were also efforts made to articulate the nature of its Indianness. One form of this, as pointed out above, was to link it to the past. Another form was to claim for it a kind of rustic, mass popularity. Bhalla makes this point clearly:

> One reason why *kabaddi* is so popular in so many different areas is that it does not require a large field nor does it require expensive and complex equipment. All that is needed is a small plot of land and chalk with which to draw lines on the ground. If there is no chalk, players will often use their clothes and shoes to demarcate the boundary. And not only this, but in large cities at the end of a hard day when workers are tired and downtrodden and cannot find any open space they will simply go and play in the street or even in an unpaved walkway. (1976: 9)

Interestingly, however, there are ways in which the sport has also been linked, on a theoretical and practical level, to the practice of yoga, thus making it not just an Indian sport, but an important feature of Indian culture linked to one of the most distinctive features of Indian civilization. As Chauhan puts it, 'some scholars of sport believe that saints and sages who practiced the art of *pranayama* to enhance their power, gave birth to this sport by engaging in these breath-holding exercises' (1990: 7).

The purported link between yoga and *kabaddi* revolves around breath, the holding of breath and the way in which breath is linked to fitness, agility and strength.[15]

> The most important thing in the game of *kabaddi* is breath and the spoken word. Together, breathing and verbalization is a spiritual process in which one's

intellect is focused, awareness becomes total and one's work is completed to perfection in a single instant. In *kabaddi* one must not breathe while canting. The meaning of this is that one must hold one's breath while playing. In yoga, holding one's breath is called kumbak. By holding one's breath all of one's consciousness is focused. With the energy of this focused consciousness, one is able to accomplish anything. It is for this reason that people hold their breath while lifting heavy things. In the same way, whenever there is a really difficult task that requires concentration, one's breath is held. This is also called dam sadhana. A person who holds his breath while undertaking a task is called damdar. The breath that is held goes to the navel and triggers the great store of energy there which is then directed to the completion of the task at hand. (1982: 62)

It is worth quoting Bhalla at some length on the subject of how breathing, yoga and *kabaddi* are distinctly Indian. After a paragraph on the history of physical education in Greece and Rome; the way in which physical education helped to unite Germany; how the Olympic movement, originating in France, helped promote good international relations; and how physical education in England helped develop good character, high productivity and mutual respect among citizens, he writes the following:

India has maintained its own unique perspective. Here the body is viewed as a means to an end; as an instrument to be used. However, this does not mean that people hold the body itself in contempt or neglect it in any way. People regard it as their duty to make their bodies strong and to develop stamina because this is the only way to fulfill one's dharma. Here the interrelationship between body, spirit and the universal soul is taken for granted and building up the strength of the spirit is an important exercise.

As a result, physical education in India has developed in such a way that along with physical fitness there is both intellectual and spiritual fitness. As a result of this the whole world has benefited from the invaluable gifts of yoga and pranayama. Remarkable kinds of power are generated in the body through the practice of yoga, as is a high degree of tolerance, such that in pranayama when one gains control over the flow of breath one is able to acquire the power of a controlled and focused mind.

Looking at the great good humor, life-long good health and integrative perspective that we Indians have, it is highly appropriate that we play *kabaddi*. And there is no question but that in a few years this sport will become very popular everywhere and will achieve an international reputation. (1979: 16)

Regardless of the extent to which there is a significant cultural association, or 'natural history' of the relationship between yoga and *kabaddi*, there is certainly an important discursive correlation in the history of Indian sport and physical culture. This is not as surprising or far fetched as it might seem at first, but neither is it a function of some kind of inherent, cultural logic hidden in the structure of Hindu culture. It reflects a kind of 'body culture' made possible by the history of Indian nationalism.

At the same time that *kabaddi* began to be popularized and codified in the Satara district of Maharashtra, yoga was being revived, popularized and reinvented as a distinctly Indian form of physical culture. In the first two decades of the twentieth century, the three primary centres where yoga was transformed into a type of physical education were Baroda where Professor Rajratan Manikrao had established a number of gymnasiums for the promotion of Indian gymnastics and martial arts, Bombay where some of the earliest yoga research and therapeutic centres were located, and in the town of Amravati where a small group of 'athletic nationalists' established the Hanuman Vyayam Prasarak Mandal for the development of indigenous games and the promotion of national health.[16] Along with the Vaidya brothers from Amravati, one of the most significant figures in the history of Indian physical education and sport was Swami Kuvalyananda, a disciple of Manikrao. Trained in the martial arts and schooled in the revolutionary climate of Manikrao's gymnasiums, Kuvalyananda committed his life to the promotion and development of yoga physical culture. To this end he built a large research centre for the scientific study of yoga in Lonavala between Pune and Bombay. While engaged in research, however, Kuvalyananda served as the government-appointed chairman of a number of committees on physical education, and from 1938 to 1950 as chairman of the State Board of Physical Education, Bombay. In 1948 he became a member of the Central Advisory Board of Physical Education and Recreation. He was also the main architect of the Government College of Physical Education at Kandavali that was started in 1938. In all of these positions Swami Kuvalyananda promoted indigenous sports and Indian forms of physical training. He successfully integrated yoga as physical education into the school curriculum of the Bombay Presidency (Gharote 1975; Sathe 1975; Wakharkar 1975, 1984).

In other words, from the perspective of Kuvalyananda and a large number of other proponents of indigenous sports and games, yoga was not in the least a mystical, spiritual, metaphysical philosophy, but a kind of synthetic mind-body athletic regimen. In his primary work on the subject entitled simply *Asanas*, Kuvalyananda outlines a 'short' and 'full' course in 'yogic physical culture' with the exact number of each pose stipulated and the length of time to stay in each pose calibrated to fractions of a minute (1933 [1993]: 109-19). Deep breathing and *pranayama* exercises are regulated in much the same way. In this light, the distance – and cognitive dissonance – between yogic breathing and *kabaddi* is dramatically reduced and the comments by Chauhan, Bhalla and Pande make more logical sense.

Kuvalyananda was an outspoken nationalist as were the Vaidya brothers who founded the Hanuman Vyayam Prasarak Mandal (HVPM) in Amravati (Jodh 1983: 123). Shri Ambadas Krishna Vaidya was a follower of the revolutionary Shri Veer Vamanarao Joshi, and, as Jodh writes, he inspired a number of younger revolutionary figures and,

> dedicated his entire life to the cause of physical betterment of the younger generation of which he has become a great pioneer and source of infinite strength. He brought to bear upon the HVPM his vast experience and superb skill

achieved by him in physical exercises, but much more invaluable was that which was his contribution in imparting a scientific and modern aspect to the national system of physical education . . . It was with this view in mind that he started mass drills and exercises maintaining the old spirit and yet giving them such forms as to bring them into consonance with modern conditions. (Jodh 1983: 132)

Although Kuvalyananda started out as a militant revolutionary, once he took up the cause of yoga he became less violent and less militant. Throughout his career he remained staunchly patriotic in his advocacy for the improved health of young men and women, but there is no indication that his patriotism was based on religious or sectarian ideals. The same is true for the Vaidya brothers who advocated reform through gymnastic drills and scientific physical training, and like Kuvalyananda, became, through time, sympathetic to the Gandhian ideals of social reconstruction and political nonviolence and the Nehruvian ideal of rational, scientific, secularism. In many ways, therefore, although Kuvalyananda, the Vaidyas and Buck were motivated by very different values and came onto the national stage through different configurations of history, they were all doing more-or-less the same thing – trying to organize, formalize and regiment physical education and sport in India in order to improve health and build character through modern means.

In 1920 the recently founded HVPM was invited to send a team to perform Indian gymnastics and indigenous games at the second Lingiad in Europe (Vaidya 1951). Like the Olympics upon which it was based, the Lingiad brought together nations from around the world, but instead of sports competition the emphasis was on gymnastics and physical culture demonstrations. The HVPM team was called on to perform Indian gymnastics, of which the primary ones were yoga and a permutation of yoga postures and wrestling grips called *mallkhamb* performed on a 'wrestlers' pillar. Based in part on this experience, and in larger part through their association with the MSSM and its effort to modernize *kabaddi*, the HVPM arranged to send a team to the Berlin Olympics of 1936 to demonstrate various indigenous games. Of these, *kabaddi* was held up as the signature sport of India. It was only after this that *kabaddi* was introduced as a full-fledged sport in the Indian Olympic Games held in Calcutta in 1938. To some extent, then, *kabaddi* became fully Indian – in a symbolic sense – by way of its export to Europe under the auspices of a nationalist organization.[17]

Overall, the history of *kabbadi's* development is presented in two dimensions. On the one hand it is a history of increasing standardization and modernization in explicitly international terms. To the extent that this is what Elias refers to as a civilizing process for which the bases of civility are distinctly European values and European forms of regulation, the standardization of *kabaddi* may be seen as a form of neo-colonization through the imposition of strictly delineated criteria for the control of space, time and body movement (see Eichberg 1998: 100-7; 142-5). On the other hand, however, this same history ascribes to *kabaddi* a kind of innate Indianness. These two histories come together in the Berlin Olympics of 1936 where modern, rule-bound and technically elaborate *kabaddi* is played on an international stage for a global audience because it is thought to be uniquely Indian. In Maharashtra, at about the same time, the modern form of the sport was being retaught to the 'sons of the soil' who had inspired the game's revival in the first place.

In one sense, then, *kabaddi* has been modernized in a similar way and over about the same course of time, that cricket has been modernized in India. The vernacularization of cricket is counterpoised by the translation of *kabaddi* into the official language of international competition. In the case of *kabaddi*, however, this self-directed, self-conscious transnationalization of the sport was motivated by explicitly nationalist forces. Thus, ironically, *kabaddi* became a national sport at the same time that it became less distinctively Indian, whereas India gained international recognition in cricket as the sport itself became more and more distinctively Indian. Wrestling is a different story that can only be alluded to here. As I have written elsewhere, 'India' – more as an imagined community than as a jewel in the Empire's crown – fielded a number of competitors in the World Championship tournament of 1910 in London (Alter, n.d.). Gama, a relatively poor, illiterate Muslim boy from the Central Provinces won the title in a dramatic fight with Zybysko, the much bigger and older reigning champion from Poland. In 1928 Gama defended his title in an earthen pit in the princely state of Patiala. But although Gama became World Champion, wrestling in India remained a largely lower-class, provincial, 'traditional' sport that was manipulated in various ways by aristocrats and middle-class nationalists to make various claims about the nature of Indian manhood and strength. Moreover, the rather haphazard and unregulated World Championships soon gave way to the Olympic standard of freestyle and Greco-Roman grappling in the late 1920s and 1930s. This left Gama with a title he could defend but no longer really claim after about the mid 1940s or so when the Olympics effectively took over the world of sport and helped turn Gama into a somewhat ambiguous, anachronistic, colonized person; a person with great fame, to be sure, but a hero whose ethnicity, along with his class, national and global status, had become increasingly problematic.

Through its early association with the Swadeshi movement, *kabbadi* has often been linked to the politics of nationalism on a number of different levels. As Bhalla points out

> Before independence when people were imprisoned by their infatuation for the depravities of Western civilization there were some people who said that *kabaddi* was a low-class village game. But now that we Indians have cast off the yoke of Westernization and have given birth to a new patriotic spirit this sport is finally receiving the recognition it deserves. It is being looked at in a new light and is finally coming into its own in schools, colleges and universities. (1979: 9)

In light of this anti-Western nationalism, however, what is significant is the expressly regional and sub-regional development of *kabaddi* into a national sport. Although said to be played by everyone everywhere in many different ways, in fact the sport was popularized by small organized groups of middle-class men in the western part of Maharashtra, specifically in Pune, Bombay and Satara.[18] In any case, what was going on from the early 1920s through 1950 was in all probability as much an articulation of regionalism as it was an expression of nationalism. Soon after independence however, the popularity of the sport became viewed as dependent on its delocalization as reflected in the need at first for a Bombay federation and then an all India national federation. The degree of conflict over the 'rules' of play was in all likelihood a conflict over articulations of regional identity manifest in the word or words that were designated as legal or fair to cant. In effect, a team could be disqualified for speaking its own language. I would suggest that these regional differences were strong enough to prohibit the final standardization of play until after independence and the formal unification of the new Republic.

From independence in 1947 until about 1952 the critical question with regard to *kabaddi* was the standardization of rules. Subsequently what has become more of an issue is the extent of the game's popularity in relation to other sports and an increasing technicalization, sophistication and disciplinary articulation in how the sport should be played. Both of these dimensions are reflected in the publication of books that not only spell out the rules, but stipulate a range of training methods, strategies, coaching guidelines, refereeing techniques and physical exercises that can be done to develop the right kind of fitness for the best possible performance. As one might guess, a significant number of these books on *kabaddi* are published in Maharashtra, some in Marathi (Dabholakara 1980; Gandhe 1962; Kandhe 1987) but a number in Hindi and English as well (Bapat 1966). Many are published by the Maharashtra State Kabaddi Association (MSKA) (Bapat 1968; Ghurye 1971; Gole 1978a, 1978b; MSKA 1972, 1977). Despite their regional basis, however, these publications are not significantly different from a number of others that are published independently (Chauhan 1990; Pande 1982) or under other auspices, most notably the Sports Authority of India in New Delhi (de Mellow 1987) and the National Institute of Sports in Patiala (Rao 1971).

Popularity as such is a very difficult thing to gauge, particularly in the case of a sport such as *kabaddi* where state and national federations have a vested interest in claiming that large numbers of people enjoy playing the game and larger numbers enjoy watching it. According to a publication by the Sports Authority of India, there are 'thousands of *kabaddi* clubs all over India and tournaments are held at village, town, school, university and state levels' (de Mellow 1987: 3.4). As with many other sports, various public sector units of the government such as the railway and post and telegraph have *kabaddi* associations that are affiliated to the AIKF (Arlott 1975: 556). In 1988 a regional tournament was sponsored in which a large number of local teams participated and the number of spectators on average seemed to be counted in the hundreds. Regardless of its institutionalized prevalence throughout the country, it is clearly apparent, from even a cursory ethnographic perspective, that *kabaddi* is not in the least bit as popular as cricket. And here I must briefly digress.

Traveling between Pune, Delhi and Dehra Dun in the summer of 1998 I watched cricket games being played everywhere and anywhere on patches of open and not-so-open ground by boys and young men of almost any age. Beneath the level of international test cricket, globally televised one-day matches and the stardom of India's international champions, the game has been popularized and vernacularized in the full sense of these terms, being played, it would almost seem, by anyone and everyone who is male everywhere and anywhere. Or perhaps it would be more accurate to say that cricket is being played by too many people in too many places too much of the time. I made note of a number of instances where groups in the wealthier areas of South Delhi have organized themselves to prohibit young boys from playing cricket in neighbourhood parks, in the interest of controlling crowds, maintaining lawns and preserving space for less plebeian activities. On the roadside between Bombay and Pune, not far from Satara, I must have counted 30 games in progress, and between Delhi and Dehra Dun in the midst of one of the hottest Junes on record – and directly under the noonday sun – I counted no less than twenty games being played in school yards and public parks, on roadways, fields, old basketball courts and canal banks and in almost any one of the empty 'unused' spaces marked off by the construction of urban, semi-urban, peri-urban and rural buildings and roads.

Walking away from the Jumma Masjid in Old Delhi toward the Red Fort on a Sunday afternoon there were at least ten games in progress on the expansive, dusty lawns alongside the dry fountains between the fish market to the south and the ready-made clothes market to the north. These games, as with most others I watched, were vigorous, highly contentious affairs. No pads of any kind were worn, bats were old and often taped together, stumps were replaced by a pile of bricks, the pitch was bumpy and therefore very dangerous, balls were often bowled at full velocity and the batting technique of choice was unambiguously aggressive as though the only thing that mattered was the furthest possible boundary – the front foot *chaka* of every boy's dream. Many of the games I watched, even for a few minutes, contained episodes of violence: a slap to the head by a fellow teammate for being bowled, a hard kick to the backside to resolve a dispute over the length of an over and an almost constant string of loud, passionate, abusive language verging on the border between anger, frustration and elation.

If, as Appadurai points out, the Victorian ethic of the game has been stripped away at the highest level of play, and if, as Nandy argues, the game has taken root in India – again at the highest level of play – because of a congruence between the mythic structure of sport and Indian national consciousness, then what I saw being played by the working-class boys on the Masjid lawn may be understood as the cultural distillate of a long history of indigenization that is intimately concerned with class and status, civility and civilization.

But where cricket has not only been decolonized on the pitches of Bombay, Calcutta and Madras, but also 'radically subalternated' in the back streets of Pune and on the lawns of the Jumma Masjid, and thereby turned into a game with tremendous mass appeal, it has been many many years since I have seen a game of *kabaddi* being played in a similar way – simply for recreation. This is not to say that *kabaddi* is unpopular, but simply to point out that its popularity has been formalized, normalized and institutionalized, whereas cricket has not only been vernacularized but vulgarized to the extent that it is played 'against the rules' in much the way the authors who write about *kabaddi* imagine *kabaddi* to have been played 'by strong and healthy folk' (Gole 1978a: 8) and 'sons of the Indian soil' (Bhalla 1979: 9) before it was 'civilized' in the early part of this century.

Technical Language and the Grammar of Nationalism

Following the standardization of rules, the progressive civilization of *kabaddi* up to the present is manifest in the articulation of technical details, the delineation of specific skills and techniques for gaining a competitive edge, and fairly detailed discussions about the kind of physical fitness required for play and derived from playing. Although anthropologists sometimes criticize sports sociologists and sport historians for dwelling simply on these 'mechanical' features, it is important to look at the way in which apparently insignificant details – as well as seemingly meaningless, rhetorical generalizations – reveal significant cultural patterns and historical trends both in the sport and the social context within which the sport is played. For example, from an anthropological perspective the exact length, breadth, and width of a *kabaddi* field is irrelevant. So are the rules *per se*. So is the precise subdivision of the field into demarcated areas where various rules apply. What is significant is what, if anything, these measurements, rules, and subdivisions mean. What is most significant is the question of why, how and for whom the stipulation of these measurements, rules and subdivisions has become an important end in and of itself.

Obviously the mechanical details of the sport are important for those who play, but I would suggest that in light of the sport's modern, relatively short, deregionalized, out-of-the-village-into-the-city history, the intense concern with detail, precision and sophistication is very important. All the more so because almost every book that contains page after page of detail begins by saying something to the effect that it 'is a simple game that requires very little space and no equipment to speak of' (Chauhan 1990: 4; see also de Mellow 1987: 3.4; Reddy 1974: 3) and that it is, therefore, 'most suitable for the rural youth of both developed and developing countries' (Rajagopalacharya 1978: 1).

Details are such that it is difficult to give a cultural account of them without being ponderous and pedantic. Nevertheless, some sense of regimentation and exactitude can be had by looking simply at the volume of writing on certain subjects. For instance, most books define between 15 and 20 official terms such as the 'cant' which is, technically, 'the repetition of the word *kabaddi* in a loud clear voice spoken in one single breath' (Bhalla 1979: 55, see also Pande 1982: 54-7, Reddy 1974: 7-9, YMCA 1991: 304). 'Safely' is also a technical adverb meaning that 'when a raider touches (returns to) his own court, with any part of his body, without violating any rules, after crossing the chalk line he is said to have reached his court safely' (de Mellow 1987: 3.5). Although the term 'safely' does not appear on the list given in the updated and standardized twenty-third edition of Buck's Rules published by the YMCA, the term 'touch' does. It means 'contact by a raider or anti with clothing, shoes, or any other outfits on any part of their bodies' (1991: 304). Either Hindi or English terms are used, but the technical definition is almost always exactly the same. Pande lists eleven essential items for play: a stop watch, record book, paper, pad, pencil and pen, whistle, first-aid kit, water, lime or chalk along with a rope and tape measure, badges for the officials, a rule book, tables and chairs, and sawdust (1982: 67). For determining the size and shape of the field Pande labels the corners of a rectangle a, b, c, d, and then provides the following formula to calculate the bisecting length ac: ab = cd = 13 meters, bc = ad = 10 meters, ac squared equals ab squared plus bc squared, therefore ac = the square root of ab squared plus bc squared, which is the square root of 12.5 m squared plus 10 squared. This equals the square root of 156.25 plus 100, which is the square root of 256.25 which is 16.008 meters which can be rounded off to 16 (1982: 67). Measuring the distance of this bisecting line ensures that the field will form a perfect rectangle with 90 degree corner angles. Similar calculations are given by Bhalla who has a long paragraph describing the shape, construction and measurements of the sitting blocks at the two ends of the field where reserve players are seated (1979: 21-4). Consider also that players must wear a clearly visible number on both their back and front. Each number must be four inches in length. A player must, at a minimum, wear a sleeveless undershirt and shorts with either a *langot* or *janghia* underneath. Players must also keep their nails closely clipped (YMCA 1991: 308).

One could argue that rules, regulations and measurements have to be exact and exactly stipulated. However, the concern for detail seems to carry over into areas where what is more at issue is the aesthetic sense of comprehensiveness, and the image of the sport generated out of that sense, than a need for precision *per se*. What I mean is suggested by the following guidelines given by Pande for the selection and preparation of the field.

In the selection of a place to play *kabaddi* it is important to think carefully to ensure that the earth is of good quality and that there is plenty of space for spectators. One should never select a site where there are sticks and stones, thorns and branches or where the ground is all uneven. The earth should be soft, fine textured and level. In order to ensure that the earth is of the right texture one should add saw dust, a little fine-grained sand and some soil brought in from elsewhere. If you want to ensure the very best conditions you should choose a place where there is soft green grass . . . (1982: 64)

Similarly, although the need for training and physical fitness in preparation for the sport is undeniable, what is noteworthy in this regard is the degree to which the requisite skills of the game get broken down into discrete facets and component parts for which a single type of exercise is then prescribed for development. Pande, for instance, points out that since *kabaddi* requires quick reflexes it is imperative that *kabaddi* players do 'exercises that promote excellent neuromuscular coordination'. He then provides a list of eight categories of exercise including rope jumping, deep-knee bends done while balancing on the balls of one's feet, standard *dands* and *bethaks*, as well as twisting, jumping and bending routines (1982: 68).[19] Others, for obvious reasons, suggest yoga postures and, more significantly, yoga breathing exercise. Although some of these exercises are distinctively Indian, they are incorporated into a training regimen that is explicitly 'modern and scientific' (Reddy 1974; Rao 1971).

Aside from rules and regulations, most books on *kabaddi* comprise comparatively long sections that deal with techniques and skill – various kinds of attack, various kinds of defensive strategy, body positions that afford the longest reach and quickest mode of escape, holds, traps, lifts, jumps, twists, turns and kicks (Bhalla 1979: 25-56; Chauhan 1990: 21-38; Pande 68-78). Chauhan describes the 'toe touch', one of the game's signature moves, as follows:

In *kabaddi* this is a great move whereby a raider can win points for his team. As the name of the move would suggest, it is executed when the raider touches one of the anti-raiders with his foot. When the raider is close enough to an anti-raider he extends his leg outward making sure to fully 'open up' the hip, knee and ankle joints. While doing this he crouches down on his other leg with his knee bent and pointing out at right angles. He should keep his hands in front so that if an anti-raider attacks he will be able to defend himself (1990: 22).

Along these lines, Reddy and Rao's books are by far the most detailed with fifteen defensive holds described by the former, along with a training programme of general exercises broken down into twenty separate points (1974: 10-31; 48-9), and ten offensive moves described by the later along with a chapter on tactics and strategy (1971: 10-25; 41-50).

It is noteworthy that in the literature on *kabaddi* there is a proliferation of detail but not a great deal of rhetoric about the virtue of the sport *per se*, apart from what is spelled out in the sections on history and the games association with Indian nationalism. There are some references that convey a sense of the game's 'attributes', such as the following:

Kabaddi identifies with agility, co-ordination of the muscles, lung-power, speedy reflexes, intelligence and presence of mind. It is a good barometer for individual fitness. From bellying through the lines of determined defenders to carefully calibrated evasive movements, the *kabaddi* player must never lose his competitive edge, high morale or the fire and flash that stimulates his desire to excel. He plays with volcanic intensity, marked by bursts of speed, which take him past a line of defenders, like of scythe of flame! (de Mellow 1987: 3.3)

However noteworthy, these attributes remain tied firmly to the field of play and the context of competition and are not translated out of that context. Most significantly, particularly in sharp contrast with the hyperbolic rhetoric in the literature on Indian wrestling, the attributes of *kabaddi* are not embodied. One must have good character to play *kabaddi*, but the sport of *kabaddi*, unlike Indian wrestling, is not regarded as a medium through which one can develop the attributes of good Indianness, even though Gole does quote Sant Tukaram as saying that in the time of Lord Krishna the game of *ha ma ma* or *hombri*, as *kabaddi* was known, 'had a great bearing on one's actions in everyday life' (in Gole 1978a: 6). In a short section entitled 'the character of a *kabaddi* player' Pande writes:

Character and style are one. Every sport has its own style and will attract those athletes who share the character of that style. To manifest that style in his character an athlete must have confidence, natural ability and strength. He must train to develop these attributes as far as possible. Thus, a *kabaddi* player can only be someone who knows himself well and who has trained and studied hard. (1982: 72-3)

On one level, there is an obvious reason why *kabaddi* skills are not embodied as individual virtues that adhere to the person of the player. *Kabaddi* is, in essence, a team sport. Moreover it is precisely the contained contrast between team work and individual skill within the game that is regarded by many as distinctive and noteworthy. As de Mellow writes:

Fifty-six lively limbs, controlled by steel-trap minds, fighting a battle of wits. Hands reaching out to catch, hold or to encircle. This is a drama of movement, swiftly swaying, dancing and shuffling. It is the single brilliant raider, defying a whole team that is out to get him! Can the individual dupe the lot of them, and dazzle them with his prowess, speed and imaginative forays? He can, and frequently does so, in this fascinating game, which caters both for individual genius, group cohesion, and *esprit de corps*. (1987: 3.10)

It is the group cohesion and esprit de corps dimension of the game – the brilliant individual interlocked with the lively limbs and steel-trap minds of his or her team mates – that has made *kabaddi* one of the most popular forms of purposeful recreation among the local-level units of the Rashtriya Swayamsevak Sangh (RSS), a militant nationalist organization (Basu, Datta, Sarkar, Sarkar and Sen 1993: 18; see also Andersen and Damle, 1987). Since the 1920s when the RSS was founded to promote a sense of pride and purpose among Hindu youth, the game has been used as a primary means by which to promote team work and a sense of common purpose.[20] Clearly the 'innate' Indianness of the game is important here insofar as it appeals to the anti-Western ideology of the RSS. As Bhalla writes in his book published by a press sympathetic to the RSS, if not explicitly for the group as such, 'Kabaddi is India's national sport. Through it one can see the splendor of the nation' (1979: 7). More significant than this cultural component, however, is the way in which the game has been formalized so as to require a great deal of structured coordination on the part of players, and organization on the part of those who are officiating.

One of the most distinctive features of the RSS, clearly apparent in the name of its official organ, *The Organizer*, is the way in which the Sangh sees its primary role as being one of coordinating and organizing the Hindu youth of India into a powerful group with a single-minded purpose (Malkani 1980). In this regard, as I have written elsewhere, it is interesting to note that the RSS has had a rather ambivalent relationship with wrestling gymnasiums where Indianness is very clearly defined, but structured organization is often lacking or else manifest in the problematic form of a *guru-chela* (master-disciple) relationship where loyalties are hierarchically defined one to one rather than horizontally defined one with another (Alter 1994). Although for the RSS Indianness is synonymous with the culture of Hinduism, the culture of Hinduism which the organization promotes is very much the product of its imagination and its selective appropriation and invention of tradition. Consequently, following the seemingly jingoistic sentiment expressed in the sentence quoted above, Bhalla veers away from the content of culture as such to the broader structure of international representation:

> One is sure to be able to see this game being played in one form or another in all parts of the country. It is also on its way toward gaining international recognition. There is even a movement afoot to have it included as a sport in the Asian Games. (1979: 7)

As far as I am able to tell, even within the assertively masculine, militantly pro-Hindu rhetoric of the RSS, the primary link between nationalism and *kabaddi* is on the level of formal standardization, structured organization and official recognition. Although there are obviously differences in the way in which the game gets used to articulate the ideology of various groups at various times – local Maharashtrian regionalism, pan-Hindu solidarity, unity-in-diversity on a national scale, and Swadeshik self-reliance – the modern re-structuration of the game is what has made it available for articulation. Thus, what makes it Indian is not so much its past – where, if anything, it is provincially local – as the history of its modernization and the extent to which it has been elaborated as a modern, international sport. Almost all of the authors I have read point out, as de Mellow writing for the Sports Authority of India does, that *kabaddi* is now played in 'Nepal, Bangladesh, Sri Lanka, Japan, Thailand, Pakistan and Malaysia', where it is known by various names (1987: 3.10; see also Rao 1971: 4). Arlott claims that it is played in China as well (1975: 556) and Chauhan says simply that 'at the present time it is popular throughout Asia' (1990: 7). Ever since the HVPM demonstrated the sport at the Berlin Olympics there has been a concerted effort by the AIKF to 'international-ize' the sport by demonstrating it in various venues, most notably at the Asian games. Consequently, the national character of the game and its inherent Indianness is regarded as something that does not need to be explained or, much less, protected and defended as a unique facet of culture, but rather as something that can and should be freely exported on the open market of modern 'Olympic Standard' sports. Once popularized outside the country the game no longer remains an inherently Indian form of recreation, but becomes a sport of Indian origin about which the nation as a whole in South Asia, and individual Indians wherever they may be, can and should be justifiably proud. There is no need for the style of play to be characterized as distinctively Indian, as has been the case for decolonized cricket, or for the earth upon which the game is played to be Indian earth per se, as is clearly the case for the earth of wrestling pits. The game becomes more Indian as more and more foreigners learn to play and enjoy it.

Even with regard to the association between *kabaddi* and yoga, the emphasis is on pan-Asian internationalism as much as on nationalism, and on the 'origin' of tradition rather than on the substance of 'traditional' culture and its exclusive ownership. For example, writing about *pranayama*, the 'breath of life', and the structure of the five elements as this pentatic configuration defines the complex, integrated whole underlaying the indigenous games and martial arts of India, de Mellow makes the follow-ing observation which seems to invoke the mystical timelessness and harmonic holism of yogic spiritualism.

> Man can do nothing so long as he does not appreciate the visible and invisible effects of this energy or this breath, which embraces both himself and the universe. Everything is united – the moral order and the natural order, the natural and the supernatural. (1987: 2.6)

Writing just prior to this, however, he briefly explains the theory behind Chinese *t'ai chi* before making the following statement, which is expressly international.

> This sums up the probable origin of what one can call the 'Way of Breathing' and of 'Empty Hands', which is incorporated into Tae-Kwan-Do, Karate, Judo and Sumo. In India we call it pranayama or breathing control. There is little doubt that these techniques were spread all over the Far East by Buddhist pilgrims from India. (1987:2.6)

It must be noted, and underscored, that it only became possible for yogic pranayama to be construed as an elementary form of all martial arts in Asia once yoga itself had been transformed into a 'scientific' type of physical fitness training in the first quarter of this century by Rajratan Manikrao, Swami Kuvalyananda, Sri Ambadas Krishna Vaidya and Dr Kokardekar of the HVPM who sponsored a demonstration of yoga at the World Pedagogic Congress that was held in Berlin in conjunction with the eleventh Olympic Games (Jodh 1983: 124). In this sense, the yoga of tradition is, in fact, the yoga of modernity, thus making it structurally compatible with the foreignness of India's international, national sport.

Conclusion: It's Just Not Cricket

In my previous work on Indian wrestling I was struck by the extent to which the Indianness of the sport is articulated in minute detail in the popular literature on the subject. Regional differences in style and terminology are thought of as insignificant in relation to the broad cultural traits regarding diet, exercise and technique that are said to be universal throughout the country. I was also struck by the fact that although Indian wrestling is not significantly different from Olympic freestyle, there has clearly been more of an effort to distinguish Indian wrestling from international wrestling than to find common ground between them.[21] Moreover, in the literature on Indian wrestling there have been some, but relatively few, attempts made to publicize and promote the international rules of the sport in India. There have been no attempts as far as I know to popularize Indian wrestling outside of India. Indeed the very idea sounds oxymoronic. Although there are detailed descriptions of moves and counter moves in some of the literature, on the whole most of what is written has to do with the uniquely Indian character of the wrestler as a distinctive category of person.

I must also confess that in reading the literature on wrestling and listening to wrestlers talk about the country's decay, that I was somewhat sympathetic to the view expressed by many that cricket in particular – but also hockey and football – has corrupted the youth of India by enslaving them to a colonial sport that may well not be quintessentially English and affectedly elite anymore, but still does not promote the right kind of ethics, does not make the embodiment of important masculine virtues possible, and does not allow for the development of strong, healthy character. Yet despite my anti-colonial sympathies – and along with my wrestling compatriots – I was able to watch cricket matches being played in almost every park, and unable to help but notice that it fills half the sports page of every Indian daily, has numerous magazines devoted to it and is broadcast almost every day on radio and television. I was sympathetic to the critical view of nationalist wrestlers, but it took considerable effort to locate wrestling gymnasiums and wrestling tournaments. While wrestling rhetoric is very clearly defined and whereas its practice is clearly articulated, it is very difficult to link either the rhetoric or practice to any institutionalized history of nationalism in India or to any organized group with an agenda for systematic decolonization. Wrestling's nationalism is visceral, emotional and almost wholly embodied, and for this reason I have referred to it as somatic nationalism.

Cricket has been decolonized in India, and may be said to stand in opposition to the English history of the sport, but the nature of its opposition is categorically different from that of Indian wrestling. The decolonization of cricket has been both covert and subtle to the extent that it is very difficult to discern any clearly articulated nationalist rhetoric, any formalized anti-colonial agenda, or any implication of the body and body discipline as such in the regionalization of this international sport.

In many respects, therefore, the case of *kabaddi* provides an answer to – or simply a more subtle perspective on – the cultural conundrums and historical contradictions that are suggested by the sharp contrast between 'Indian' wrestling and 'English' cricket, between the East and the West, between indigenous games, modern sports and the breathless articulation of various kinds of nationalism. *Kabaddi* clearly illustrates the way in which nationalism emerges out of a transnational context of cultural intertextuality where Indianness and foreignness are not all that different and where nationalism takes its clearest shape not in the imagination of inward looking men but in a global context of mixed-up modernities. I will simply end by translating one of the *kabaddi* cants that may well have been invented during the heyday of the Swadeshi movement: *Hindustan, bara Maidan/Hindustani bare Shaitan.* India is a big playing field/Indians are wily characters. Or perhaps I should close with a vernacular intervention by explaining what was often done in the games I used to play while growing up. With the flat of your hand slap your lips, or stick your thumb into your mouth, in mid-cant, while loudly intoning the sound 'gup' thus 'swallowing' the word *kabaddi*, ending the cant, and stopping your breath all together. Then your full power is unleashed, but no one can really tell if you are breathing. In any case there are no verbal clues of origin or linguistic barriers to globalization . . . but that just wouldn't be cricket.

Notes

1. The relationship between cricket as a comparatively elitist, foreign sport and wrestling as an indigenous sport of the masses, and the fact that wrestling's common, earthy character is often juxtaposed to the big-business of cricket is similar to the relationship between wrestling and football in Turkey (Stokes 1996) and indigenous polo and official polo in Pakistan (Parkes 1996).

2. The governmental administration of sport in India is too complex an issue to go into in detail here. Kamlesh, Chelladurai and Nair provide a concise, up to date discussion of national sports policy in India (1996: 212-40). In 1950 the government of India established a Central Advisory Board of Physical Education and Recreation. Subsequently,

the All-India Council of Sports was established in 1954, and then a separate Ministry of Sports was established in 1982 within the larger framework of the Ministry of Human Resource Development. Thereafter, in conjunction with plans for India's hosting the Asian Games in 1982, the Sports Authority of India was established in 1984 'as the apex body for all sport in India' (1996: 215). However, most sports, with the notable exception of cricket, are promoted, organized and administered through national associations or federations that function primarily on the state, district and local level. All of these must be affiliated with the Indian Olympic Association, which is responsible for the promotion of amateur athletics and sports. Most of the national associations in various parts of the country receive grants from the central government for training, coaching and the organization of competitions, so although the administrative network is rather loose, the financial and political links are often very tight (1996: 215-16).

3. *Kabaddi* is officially recognized as a national sport of India by the Sports Authority of India. To the best of my knowledge, however, this does not entitle either state or national federations to any special benefits from the government. Although *Kho Kho* is also a national sport, in a Sports Authority of India publication *kabaddi* alone is delineated as 'all Indian' whereas *Kho Kho* is described as a Maharashtrian sport (de Mellow 1987: 4.1).

4. It is important in this regard that there is a Wrestling Federation of India which administers the international freestyle and Greco-Roman form of the sport as well as an Indian Style Wrestling Federation. The fact that a formal distinction is made between the two, despite the fact that athletes freely compete in both styles, signifies the symbolic significance of the Indianness of Indian wrestling, as well as the political desire of Indian wrestlers to define their sport as different from wrestling's international form. This is exactly the opposite of *kabaddi*.

5. The technical term is clearly 'cant'. However, in some English language sources the term is spelled chant (de Mellow 1987). In all Hindi language sources I have seen the transliterated form of the term used is 'kant'. In Arlott's encyclopedia the term is cant and it would seem that the dictionary definition of this noun, being a repetition of stock words in a sing-song voice, would be most appropriate to the nature of the game (1975: 554). The adjective form of the noun is canting.

6. This is true also for most if not all of the other various regional, linguistic variations of the game such as *hu tu tu* and *chedu gudu*.

7. Ram is one of the most important deities in the Hindu pantheon. In the Ramayana, an extremely popular epic poem, Lakshman is Ram's younger brother and Janki their mother. Hanuman is one of the most popular deities in the Hindu pantheon and plays an important role in the Ramayana as a devotee of Ram and a general in his army. The sounds 'hu tu tu' in fact constitute the name of the game as it is known

in Maharashtra.

8. In his encyclopaedia of *World Sports and Games* Arlott claims that there was an earlier effort in 1885, but I have found no other references to corroborate this (1975: 556).

9. A loose translation of this organization's title would be 'Victorious India Sports Club'. Although I have not been able to find documentary evidence, it would be safe to assume that the Hind Vijay Gymkhana was influenced by, if not under the supervision of, Professor Rajratan Manikrao of Baroda, a well-known physical culturist and political revolutionary.

10. Gray, Noehren and Buck all subscribed to a view that was common at the time regarding the condition of health among young Indian men. The following statement by Buck is typical. After comparing Madras, with its schools, colleges and universities, favourably to Boston, he writes

[B]ut with teachings of centuries back to the effect that all physical labour is degrading, India's boys grow up enjoying the very minimum of physical exertion. There is none of the healthy 'hardy boy' life which we know in America, and as a result students come to us with constitutions and habits which would cause grave anxiety if the same conditions prevailed among our student bodies at home. (In David 1992: 167-8.)

The motivation for promoting physical education, therefore, was to improve the constitutions and reform the bad habits of young Indian men.

11. In 1913 Gray was made full-time Physical Director. Along with his work for the YMCA, he also responded to a request from the government of India to help promote physical education throughout the country. Up until this time physical training had been conducted within the framework of military drill, but the value of Gray's American technique was in its scientific form and broad-based educational potential. In order to establish a school for training teachers of physical education and hygiene, who would subsequently become physical educators to serve in all of the various states, the government gave a grant of Rs 160,000 to the YMCA.

12. In 1923 the college became the government's official training and certification centre. By 1925 over 146 qualified physical directors had graduated.

13. Buck's rules for playing *kabaddi* were similar but not identical to the rules established by the Deccan Gymkhana and the MSSM. Specifically, as Gole points out, the team of seven and "lobby" did not exist, the length and breadth of the court was larger and the scissor leg hold was not allowed (1978a: 12). Bhalla claims that in district level competitions and in tournaments organized by various provinces, the MSSM rules were followed whereas in national competitions Buck's Olympic Standard was the rule (1979: 15-16). However, Bhalla goes on

to point out that persistent ambiguity remained, and that up until 1950 'the game was played in many different ways and that the rules had to be amended on a regular basis' (1979: 16). Gole writes that 'every province played according to their own rules and there was no compulsion to play by Bucks rules' (1978a: 12).

14. More could be said on the subject, but the neutralization of gender as a criterion for nationalism is reflected in Chauhan's single list of winners of the Arjun Award, a medal and prize money given to individual athletes by the central government under the auspices of the Sports Authority of India. For the years 1972 through 1989 seven medals were given out in *kabaddi*, four to women and three to men. When listing the country's most well known players from Uttar Pradesh, the names of Ms Sunita and Ms Suman Chaudhuri are given along with the names of four men by the name of Singh (1990: 38-9). Bhalla provides a list of men's and women's national championship winners from 1938 through 1979 showing that the women of Maharashtra have won every year from 1955 through 1979 except in 1975 when they were defeated by the women's team from West Bengal (1979: 119).

15. It is noteworthy that Reddy, writing under the auspices of the YMCA, and Rao, writing for the National Institute of Sport, make the claim that breath holding was a 'mechanical' technique that was introduced in order to effectively put a time limit on each raid (1974: 1; 1971: 3). Neither author makes the association with yoga.

16. Physical education and physical culture are, of course, modern disciplines based on modern distinctions between work and leisure on the one hand and pleasure and health on the other, among other things. Even so, there are a few studies of so-called traditional forms of Indian physical culture wherein various forms of recreation, self-discipline and martial training are interpreted from the perspective of contemporary physical education (Deshpande 1992; Rajagopalan, 1962).

17. It is interesting to note that it was also at approximately this time that the leaders of the MSSM and also Justice Puranik of the National Council of Physical Education and Recreation formed a group called the Akhil Bharati Sharirik Shikshan Maha Mandal that was responsible for the promotion of indigenous games and physical culture. Ironically, given *kabaddi's* rural pedigree, the urban-based MSSM apparently initiated a project in the 1930s to 'popularize the game in villages' (Gole 1978a: 11).

18. In this part of the country the game was called *hu tu tu* and it was only after the formation of the All India Kabaddi Federation in 1952 that the North Indian term *kabaddi* was made official. The AIKF in fact grew out of the Bombay Provincial Kabaddi Federation that was established in 1945 in order to 'to safeguard the interests of the various hu tu tu clubs and to foster the spirit of unity and development of the game' (Gole 1978a: 14). An earlier attempt had been made to achieve the same end by the Bombay Sharirik Shiksha Mandal in 1935, how-

ever there was apparently too much disagreement and conflict between the clubs to enable the federation to function. Nevertheless, as Gole points out, a good deal of credit for the sport's popularization should go to regional Bombay clubs such as the Rashtriya Hu tu tu Sangh, the Sri Krishna Hu tu tu Sangh, Shri Hanuman Sangh, and the Shivaji Sangh as well as various others (Gole 1978a: 14). Unfortunately not much information is available on these *sanghs* apart from the fact that they played *kabaddi* against one another and often got into conflict over the rules of play.

19. *Dands* are a kind of jackknifing push-up whereas *bethaks* are deep-knee bends.

20. Although *kabaddi* is clearly one of the most popular games played by *shakhas*, it is important to note that in two of three training manuals on physical education and gymnastic drill training the game is only mentioned in the context of a long list of other games – 14 'fighting' games, 14 games where only one person wins, 14 'team' games and 14 'stick' games – that are designed to be fun and entertaining but also 'develop competitiveness, coordination, [and] team work' (RSS, vs1914a: 34; vs1914b; vs1901). Based on their names, a number of these games would appear to be indigenous – *chor sipahi, sarap nidra, ram/ravana, urdti machli* – but an equal number are played with balls, ropes, stick, handkerchiefs and rings that are given only descriptive titles – rope pull, ball throw, long jump – and are of ambiguous origin. Counting the gymnastic routines and mass drill exercises along with such games as 'dodge ball', 'foot ball' and 'musical chairs' where the names appear in English, a significant number of the RSS training activities are derived from foreign sources. It is interesting to note, however, that although a diagram of the 'official' *kabaddi* playing field is given in the 'first year' manual, there is also mention of a 'folk' variation called 'horse kabaddi' as one of the 14 team games. Each team designates one player as the horse. The horse is 'locked up' in the enemy camp and the object is to try to free the horse in a single breath without being captured (RSS, vs1914: 76).

21. This is most clearly evidenced by the fact that there are separate federations in India for international-style wrestling and Indian-style wrestling. See note 4.

References

Alter, Joseph S. (1992), *The Wrestler's Body: Identity and Ideology in North India*, Berkeley and Los Angeles: University of California Press.

— (1993), 'The Body of One Color: Indian Wrestling, the Indian State and Utopian Somatics', *Cultural Anthropology* 8(1): 49-72.

— (1994), 'Somatic Nationalism: Indian Wrestling and Militant Hinduism', *Modern Asian Studies* 28(3): 557-88.

— (1995), 'The Celibate Wrestler: Sexual Chaos, Embodied Balance and

Competitive Politics in North India', *Contributions to Indian Sociology* (n.s.) 29(1 and 2): 110-31.

— n.d. *Subaltern Somatics: Gama the Great and the Heroic Indian Body*, (manuscript).

Appadurai, Arjun (1995), 'Playing With Modernity: The Decolonization of Indian Cricket', in Carol A. Breckenridge (ed.), *Consuming Modernity: Public Culture in a South Asian World*, Minneapolis and London: University of Minnesota Press, pp. 23-48.

Arlott, John (1975), *The Oxford Companion to World Sports and Games*, London, New York and Toronto: Oxford University Press.

Bale, J. (1994), *Landscapes of Modern Sport*, Leicester: Leicester University Press.

Bale, J. and Sang J. (1996), *Kenyan Running: Movement Culture, Geography and Global Change*, London: Cass.

Bapat, Vinayak Dhundiraj (1966), 'A Psychological Study of the Methods of Measurement and Prediction of Athletic Ability in Kabaddi and Kho Kho', Ph.D. dissertation, University of Bombay.

Basu, Tapan, Pradip Datta, Sumit Karkar, Tanika Sarkar, and Sambuddha Sen (1993), *Khaki Shorts and Saffron Flags*, New Delhi: Orient Longman.

Bernett, H. (1985), *Sportunterrichet an der nationalsozialistischen Schule: der Schulsport an den hoheren Schulen Preussens 1933-1940*, Sankt Augustin: H. Richarz.

— (1978), *Der Judische Sport Im Nationalsozialistischen Deutschland, 1933-1938*, Schorndorf: Hofmann.

Bhalla, Ajay (1979), *Rashtriya Khel Kabaddi* (National Sport Kabaddi), New Delhi: Saruchi Sahitya.

Blecking D. (1987), *Die Geschichte Der Nationalpolnischen Turnorganisation 'Sokol' Im Deutschen Reich, 1884-1939*, Munster: Lit.

Blecking, D. (1991), *Die Slawische Sokolbewegung: Beitrage Zur Geschichte Von Sport Und Nationalismus in Osteuropa*, Dortmund: Forswchungsstelle Ostmitteleuropa.

Brownell, Susan (1995), *Training the Body for China: Sports in the Moral Order of the People's Republic*, Chicago: University of Chicago Press.

Cashman, Richard (1980), *Patrons, Players and the Crowd: The Phenomenon of Indian Cricket*, New Delhi: Orient Longman.

Chauhan, V.S. (1990), *Bharatiya Khel – Kabaddi* (Indian Sport – Kabaddi), Lucknow: Sindhal Agencies.

Dabholakara, Narendra Acyuta (1980), *Kabaddi*, Mumbai: Maharashtra Rajya Sahitya Sanskriti Mandala.

Deshpande, S.H. (1992), *Physical Education in Ancient India*, New Delhi and Varanasi: Bharatiya Vidya Prakashan.

de Mellow, Melville (1987), *Indigenous Games and Martial Arts in India*, New Delhi: Sports Authority of India.

Diawara, Manthia (1990), Englishness and Blackness: Cricket As Discourse on Colonialism, *Callaloo* 13(2).

Dunning, Eric (1986), 'The Dynamics of Modern Sport: Notes on Achievement-Striving and the Social Significance of Sport', in Norbert Elias and Eric Dunning (eds), *Quest for Excitement: Sport and Leisure in the Civilizing Process*, Oxford and New York: Basil Blackwell, pp. 205-23.

Eichberg, Henning (1998), *Body Cultures: Essays on Sport, Space and Identity*, London and New York: Routledge.

Elias, Norbert (1986), 'The Genesis of Sport As a Sociological Problem', in Norbert Elias and Eric Dunning (eds), *Quest for Excitement: Sport and Leisure in the Civilizing Process*, Oxford and New York: Basil Blackwell, pp. 91-125.

Elias, Norbert, and Eric Dunning (1986), *Quest for Excitement: Sport and Leisure in the Civilizing Process*, Oxford and New York: Basil Blackwell.

Gandhe, Srikrishna Viththala (1962), *Hututu*, Nagapura: Hindi Marathi Prakashan.

Gharote, M.L. (1975), 'Swami Kuvalyananda – His Life and Mission', in *Kaivalyadhama: Golden Jubilee Year Souvenir*, 1975, Lonavala: Kaivalyadhama, part 1, chapter 13.

Ghurye, B.P. (1971), *Know the Game Kabaddi*, Bombay: Maharashtra State Kabaddi Association.

Gole, Y.A. (1978a), *Handbook on Kabaddi*, Bombay: Maharashtra State Kabaddi Association.

Gole, Y.A. (1978b), *Kabaddi Referee's Manual*, Bombay: Maharashtra State Kabaddi Association.

Harsha, Ambi (1982), Development of Physical Education in Madras, 1918-1948, Madras: Institute for Development Education, Christian Literature Society.

Jarvie, Grant (1991), *Highland Games: The Making of a Myth*, Edinburgh: Edinburgh University Press.

Jodh, K.G. (1983), *Amravati Cradles the Nationalist Movement*, Amravati: All Indian Languages Literary Conference.

Kamlesh, M.L., P. Chelladurai, and U.S. Nair (1996), 'National Sports Policy in India', in Laurence Chalip, Arthur Johnson, and Lisa Stachura (eds), *National Sports Policies: An International Handbook*, Westport, CT and London: Greenwood Press, pp. 212-40.

Kuvalyananda, Swami (1933), *Asanas*, Lonavala: Kaivalyadhama.

MacAloon, John J. (1981), *This Great Symbol: Pierre De Coubertin and the Origins of the Modern Olympic Games*, Chicago: University of Chicago Press.

MacClancy, Jeremy (1996), 'Nationalism At Play: The Basques of Vizcaya and Athletic Bilbao', in Jeremy MacClacy, (ed.), *Sport, Identity and Ethnicity*, Oxford and Herndon, VA: Berg, pp. 181-99.

— (1996), *Sport, Identity and Ethnicity*, Oxford and Herndon, VA: Berg.

Maharashtra State Kabaddi Association (1972), *Kabaddi in the Context of Other International Games: A Report on the Symposium Organized by the Maharashtra State Kabaddi Association*, Bombay: Maharashtra State Kabaddi Association.

— (1977), *Our National Game: an Informative Folder*, Bombay: Maharashtra State Kabaddi Association.

Malkani, K.R. (1980), *The RSS Story*, New Delhi: Impex India.

Mangan, J.A. (1986), *The Games Ethic and Imperialism*, London: Cass.

Nandy, Ashis. (1989), *The Tao of Cricket: On Games of Destiny and the Destiny of Games*, New York: Viking.

Pande, Lakshmikant (1982), *Bharatiya Khelon Ki Mimunsa* (An Examination of Indian Games), New Delhi: Metropolitan Book Company.

Parkes, Peter (1996), 'Indigenous Polo and the Politics of Regional Identity in Northern Pakistan', in Jeremy MacClancy (ed.), *Sport, Identity and Ethnicity*, Oxford and Herndon, VA: Berg, pp. 43-68.

Rajagopalan, K.A. (1962), *A Brief History of Physical Education in India*, Delhi: Army Publishers.

Rajagopalacharya, T. (1978), 'Forward', in Y.A. Gole, *Handbook on Kabaddi*, Bombay: Maharashtra State Kabaddi Association, pp. 1-4.

Rao, C.V. (1971), *Kabaddi: Native Indian Sport*, Patiala: National Institute of Sports Publication.

Rashtriya Swayamsevak Sangh (vs1901), *Sharirik Shikshakram: Teachers Manual*, Nagpur: Rashtriya Swayamsevak Sangh.

— (vs1914a), *Sharirik Shikshakram: First Year*, Nagpur: Madhav Prakashan.

— (vs1914b), *Sharirik Shikshakram: Third Year*, Nagpur: Madhav Prakashan.

Reddy, B.R. (1974), *Scientific Kabaddi*, Madras: Ramon's Print Press.

Roberts, Michael (1985), 'Ethnicity in Riposte at a Cricket Match: The Past for the Present', *Comparative Studies in Society and History* 27: 401-29.

Sathe, R. V. (1975), 'Swami Kuvalyananda and His Mission', in *Kaivalyadhama: Golden Jubilee Year Souvenir*, 1975, Lonavala: Kaivalyadhama, part 1, chapter 1.

Stoddart, Brian (1988), 'Cricket and Colonialism in the English-speaking Caribbean to 1914: Towards a Cultural Analysis', in J.A. Mangan (ed.), *Pleasure, Profit and Proselytism: British Culture and Sport At Home and Abroad 1700-1914*, London: Cass, pp. 231-57.

Stokes, Martin (1996), 'Strong As a Turk': Power, Performance, and Representation in Turkish Wrestling', in Jeremy MacClancy (ed.), *Sport, Identity and Ethnicity*, Oxford and Herndon, VA: Berg, pp. 21-42.

Stuart, Ossie (1996), 'Players, Workers, Protestors: Social Change and Soccer in Colonial Zimbabwe', in Jeremy MacClancy (ed.), *Sport, Identity and Ethnicity*, Oxford and Herndon, VA: Berg, pp. 167-80.

Sugden, John, and Alan Bairner (1993), *Sport, Sectarianism and Society in a Divided Ireland*, Leicester: Leicester University Press.

Vaidya, A.K. (1951), *We Go to the Lingiad*, Amravati: Hanuman Vyayam Prasarak Mandal.

Wakharkar, D.G. (1969), *Kabaddi*, Bombay: Maharashtra State Kabaddi Association.

— (1975), 'Swami Kuvalyananda – An Architect of Physical Education Movement in Maharashtra', in *Kaivalyadhama: Golden Jubilee Year*

Souvenir, 1975, Lonavala: Kaivalyadhama, Part 1, chapter 12.

— (1984), 'Swami Kuvalyananda – His Contribution to Humanity', in *Swami Kuvalyananda Birth Centenary, 1883-1983*, Lonavala: Kaivalyadhama, pp. 3-8.

Young Mens Christian Association (1991), *Book of Rules of Games and Sports*, New Delhi: National Council of YMCAs of India.

5

Soccer and the Politics of Culture in Western Australia

Philip Moore

Football, it has often been proclaimed, is 'the world game', and while this phrase possesses the ring of a clever marketing slogan, there is much truth to it. No other game is played by as many people, and no other sport has the numbers of spectators that this sport attracts. As a measure of its place in world sport there now exist accounts from every region where the game is played and this literature includes some of the most sophisticated social analyses and interesting interpretations of any sport. Football is indeed the world game and nowadays it has a global academic literature trying to make sense of it (Tomlinson and Whannel 1986; Giulianotti, Bonney and Hepworth 1994; Wagg 1995; Archetti 1997; Armstrong and Giulianotti 1997). Yet as a global sport 'the world game' is not known and experienced merely as some abstract globalized form shared equally and homogeneously by all; rather, what this literature shows is that the game is known and experienced intimately within national and local communities in terms of particular traditions and styles of play.

The world game is not necessarily the culturally dominant sport everywhere it is played. In Australia the game is marginal and is known as soccer, in part because it has since the nineteenth century competed less successfully with two codes of rugby and with Australian rules football, the game that has captured national control of the unmarked name 'football' in Australia. Soccer does have a following in Australia, but it is not sufficiently large to command extensive attention by the media. When soccer appears on television in Australia it is not on the large commercial networks. Rather, it tends to be on state-funded channels, the Special Broadcasting Service (SBS), commonly referred to as 'the ethnic channel', or else late at night on the Australian Broadcasting Corporation (ABC). Emphasizing this marginality, the study of soccer in Australia has thus far been carried out primarily in terms of an ethnic involvement with the game. While it is certainly true that most of the clubs currently playing in Australia have grown out of the social clubs of post-Second World War immigration, the reduction of the game to merely an ethnic sport does not do justice to the social and cultural complexities of the game as it is organized, played and supported by an Australian soccer community. Nor does such a reduction do justice to the history of the ways in which cultural differences have been marked in Australia. A recognition of cultural differences must be woven into any account of the game but identifying such differences as ethnic, to the exclusion of the other sorts of engagements with this sport, comprises one way that Anglo-Australian dominance is written into the sporting history of Australia and so maintains the marginality of the world game.

In this chapter I examine the way soccer has been played, organized and understood in Perth, Western Australia. In recent years there has been much debate about the way that the game in Perth, and indeed across Australia, has been controlled by clubs bearing ethnic names, and in particular with the impact that this control has had in discouraging others from an active interest in the local game. A central dispute within the sport has been whether or not this cultural dimension of the game should be backgrounded, or expunged, so that the sport can be further developed by tapping into a broader audience and market. In seeking to embrace a wider audience, many of those involved in the game have been concerned about losing control of the sport they have nurtured, and the potential loss of an important arena in which many Australians have chosen to celebrate their identities (Jones and Moore 1994). The argument of this paper is that an understanding of the game in Perth is not reducible solely to the play of ethnic differences. There are other important grounds for contestation that are played out through the organization and control of the game.

This account rests easily under the broad rubric of the anthropology of sport. One recent collection uses notions of sport, ethnicity and identity as three of its key orienting concepts (MacClancy 1996). The strength of the accounts in the volume edited by MacClancy comes from the willingness to emphasize local meanings for the orienting concepts. This paper adopts a similar approach and focuses on a series of events in the mid-1980s when an offer of financial support by the Labor state government in Western Australia highlighted differences amongst those in the soccer community. The dispute which emerged around this offer entailed more than just a competition among ethnic clubs. There is, on closer examination, an organizational culture (see Wright 1994) of soccer in Western Australia that has considerable influence in shaping the way the game is organized and the ways in which disputes and disagreements are handled. Soccer in Perth is best understood as a loose federation of leagues, teams and interests that lacks strong central governing body, so that the various interests within the game do not have to give up their own autonomy to a powerful central authority. This organizational culture makes attaining consensus about the direction of soccer in Western Australia (WA) a contentious and difficult matter to realize.

The anthropology that guides this account is founded on a concern with the politics of culture. Ethnicity has been defined as 'the *politics* of culture' (Paine 1984: 212, emphasis added) but this is far too limiting. Ethnicity alone should not be taken as definitive of all cultural politics. All culture is necessarily produced and reproduced under social conditions in which dispute and disagreement are every bit as important as consensus and agreement. More generally, within anthropology there has been for some time a growing recognition that notions of culture, power and history are woven into all social activities (Dirks, Eley and Ortner 1994). Perhaps most clearly articulated as the 'politics of culture' this phrasing provides a clear focus for such a changing perspective (Dirks 1996: 19-20), for where there is power there must also be politics as people seek to exercise it or protect themselves from its exercise. Forceful in framing the anthropological results of such a recognition is Ortner's (1996) notion of 'ethnographic refusal'. Formulated in the first instance in relation to the literature dealing with resistance, the notion has much broader applicability than this one context. Her argument is that in characterizing the activities of some groups as acts of resistance, anthropologists have then entered into an 'ethnographic refusal' to engage with the internal politics of resisting groups. This comprises a misrepresentation of the politics of culture among such peoples, which denies to them the rights to a range of disagreements and disputes within their communities. The result of this is that any group so identified tends to be represented in ethnographic terms that give emphasis to the community as culturally homogeneous rather than internally diverse with its own politics. It is my contention that the characterization of soccer in Australia as an ethnic game comprises an ethnographic refusal to allow for or to treat as serious the range of cultural complexities that are woven into the local organization and understandings of the sport.

The World Game in Australia

Soccer attracts considerable research interest in Australia, particularly from historians and sociologists (see Hughson 1997a, 1997b; O'Hara 1994; Vamplew 1994; Murray 1995; Mosely 1992, 1995; Mosely *et al.* 1997). This has not always been the case. In 1981, when Pearson and McKay (1981) provided an overview of the sociology of sport in Australia soccer was deemed to be insignificant. In Stoddart's historical account of sport in Australia he subsumed soccer within the penultimate chapter, evoking and criticizing the assimilationist sentiments of an earlier time in Australian history by encouraging players to 'play an Australian game, mate' (Stoddart 1986).

The dominant organizing theme running through recent accounts of Australian soccer identify it is an ethnic sport. However, the notion of ethnicity being used, or constructed, is left relatively unexamined. There is little serious engagement with the varieties of theorizing that have made ethnicity such a powerful notion in the social sciences and there is no well-developed historical sensitivity to the local appearance and use of this concept. It is true that Mosely (1995) does locate the notion of ethnicity within a broad historical context, by emphasizing that cultural relationships are never static and that ethnicity is always to be found in the processes of its negotiation. However, rather than embracing these histor-ically unfolding bundles of relationships, and dealing with the notions in use at various times, he finds in the end that it is easier to simply fall back onto an unproblematical use of 'ethnic' to categorize and organize his understandings of cultural differences. His opening sentence, 'Australia has always had a rich history of ethnic diversity' (1995: 1) sees him write a contemporary and popular notion of ethnicity backwards into the past. I do not deny the presence of a variety of forms of cultural difference in the Australian past. However, privileging them as ethnicity in such a timeless and uncontextualized fashion is not particularly helpful. Ethnicity in such accounts is removed from its popular use, transformed into an organizing and analytical theme, and yet not dealt with historically as it has emerged and developed as one way of marking cultural differences. While the word 'ethnic', or any of its many variants, has a long history (Williams 1988: 119-20) it has not always had wide currency in popular discourse. When paired with the notion of sport, ethnicity has come wrongly to encompass almost the entire range of social and cultural possibilities taken as relevant in accounts of soccer in Australia.

In Australia of the 1950s, for example, talk of the cultural differences of the numerous European migrants to Australia was carried out in a differ-ent register. They were, politely, 'new Australians' who were expected to embrace the Australian way of life, to assimilate and become just like everyone else. Evans begins her account of the history of soccer in Collie with a quote from the 1950s Department of Immigration's newsletter, the *New Australians*, noting that 'New Australians are now taking their part in many sports' (in Evans 1997: 51). Less politely, those identified as new Australians have been known in the past by a number of derogatory names, including 'slavs', 'dings' and the generic 'wogs'. With their consid-erable interest in the game, soccer became known occasionally as 'wog ball' to differentiate it from the local football codes. Soccer is still occa-sionally referred to in this way (Vamplew 1994).

By 1972 the federal government accepted that the assimilationist posi-tion of the postwar years had been unsuccessful. It was only then, with the formulation of multiculturalism as the official government position, that ethnicity came to be a more common and accepted way of describing and referring to cultural differences in Australia. There appeared a number of so-called 'hyphenated' Australians, who identified both with the home they had left and the home to which they had come: Greek-Australians, Italian-Australians and so on. And as multiculturalism became entrenched, ethnicity, as 'the primary organizing category of multicultur-alism' (Kapferer 1996: 163) also rose to popular and widespread currency. Ethnicity becomes a significant category in the formulation and discussion of cultural differences because, within multiculturalism, such cultural dif-ferences were to be made less value laden and the maintenance of tradi-tions from other nations was to be supported. The social and cultural harmony of the nation was to be constructed not on cultural similarities

Figure 5 Globalisation: many jerseys in the Perth Glory crowd [Roy Jones]

but rather on the recognition of, and respect for, all of our varied and different cultural heritages. Nation building ceased to feature assimilating newcomers into some existing Australian way of life and came instead to be a project of bringing together a population of disparate cultural groups into a nation built on difference.

Multiculturalism has travelled a rocky road in Australia. From its appearance in the early 1970s through to the present day, it has changed through time as various politicians and governments have reworked and redefined it to serve their understandings of the social, cultural and economic needs of the day. Perhaps most obvious in the way that multiculturalism was reworked was how it became part of the economic platform of the Hawke federal government in the late 1980s (Kelly 1992). Nowadays there are many who see the word and the policy direction it has provided as maintaining social and cultural differences and inhibiting the unification of the nation (Kelly 1998). Governments in Australia have had difficulty in supporting the ideology of the policy while, at the same time, not wanting to be seen to be providing unequal funding or support to particular groups in society merely on the grounds of their cultural differences. This has meant that the maintenance of cultural traditions has been supported as long as no material advantages accrue from those traditions.

Cultural differences have long been a significant part of the game. For some, ethnic identification in the game has been an impediment to the game's acceptance by a broader Australian community. In the late 1970s unsuccessful moves were made in Victoria to remove the ethnic names of the clubs. Ethnic names were seen as giving the game a bad image through the violence amongst various supporters from different European nationalities residing in Australia, and by making others feel unwelcome at matches. A proposal to remove the ethnic identifiers from team names was a 'heated issue debated quite fiercely' (Unikowski in Harrison 1979: 31). A footnote in Unikowski's account of 'migrant organizations in Melbourne' notes that 'The essential importance about this debate is the ethnic importance still attached to the clubs a quarter of a century after their formation and which at least equals the importance attached to sporting achievement' (Unikowski 1978: 49, footnote 1, in Harrison 1979: 31).

The disagreement over whether the ethnic names and organization of the game has helped or hindered the growth of soccer has continued until the present day. Throughout the 1980s and 1990s those interested in soccer in Australia have continued to debate the importance of ethnic club names. Jeff Wells, a sports journalist for the national newspaper, *The Australian,* has been one of the strongest critics of the 'tribalism' of ethnic soccer in this country. In his account of the 1992 Grand Final, Wells framed the contest between the supporters of Adelaide City and Melbourne Croatia as a battle waged between the Italians supporting Adelaide and the Croatians supporting the Melbourne side even as he notes 'as far as I know Italy and Croatia are not at war at the moment.' Sprinkled with words like 'rogue citizenry', 'hooligans' and with references to flashpoints and conflicts around the world, Wells concludes that '[w]hile sport has helped you with racial understanding, we offset our efforts with a football code which encourages our citizens to forget that they are Australians and harass each other with old banal European grudges' (Wells 1992). In 1998 when David Hill resigned his position as head of Soccer Australia to pursue a political career, media accounts noted that he will be remembered as the man who did finally succeed in having the ethnic names changed, even if what constitutes an ethnic name remains unclear. In removing the ethnic names, and substituting them with regional titles, the English have moved out of the ethnic arena so that names like 'City' and 'United' are now no longer seen as ethnically marked.

Soccer in Western Australia

The study of soccer in WA is not as well developed as the study of the game in the eastern states of the country. Most of what has been written about the game in WA is written by insiders for insiders. Some years ago Reynolds (n.d.) produced an account of the local game. It has thus far remained unpublished. More recently, Kreider has produced a popular and useful account of the local history of soccer in WA, writing as an insider to the game. Both authors seem concerned primarily with getting the names correct and reporting the facts. There are few accounts that have sought to go beyond writing from within the game and to engage in social analysis (Brabazon 1998; Evans 1997; Jones and Moore 1994).

Soccer arrived in WA in the 1890s and remained localized around the mines and coalfields being worked by migrant labour from the UK. An attempt was made to organize the game in Perth in 1893, but this attempt lasted barely ten weeks. It was not until 1896 that another attempt was made (Reynolds n.d.). The game continued to be played in WA throughout the twentieth century, particularly with the arrival and settling of the European migrants after the Second World War, but the game has never been considered a culturally significant sport within the broader community. It was the fervour for the game brought with these migrants which has seen the game supported and nurtured since the war. It was the social clubs of these migrants that took up the organization and management of the game. These clubs established full development programmes in order to provide youths the experience of playing the game and to provide a pool of potential players for the major league competition. Soccer has, for most of the past 50 years, provided an arena in which various migrant associations could compete on equal terms with each other for recognition and respect. And in the organization of the game the English migrants who shared the attachment for soccer played side by side with other migrants to Australia. This rendered the 'poms' (English migrants) in this competition just one more ethnic group. Even locally born Australians who became involved in the game were given a distinct and equivalent social identity and referred to as 'kangaroos' or 'roos'.

With the growth of the semi-professional state league, and the expansion in various forms of the professional national league, the competition and disputes within the sport in WA became even more pronounced. As those leading the way to professionalisation and commodification sought to control the sport, in order to further the interests of game at its highest level, those who had commitments to the amateur competitions, grounded firmly in notions of community and participation, found themselves confronted by a new set of difficulties. The pull to professionalization and commodification was not easily made consonant with the commitments of many involved in the game. Jones and Moore (1994) argue that these two dimensions of the game lead to an uncomfortable tension between those who wish to give emphasis to community, by fielding a team with players drawn primarily from within the social club, and those who stress competition and fielding the best team possible in order to win, no matter what the social and cultural backgrounds of the players. This struggle between community and competition has served as a focal point in the organization of soccer.

One of the difficulties faced by amateur soccer in Western Australia is the changing participation base for the sport. Dreher and Palmer note that in one twelve-year period, between 1978 and 1990, the participation rate for the sport declined by 37.52 per cent and that between 1984 and

1990 the decline was 18.86 per cent (1991:17). In real numbers, soccer in WA fell from a high of some 19,507 registrations in 1978 to some 12,188 registrations in 1990. Dreher and Palmer sum up their analysis with the comment that soccer 'seems to be the most consistently declining sport of the popular team sports' (1991: 16). It is a common refrain to hear those who have supported and maintained the amateur game complain that the elite organization of the sport has done little to build broad community interest and support for soccer.

In examining the sources of finance for the game, Dreher and Palmer show that soccer receives most of its income from fees and realizes very little income from government funding or sponsorship (1991:18-20). The game receives less than one per cent of its income from the government, unlike forty-three of the forty-five sports included in their comparison. The lack of financial support and sponsorship for soccer is not felt equally across all forms of the game. The clubs with elite teams have maintained these teams by using income from entrance fees, some local community sponsorship and often through the selling of products associated with the social club. There has been little in the way of economic support for the amateur game from the elite, semiprofessional game. And this has produced a tendency for the organization supporting the elite teams to grow further and further away from the organization of the amateur game. Instead of one association looking after the interests of all of soccer there have developed special interest groups which look after their own narrow interests in the sport. These interest groups often cast themselves as being in competition with each other and have not easily accepted the possibility of a collective organizational structure for soccer.

In recent years, one of the most pronounced and public of these struggles within the game has been over control of the premier competition. With the tyranny of distance continually working against them, particularly when coupled with projections of small and potentially uneconomical local crowds, a WA entry was seen as not viable by eastern states teams. Several attempts to gain entry into the national competition were made by local teams or consortia of teams. In 1988, for example, several of the Italian teams in the Perth competition combined to make a single application, offering the national competition a competitive team with sound financial backing. This overture was rejected. Through all of this the national competition itself was repeatedly experiencing its own organizational convulsions as it was regularly refigured, reorganized and renamed in line with the demands of sponsors and the financial prospects of its changing constituent teams. Perth Glory finally entered the national competition in 1996.

The game in WA has never been organized without disagreement and dissent. Kreider's account of the first century of the game records as quite typical many differences, disagreements, breakaways, along with a repeated recognition of the need to work together. Names have changed and the alignment of interests have altered as individuals and particular groups within the code worked to maximize their own importance and control (Kreider 1994: 63-100). It is within this history of the game in WA that the events of the mid 1980s must be placed.

The Task Force of 1986

In the lead up to the 1983 WA state election the Labor Party aspirant for the Premier's job, Mr Brian Burke, first offered hope of government support and private sponsorship for soccer in WA. It was noted that '[f]or a number of years Mr Burke has held a soft spot for soccer through the success of his sons who have represented WA at various under-age levels' (16 February 1983).[1] The Liberal Premier of WA, Ray O'Connor, was outraged at Burke's suggestion of sponsorship tied to the election of the Labor Party and accused Burke of trying to 'buy votes'. Labor won the election and Burke was called upon to provide soccer with more than the 'poor deal' it had previously received from government.

Little changed immediately in WA soccer. In February 1984 Dick Radica, the outgoing President of the Osborne Park Galeb Club, noted that he saw little future for soccer in WA if it did not change. 'To be frank,' he said, 'one of the main reasons I have quit the game, at least for the time being, is because I see little future for it if it continues along the present path' (16 February 1984). While he was concerned about the prevalence of ethnic politics in the game, Radica placed his emphasis elsewhere: '[w]e seem content to stagger from one season to another with periodic bouts of self destruction because of individual ambitions.' It was, however, his call to end the control of the game by ethnic associations that received most attention. Paul Temev, who had been president of West Perth Macedonia, 'condemned Radica's stance as an attempt to degrade nationalities' (1 March 1984). After noting the contribution that ethnic communities had made to Australian life, and to soccer, Temev asserted: 'Mr Radica has waited until he has left office at Galeb before making this far-reaching statement, but he fully supported the ethnic principle till this year.' Radica was cast as bearing a grudge and as someone espousing a position not previously held. While many continued with calls to end ethnic identifications within the game, those with years invested in the organization of the sport were more divided in their opinions. Radica's identification of individuals as responsible for much of the disunity in the game was largely unheard or ignored.

In September 1985 the government and the executive of the Soccer Federation of Western Australia (SFWA) agreed to a task force 'to investigate the establishment of a new headquarters for WA soccer' (28 September 1985). While responsibility for the task force fell to the Minister for Sport, the Premier remained publicly interested in the outcome. It was the Premier whose good news announcement confirmed that the government would provide a grant of $750,000 for a headquarters for soccer. Over the next few weeks Andrews, one of the few newspaper reporters in WA who covered soccer, was to present an account of what the task force would consider. Although the siting and construction of a head-quarters was central to this discussion, and deemed a simple matter even 'though there might be differing opinions on how or where it should be established' (5 October 1985) it also became clear that changes to the administration of the game in WA would be much more difficult to achieve. Andrews summed up the complex organization of the game by noting that:

> Soccer is ruled by vested interests - be they the representatives of the various leagues of management or the so-called independents who have maintained a close connection with their clubs, mainly in the state league. It is imperative to attract people completely independent and highly respected in the community to direct the sport. Every aspect of the code, whether semi-professional, ama-teur, social, women, coaches, referees and players must be consulted. A head-quarters, well established for both administration and competition, would become the first step in rebuilding personality. But it is equally important that soccer develops a strong leadership that cares for soccer and its future without fear or favour. Hard decisions will have to be taken that may upset some in the short term. But, if soccer is ever to become a serious aspect of WA sporting life, they must be taken. Anything less and the encouragement the State Government is offering can be forgotten. (Andrews 1985)

Recognizing that the game lacked a central body with the accepted authority to govern all soccer, the task force was seen as an appropriate way to make the sport over into an organization that could receive public funding. This meant pushing for the various interests in the game to embrace a collective good rather than merely pursuing their individual interests. By December 1985 the task force was set and responsibility for the future of the game was 'in the hands of the soccer fraternity' (17 December 1985). The government distanced itself from any appearance of overt control of the outcome. A spokesperson noted that 'the govern-ment was not intent on imposing change in the code but assisting the game in the best direction to proceed.' The task force was expected to call for submissions from all sections of the code.

Steve Stacey, a former professional player with 18 years experience in the UK, was given the challenge of chairing the task force. Stacey was seen by many as being unaligned to existing sectional interests in WA soccer. There was not unanimous support for the task force and its members from within soccer. The executive of the SFWA sought to have the terms of ref-erence and composition of the task force altered so that they would retain greater control of any recommendations that might follow. Jack Soer, sec-retary of the Inglewood Kiev club, noted the game's traditional 'negative response to such ideas' (21 December 1985). While there was some enthu-siastic support, claiming that it was time for reconstruction in order to set the game on the right track and to reduce the declining interest in the game, there were many who remained opposed to any change. Some sim-ply remained pessimistic that any change would result. Harry Bush, president of the junior association, noted hopefully that any proposed changes might result in soccer becoming the focus rather than the individuals who controlled the game (21 December 1985). Optimistically, some hoped for positive results 'like opening a window and letting in a breath of fresh air' (21 December 1985).

The task force received some 135 submissions from individuals and organizations in the form of sixty written submissions and seventy-five oral representations. The task force itself estimated that the submissions represented 'the opinions of in excess of 90% of all those currently involved in soccer in Western Australia' (Task Force 1986: 2). The task force reported back in November 1986 and presented its findings to the Annual General Meeting of the Soccer Federation of Western Australia in December of that year. The report, 34 pages in length with several appendices, was described by one optimistic observer as 'a flash of light at the end of what has been a very dark WA soccer tunnel' (20 December 1986). Recommendations were presented in six broad categories: organizational and administrative structures and processes, a new administrative headquarters for the code, cost structure and revenue raising policy, marketing and promotional strategies, development of grounds and facilities and, finally, the improvement of coaching and development provisions for all of local soccer (Task Force 1986: Appendix 1). The organization of all soccer in WA was to be reorganized under a new soccer commission that would be charged with overseeing the varied operations of the code in WA.

Central to the recommendations was that a complex be constructed to provide a headquarters for administration and a venue for playing the game. This was to be called 'Soccer City'. The task force also recommended that a Western Pro League competition be established, with its own administration, and that the SFWA remain in control of the amateur game. It also recommended that the names of clubs be changed so that teams would be seen to represent regional districts in the city rather than ethnic communities. As part of the deal for the reorganization of the game the state government was prepared to commit $A5 million and to help organize corporate sponsorship to raise funds to $A10 million. Premier Burke sang the praises of the world game as:

> [it] is the world's biggest sport but it struggles in Australia for a number of reasons, some peculiar to itself. The time has come for soccer to appeal to a broad spectrum of the Australian community instead of the sectional interests it has served in the past. (9 December 1986)

The economic commitment from the WA Government would have been sufficient to reorganize the sport and to provide for the Soccer City development.

When the task force's report was made public so too became the brawling over the recommendations. Early reports had suggested that setting up the task force had met with 'strong approval of code officials' (21

December 1985) and that adoption of the recommendations would improve a game that had 'languished in the gloom of mediocrity for the past five years' and would allow a local Perth team to gain the long-sought-after entrance into the national competition (10 December 1986). This early optimism would not last. The task force proposed a time frame for the implementation of the proposed changes so that the code could quickly begin the process of establishing itself as a major sport in WA (Task Force 1986: 32). A sense of urgency was created as little time was allowed for negotiations, rendering the option for the code just a matter of implementation. In its programme for the 'time frame of implementation' of the proposed changes, the task force suggested that following the release of the report in November 1986 a meeting of the SFWA in December would be required 'to accept in principle the recommendations contained in the Task Force Report' (1986: 32). The SFWA, unwillingly, scheduled a meeting.

Those in favour of the changes proposed by the task force repeatedly asserted both privately and publicly that they spoke for '90% of the code' (10 December 1986; 14 January 1987; 19 January 1987). The SFWA had opposed the task force from the outset. The SFWA had not made a submission and had lobbied for direct representation on it. Their request for representation was rebuffed. Joe Lacerenza, the president of the SFWA, responded to the call for an extraordinary meeting of the organization by claiming that more time would be needed to discuss the proposals of the task force. This was seen as a delaying tactic as Lacerenza had 'made no secret of his animosity to the ideas outlined in the report' (14 January 1987). There was much discussion within the soccer community about how this impasse would be worked out.

The government continued its public support of the task force. Premier Burke noted that the government sought to provide the means for 'placing soccer among the elite sports of WA'. He noted that while there was some room to negotiate some of the recommendations, the government would not 'throw good money after bad, and certain moves will have to be put in place for soccer's development, otherwise in 10 years' time we will be back here again asking what can be done to improve the game' (19 January 1987). In a meeting of the task force and the SFWA, chaired by Joe Lacerenza, members of the task force were asked questions about their recommendations. After answering some thirty questions posed by the SFWA, Alister Norwood of the task force sought the wishes of the meeting, through a show of hands, regarding the recommendations. His attempt was deftly thwarted by Joe Lacerenza who ruled such a move unconstitutional. Lacerenza was, against his wishes, forced to accept a motion from the floor requiring an extraordinary meeting of the SFWA during which the recommendations would be considered.

The SFWA delayed scheduling the meeting and instead attempted to neutralize the task force by producing a document with a number of proposals from the executive. As a prelude to the extraordinary meeting, the task force in turn invited all members of the SFWA, including the executive, to a meeting to discuss the matter. It did not go smoothly for the executive of the SFWA. There was general agreement that the recommendations of the task force would be good for the game. At the following extraordinary meeting of the SFWA an attempt to remove the executive committee of the organization and to endorse the proposed changes would be made. When the extraordinary meeting was held Joe Lacerenza was in the chair and he used his position to control the outcome of the meeting. He refused to allow members of the task force to address the meeting, as they were not members of the SFWA, and sought to allay the SFWA's fears that the rejection of the task force would threaten the government's offer of financial support. Lacerenza assured the meeting: 'Don't worry about Burkie [the Premier], we'll get the money' (21-22 February 1987). Lacerenza received criticism for his actions, but the task force was effectively sidelined.

There was action from within the game. In their own meeting to consider the recommendations, the League of Management of the State League passed a motion of no confidence in Lacerenza. He threatened legal action over their move. The state director of coaching, Ron Tindall, resigned his position without reasons being publicly offered or sought. By April, the State League of Management was talking publicly of setting up their own competition, outside of the confines of the SFWA. It would affiliate with the SFWA but remain quite separate. In doing this, the State League of Management would seek its own links to other soccer bodies in the state, embrace the recommendations of the task force and, hopefully, realize some of the financial support offered by the government. By June 1987 concern about the recommendations by the task force was still very much present in the soccer community. Members of the junior association collected enough support, 26 of 48 clubs and affiliates, to call for another extraordinary meeting of the SFWA in July to consider again the recommendations of the task force. The junior association sought to form a committee with representatives from the various parts of the game, including the task force and the SFWA, to look into ways of implementing the recommendations. Lacerenza rejected their call, arguing that the common seals of all incorporated bodies who had signed the submission were not affixed. This was not a legal requirement of the SFWAs constitution (18 June 1987). The junior association called Lacerenza on his faulty claim and resubmitted their application. They would, according to their president Harry Croft, have the meeting with or without Mr Lacerenza (23 June 1987). In the 1 July 1987 issue of *Australian Soccer Weekly* the SFWA responded by announcing that they were continuing to review the current status of soccer in WA and that meetings regarding various aspects of the game were being held and that a new state coach had been hired. Between submissions by the junior association, signatures from two second division clubs were withdrawn and support fell to 24 clubs and affiliates. Croft continued with his submission on the grounds that the first submission was legal, and personalized the action: 'It is amazing that Mr Lacerenza and his executive continue to adopt obstructive tactics to this meeting which is seeking to involve the whole code in a review of the task force recommendations' (3 July 1987).

In an ironic twist, Harry Croft noted at a press conference the following day that the SFWA was apparently in breach of the Associations' Corporation Act in that it had not, as required, lodged changes to its constitution or the executive officers since 1979. On being informed of the claims by Mr Croft, Lacerenza advised that he had not read the legal opinion and suggested that he 'would have thought it would have been common courtesy' to give him prior notice of the claim (4 July 1987). Shortly after this the SFWA declared the breakaway Soccer Council suspended from the SFWA noting that it therefore had no right to call for an extraordinary meeting. Brandishing a legal opinion, Lacerenza announced that the SFWA now had its house in legal order. He advised that the meeting called for by the council was 'unauthorised and illegal' (8 July 1987). The SFWA suspended a number of its affiliates over this matter. While the suspended affiliates continued to receive support for their programmes, they lost all 'rights and privileges conferred on them by the federation's constitution and bylaws' (5 August 1987). The suspensions were to remain in force at least until those suspended met with the SFWA. Lacerenza noted that they could have expelled the offending affiliates but deliberately chose a gentler approach. Meetings were scheduled to deal with the issue but both the junior and the coaches' associations were cynical about the ploy by the SFWA. These associations denied that the SFWA was truly representative of all of soccer in WA.

The recommendations of the task force were debated and argued fiercely. Finally, the offer of economic support from the state government was rejected. Attempts were made to revive the offer, to embrace the recommendations of the task force, but the SFWA opposed all such moves. Kreider notes, rather tactfully and in impersonal terms, that 'It is believed the primary reason for the rejection was that the clubs were fearful of losing control' (1994:93). The rejection of the government's offer did not see the collapse of soccer as a sport in WA. It led to a number of initiatives from within the game to revitalize the sport and make it more attractive to the wider community. The organizational culture of soccer in WA makes it difficult to attain the necessary organizational support for change. The attempt to create agreement about the sorts of changes that would make the game a more attractive sport in the broader community was bedevilled by those who perceived that any change might alter their ability to retain autonomy within the game. The cleavages among the participants were so well entrenched that individuals, clubs and leagues could successfully subvert the possibility of change.

Conclusion

Since first played in WA, soccer has never been free of the practice of some sort of politics of culture. From its arrival as a game associated with migrants from Great Britain to the mass migration of Europeans after the Second World War, the game has always been identified with those who were socially and culturally different. For a long time the social clubs that organized the game competed with one another, working to maintain soccer as an arena that they controlled. While there was great strength in their control of the game, it also saw the marginalization of the game and its followers through such derogatory terms as 'wogball'. Following Australia's adoption of multiculturalism in the early 1970s the cultural differences associated with soccer became articulated in a less evaluative way, as 'ethnic' differences. Claims about ethnicity in Australian soccer need to be understood as grounded in a cultural category rather than based on ethnicity as a timeless analytical category. Too often 'ethnicity' is used to identify cultural differences in ways that are essentialist and that impede our ability to understand the social processes that are involved in shaping social and cultural differences. Ethnicity, as one way of marking cultural difference, needs to be understood contextually.

When the state government offered financial support in the 1980s, it was done within the context of Australia as a multicultural society. Without overly worrying about multiculturalism, the task force accepted that the ethnic names identifying clubs were holding the game back and recommended that they should be dropped in order to attract a broader audience. This move, adopted in order to make possible public funding for the game, served to mobilize internal tensions among factions within the soccer community so that the recommendations of the task force could not receive broad support from across the soccer community. This was not the only source of tension for the soccer community. The relationship among various interests within the game would have been refigured, advantaging some and disadvantaging others. The tensions amongst individuals, within the SFWA and its various members and affiliates, and those with differing views of the potential future for the game entail a variety of cultural differences that cannot be understood by reducing all to ethnicity. As the responses to the task force show, the internal differences and politics of culture within the soccer community comprise interests that move well beyond those typically characterized as ethnic. The organizational culture of soccer in WA is not reducible to any play of ethnicity.

Identities forged through soccer in WA are constructed in a socially and culturally complex and contested arena. This is surely the case everywhere. The game itself does not reveal identity but rather serves as a vehicle for both the construction and revelation of identity. Through an engagement with soccer, persons can use their involvement in many different ways. Identity is not found simply in the ethnic affiliations of those involved but rather ethnicity is one way in which cultural differences are expressed. The world game is particularly useful in this complex process because it always sets in opposition, both on and off the pitch, the possibilities of a variety of local and national identities. For anthropology, what are particularly interesting are the local things that people do with this global game.

Acknowledgements

Research for this chapter was supported by a small Australian Research Council Grant, administered by Curtin University of Technology, and by a small grant from the Division of Humanities (then the Division of Arts, English and Social Sciences). Ian Andrews carried out the search of the SFWA press clippings. I appreciate all of the time and effort given to this project by those involved in soccer in Western Australia. I thank Noel Dyck for his comments on this chapter. All faults, of course, remain my own.

Note

1. I have noted only the date from which the clipping appeared unless the point being made was substantial. I have then entered it in the references. All clippings are from *The West Australian*, *The Daily News*, *The Western Independent* or *The Australian* and *The Sunday Times*.

References

Andrews, David (1985), 'Tasks that Need Doing', *The West Australian*, 5 October, p. 87.

Archetti, Eduardo P. (1997), 'The moralities of Argentinian football', In Signe Howell (ed.), *The Ethnography of Moralities*, London and New York: Routledge, pp. 98-123.

Brabazon, Tara (1998), 'What's the Story Morning Glory? Perth Glory and the Imagining of Englishness', *Sporting Traditions* 14(2): 53-66.

Dirks, Nicholas B. (1996), 'Is Vice Versa? Historical Anthropologies and Anthropological Histories', In Terrence J. McDonald (ed.), *The Historic Turn in the Human Sciences*, Ann Arbor: The University of Michigan Press, pp. 17-51.

Dirks, Nicholas B., Geoff Eley and Sherry B. Ortner (eds) (1994), *Culture/Power/History: A Reader in Contemporary Social Theory*, Princeton: Princeton University Press.

Dreher, Heinz and John Palmer (1991), *Soccer: Its Place in WA Society in the 1990s. A Report for Soccer Administration of Western Australia Incorporated*, Perth: School of Information Systems. Curtin University of Technology.

Evans, Kerry (1997), 'From Grom to Wisla – Soccer in Collie 1950-1971', *Perspectives on Sport and Society. Studies in Western Australian History*, 18: 51-63.

Giulianotti, Richard, Norman Bonney and Mike Hepworth (eds) (1994),

Football, Violence and Social Identity, London and New York: Routledge.

Harrison, Graham (1979), 'What's in an ethnic name? Soccer clubs in Australia', *Canberra Anthropology*, 2(2): 23-35.

Hughson, John (1997a), 'The Bad Blue Boys and the "Magical Recovery" of John Clarke', In Gary Armstrong and Richard Giulianotti (eds), *Entering the Field: New Perspectives on World Football*, Oxford and New York: Berg, pp. 239-59.

— (1997b) 'Football, folk dancing and fascism: diversity and difference in multicultural Australia', *Australian and New Zealand Journal of Sociology*, 33(2): 167-86.

Jones, Roy and Philip Moore (1994), '"He only has eyes for Poms": Soccer, Ethnicity and Locality in Perth, WA', In John O'Hara (ed.), *Ethnicity and Soccer in Australia*, ASSH Studies in Sports History No. 10, Sydney: Australian Society for Sports History, pp. 16-32.

Kelly, Paul (1992), *The End of Certainty: The Story of the 1980s*, Sydney: Allen & Unwin.

— (1998), 'The Curse of the M-word', *The Weekend Australian*, Saturday 18 February, Focus, pp. 21-2.

Kreider, Richard (1996), *A Soccer Century: A Chronicle of Western Australian Soccer from 1896 to 1996*, Perth: West Coast Media.

MacClancy, Jeremy (ed.) (1996), *Sport, Identity and Ethnicity*, Oxford: Berg.

Mosely, Philip (1992), 'Soccer', In Wray Vamplew, Katharine Moore, John O'Hara, Richard Cashman and Ian Jobling (eds), *The Oxford Companion to Australian Sport*, 2nd edition, Melbourne: Oxford University Press, pp. 385-8.

— (1995), *Ethnic Involvement in Australian Soccer: A History 1950-1990*, Scientific Report Published by the National Sports Research Centre for the Australian Sports Commission.

Mosely, Philip and Bill Murray (1994), 'Soccer', In Wray Vamplew and Brian Stoddart (eds), *Sport in Australia: A Social History*, Cambridge: Cambridge University Press, pp. 213-30.

Mosely, Philip A., Richard Cashman, John O'Hara and Hilary Weatherburn (eds) (1997), *Sporting Immigrants. Sport and Ethnicity in Australia*, Crows Nest, NSW: Walla Walla Press.

Murray, Bill (1995), 'Cultural Revolution? Football in the Societies of Asia and the Pacific', In Stephen Wagg (ed.), *Giving the Game Away: Football, Politics and Culture on Five Continents*, London and New York: Leister University Press, pp. 138-62.

O'Hara, John (ed.) (1994), *Ethnicity and Soccer in Australia*, ASSH Studies in Sports History No. 10, Sydney: Australian Society for Sports History.

Ortner, Sherry (1995), 'Resistance and the Problem of Ethnographic Refusal', In Terrence J. McDonald (ed.), *The Historic Turn in the Human Sciences*, Ann Arbor: The University of Michigan Press, pp. 281-304.

Paine, Robert (1984), 'Norwegians and Saami: Nation-State and Fourth World', In Gerald L. Gold (ed.), *Minorities and the Mother Country Imagery*, St. Johns, Newfoundland: Memorial University of

Newfoundland, Institute of Social and Economic Research Papers No. 13, pp. 211-48.

Pearson, K. and J. McKay (1981), 'Sociology of Australian and New Zealand Sport: State of the Field Overview,' *Australian and New Zealand Journal of Sociology* 17(2): 66-75.

Reynolds, Peter (n.d.), *The New history of Soccer in Western Australia*, Volume 1, Unpublished report. Prepared for the Soccer Federation of W.A. (Inc).

Tomlinson, Alan and Garry Whannel (eds) (1986), *Off the Ball: The Football World Cup*, London: Pluto Press.

Stoddart, Brian (1986), *Saturday Afternoon Fever: Sport in the Australian Culture*, North Ryde, NSW: Angus & Robertson Publishers.

Vamplew, Wray (1994), 'British Football, Wogball or the World Game? Towards a Social History of Victorian Soccer', in John O'Hara (ed.), *Ethnicity and Soccer in Australia*, ASSH Studies in Sports History No. 10, pp. 44-79.

Wagg, Stephen (ed.) (1995), *Giving the Game Away: Football, Politics and Culture on Five Continents*, London and New York: Leister University Press.

Wells, Jeff (1992), 'Wake up, and end ethnic nonsense', *The Australian*, 6 May, p. 96.

Williams, Raymond (1988), *Keywords*, revised and expanded edition, London: Fontana.

Wright, Susan (ed.) (1994), *Anthropology of Organizations*, London: Routledge.

Part III

The Meaning of Sport for Families, Children and Youth

6

Parents, Kids and Coaches: Constructing Sport and Childhood in Canada[1]

Noel Dyck

Introduction

Organized community sport activities for children and youth in Canada not only attract high levels of participation but also represent a major form of social investment. The ongoing operations of a large number and broad range of sport clubs, leagues and competitions outside the confines of existing physical education and competitive sports programmes in schools require the construction and maintenance of diverse sport facilities, the expenditure of substantial amounts of organizational funding and the contribution of countless hours on the part of volunteer coaches, paid and (mostly) unpaid sport officials, child and youth athletes, and, not least, the parents of these athletes. By any measure, the continuing support of organized sport for children represents a significant set of social commitments on the part of individuals, families, communities and governments. From an anthropological perspective, children's sport entails densely packed networks of activities and relationships that are promulgated on the premise that these are 'good for children'. In short, the organization of children's sport constitutes an ethnographically rich and analytically complex field of investigation that has, nonetheless, received less attention from anthropologists and other students of the social and cultural dimensions of sport than it warrants.[2]

This chapter addresses some of the contributions that anthropological examinations of children's sport might make to broader social science understandings of sport, childhood and relations between children, parents and sport organizations in contemporary Western societies. The argument developed here is that an emerging anthropology of sport can learn much by noting and responding to the impressive theoretical and ethnographic achievements registered in recent years within the growing literature on the anthropology of childhood and youth[3] as well as analyses of changing family relations in the context of the fundamental socioeconomic restructuring currently taking place in Canada and elsewhere in the Western world. Substantively, the chapter will identify factors that, for many parents, make sport not only an attractive means of augmenting family childrearing stratagems but also of constructing identities for themselves and their children. What will also be elucidated are subtle and not-so-subtle disjunctures between the ideological justifications for measures taken on behalf of children and actual, commonplace experiences generated by children's sport in Canada.

The ethnographic aim of the chapter is to show how children's and parents' experiences of sport are constructed in terms of the overriding organizational interests, cultural interpretations and models of childhood marshalled by adults in managing children's sport activities. This is accomplished by considering two interrelated questions. Why do so many Canadian parents 'buy into' children's sport and invest so much of their time and money in supporting these activities? More important, why and how do parents continue to sustain their sons' and daughters' participation in organized sports, as well as their own involvement as supportive parents, when so frequently, for various reasons, smaller and larger gaps begin to appear between what parents wish to see happen for their children and the often discomforting experience of these activities by either children, parents or both?

An inquiry such as this poses special challenges for an ethnographer (such as myself) working within his or her own country. As Löfgren (1987: 91) notes in his study of middle-class culture building in Sweden, most anthropologists are members of the middle classes, so for them such studies involve a difficult sort of home coming. Any investigation of middle-class lifestyles and worldviews potentially turns the anthropologist into a key informant. The problem is, as Löfgren notes, 'that much of our anthropological discourse is rooted in a middle-class version of reality: a way of perceiving, classifying and organizing the world. Many of our analytical tools have been produced or redefined in this intellectual setting' (Löfgren 1987: 91). Löfgren's strategy for resolving this potential for 'home blindness' has been to adopt a historical-comparative perspective in order to facilitate his deconstruction of 'Swedishness'. I have written elsewhere (Dyck 2000) about my own efforts to come to terms methodologically, analytically and ethically with the advantages and problems associated with conducting ethnographic research 'at home'. In this chapter I seek to establish a critical analytical distance from the playing fields and children's sport activities that I have known for more than a decade as a parent and coach and, latterly, investigated as an anthropologist. My approach here is to look away from the fields of play in order to take account of the cultural dynamics that lead parents and children to organized sport and that govern their participation once they arrive there.

Structuring Children's Sports

The substantial structure of clubs, leagues and sport organizations that embodies children's out-of-school sport in Canada reaches from local communities to provincial and national levels. Although the resourcing and organizing of children's sport is accomplished for the most part at the local level, provincial and national sport organizations determine policy and are empowered to exercise control over the management of this sphere of activities. Local community sport organizations are, accordingly, components of a larger bureaucratic field. On one side of this field stands the sport industry that comprises national and provincial amateur sport organizations, businesses, consultants and paid coaches who work with children and youth. Various federal and provincial ministries and agencies involved in sport, as well as municipal departments of recreation, occupy the remainder of this field. Children's sport is, thus, not only an object of community and professional concern, but also a matter of state policy.

This is clearly exhibited in the report of the Canadian Task Force on Amateur Sport Policy that was commissioned in the wake of a formal inquiry – sparked by the Ben Johnson scandal at the 1988 Olympic Games in Seoul[4] – which investigated the extent of use by Canadian athletes of prohibited drugs. The report, entitled 'Sport: The Way Ahead' (Minister's Task Force on Federal Sport Policy 1992) addressed a variety of issues, including the place and purpose of sport in Canadian society, the values and ethics that should shape its conduct, the roles and responsibilities of national sport governing bodies and the government's future role in sport policy and programmes. The task force made a number of bold claims. It presented sport as a solution for all manner of societal problems, challenges and concerns. What is required, according to the report, is a fundamental reform of the sport system in Canada because of:

> the importance of sport in our society. For example, [the task force] learned that 'a majority of Canadians (90%) agree that sport is just as much an element of Canadian culture as music, films or literature' . . .

> Sport is pervasive. It is the topic of conversation around the water cooler at work. At times it dominates the airwaves and forms a major portion of our daily newspapers. The literal pervasiveness of sport is clear . . .

> Competitive sport is an expression of our nature, our search for fun and fair play and of our national character as we challenge the land, water, snow, ice and mountains of Canada. This part of daily life is deeply valued by Canadians.

> On an individual level, sport gives us the opportunity to test and develop ourselves – physically and personally – and to pursue and achieve excellence. At the community level, sport is a basis for social interaction, community building, developing intercultural relationships and local pride. At the national level, sport plays an important role in developing feelings of national unity and pride.

> Sport also helps Canadians face the reality of globalization by developing competitive skills and behaviours that are rapidly becoming essential to our economic survival. As well, on the economic side, sport is a multi-billion dollar industry providing jobs to thousands of Canadians.

For all these reasons, the Task Force concludes that sport – from recreational sport through organized competitive sport to high performance sport – must be promoted and accessible to all Canadians. (Minister's Task Force on Federal Sport Policy 1992: 9-11)

Concerning children's sports, the report of the task force says:

Traditionally, values and ethics have been instilled in children through parenting, church and formal education. Today, however, with the realities of single [parent] families, working parents and difficult economic times, the stresses placed on family life leave less time for values and ethics development. The church's position as a teacher of ethics and morals has diminished. In schools, less time is devoted to sport and physical education and to building discipline, learning fair play and following rules. Educational budgets have decreased; class size and composition cause stress on teachers, leaving them with less energy for extracurricular sport activity. All these factors, the Task Force concludes, have combined to erode the moral development of Canadian youth at a time when this development is becoming more critical.

The Task Force says that sport is beginning to address this societal gap by accepting a leadership role in instilling values and ethics in Canadian youth. (Minister's Task Force on Federal Sport Policy 1992: 22)

This curious ordering of claims is reflected not only in this report, but in most pronouncements issued by representatives of the sport industry. Sport is almost invariably mooted as being 'good for kids' and is touted as a 'solution'; thereafter, attention is given to identifying 'problems' or 'needs' of Canadian children that could be suitably rectified by sport. Implicit in this formulation is the notion that the rearing of children in contemporary Canada will remain incomplete and faulty unless supplemented by the beneficial effects of participation in organized sport. What is also implied is that traditional institutions for ensuring appropriate socialization of children – families, schools and the church – are, if left to their own devices, no longer capable of preventing the moral erosion of Canadian children and youth. The familiar model of child socialization long promoted by developmental psychology is not questioned or criticized but rather is utilized to support the claims of the sport industry and to sanction the extension of its highly organized involvement in the lives of a significant number of Canadian children and their families.

The extent of this involvement through the operations of community sport organizations for children is, to say the least, far reaching. A study of local sports clubs mounted in order to obtain an informed assessment of the scope of organized community sport for children in one suburban area of the Greater Vancouver Regional District of British Columbia (Dyck and Wildi 1993) revealed that almost 15,000 of the 40,500 children under the age of 19 years in these communities took part in community sport activities organized outside of school programmes. They represented just under half of all children in the district between the ages of five and 18 years.

The minimum cost for personal sporting equipment for these child and youth athletes amounted to some $1.6 million per season, and the forty-five clubs in the district (which together offered twenty different sports)[5] had operating budgets during the 1992-3 season of $1.9 million. These clubs held an additional $1.2 million in accumulated capital equipment assets, not counting the extensive municipal sport facilities (in the form of playing fields, gymnasia, swimming pools, ice rinks and other facilities provided by local governments) used by these clubs for practices, competitions and tournaments.

In addition to these resources some 3,500 adults served as club officials, coaches, managers, referees and judges. Few received any form of payment for their efforts, let alone expenses to cover incidental costs for local travel. Although it was not possible to obtain detailed figures concerning the numbers of hours contributed by these volunteer officials, it is safe to conclude that 100 hours per season per volunteer comprises a decidedly conservative estimate of the time donated to organized children's sport activities in this locality. Nor does this figure take into account the support of parents who routinely drive their children to and from practices and competitions, who watch and cheer from poolside or the sidelines and who participate in fundraising activities mounted by ambitious coaches. The extent of overall investment in children's sport, including not only actual financial expenditures but also the enormous amounts of time volunteered by adult sport officials and parents, speaks to the significance invested in these activities by adults.

Why, then, do so many Canadian parents choose to invest so much of their discretionary time (and that of their children) and money in supporting these activities? This is one of the questions asked in a Sport Parent Survey commissioned by the British Columbia Government in 1994 (SOAR International1994). This survey of over 650 parents whose children were involved in sport was administered at different locations in the province and across eleven different sports. Most of the parents surveyed[6] had children under the age of twelve years then playing sport. What is particularly interesting is the preselected list of reasons for parents to enrol children in sports, out of which parents were asked to rank their top five reasons.[7]

- To build self-esteem
- To develop skills
- To make new friends
- To have fun
- To increase fitness
- To go to the Olympics
- To win awards
- To have a professional career
- To play on a winning team
- Other

The most important reason listed by the parents surveyed was the first one on the list – that of building children's self-esteem (followed by having fun, developing skills, increasing fitness and making new friends). By no means a transparent concept, either in theory or practice, the nature of 'self-esteem' and the basis of its considerable appeal to Canadian parents is examined later in this chapter. Nevertheless, an equally telling part of the otherwise quantitatively based survey report is a qualitative appendix that reports the verbatim comments of various parents concerning their experience, as well as that of their children, with the sport system. There is little consistency in these comments, which range from general observations to highly particular and personal experiences. But the fact that some parents of child and youth athletes harbour a significant degree of dissatisfaction and disagreement with various facets of organized sport readily emerges from this appendix, along with a diverse set of proposals for rectifying these problems:

It really is a joke sometimes the people that end up coaching (often because no one else will). If you have a baseball cap and a whistle you 'qualify' . . . Coaching needs to become a RESPECTED profession – so much is at stake with our children – coaches are often the moulders of character – a foul mouth (swearing) cigarette smoking coach is a great role model (not!). Associations need to get some backbone and get rid of some coaches if they don't '[shape] up'. We evaluate referees yet I've never seen coaching evaluations done on coaches at this level. (*Respondent #135*)

Some coaches are losing sight of what the reason is for young children's sport involvement. Too competitive, biased [refereeing], doing anything necessary to win. These coaches should not be allowed to coach. They not only ruin the sport for their own teams, but also for their competitors. (*Respondent #162*)

I think it's very unfair and in poor taste that the ____ team stacked their team with players from [another team]. By doing this, our daughter . . . got bumped from the team and had to play for [another] team. (*Respondent #164*)

I know this has nothing to do with the [survey questions], but I don't know how else to have my feelings be heard: I RESENT having to pay to watch my children compete at a tournament. We spend enough to get them involved in the sport, to travel to the event, to be housed and fed while attending the event . . . Could we not be given complimentary tickets so we can enjoy their performance and cheer them on? (*Respondent #207*)

I have two sons both in hockey, soccer, track, cross country and baseball. One son reached provincial level in soccer this year. The team was not played as a team from its inception three years prior (age 8-11) i.e. not equal time for players. I was glad they lost the final because one of the stars was not playing. It proved a point – the team lacked 'team' cohesiveness – it was competitive among themselves. (*Respondent #391*)

(1) Coaching selection should be taken out of the political local arena and have certification rules applied straight across the board, provincially. (2) Children who want to play outside of their division should have their skills tested by someone outside their local district. (3) Local clubs are a political quagmire. Structure has to be changed. (4) Team selection should not be left to the coach. A panel of non-affiliated people should be asked to select a team and the coach can then proceed. (field hockey) (*Respondent #486*)

Better [referees] are DESPERATELY needed. UNFAIR refs ruin a good sport and teach kids to be unfair. (*Respondent #561*)

Games out of town i.e. New Westminster vs. Mission, Abbotsford, Chilliwack[8] should NEVER be scheduled on a school night or after 7:00 pm. (*Respondent #616*)

The ambivalence and dissatisfaction expressed in many of these parental observations and recommendations is not readily reconcilable with either the rhetorical claims of sport industry and government representatives or the high levels of participation and investment in sport incurred by so many Canadian parents and their children. Although quantitative researchers might wish to measure the statistical representivity of these sentiments, a no less salient matter is why and how any parents of child and youth athletes continue to endure such ambivalence.

Constructing Childhood and Families

The on- and off-field activities that make up organized community sport for children are infused with a set of overlapping premises about the nature and needs of the child and the responsibilities and capacities of parents to address these needs. Specifically, the models of childhood and family relations invoked by the Canadian sport industry (at all levels) are informed by popular renderings of the teachings of developmental psychology. At the core of this approach, which has dominated the study of children and childhood for most of this century, rest three tenets: (1) that since rationality represents the mark of adulthood, childhood comprises a period of apprenticeship during which this capacity is acquired; (2) that childhood is a naturally occurring, biologically defined phenomenon; and, (3) that childhood is essentially universal in nature (Prout and James 1990: 10). In recent years each of these assumptions has been subjected to searching reassessment, not least by critical psychologists (for example Morss 1990; Stainton Rogers and Stainton Rogers 1992) who have challenged the propensity of the developmental paradigm to ignore not only the social and political processes that shape childhood but also those employed to promote hegemonic claims of disciplinary expertise. Although the implications of this critique have yet to filter down to the playing fields of children's sport in Canada, they have supported a systematic rethinking of the nature of childhood and family relations by anthropologists and other social scientists.

Within this new perspective (which has been aptly summarized by Prout and James, 1990: 8-9) childhood is viewed as a social construction which 'provides an interpretive frame for contextualizing the early years of human life'. Childhood, which is distinguished from biological immaturity, is seen as neither 'a natural nor universal feature of human groups' but rather as a particular structural and cultural component of many, but by no means all, societies. Thus, as a variable of social analysis, childhood cannot be conceptually isolated from other factors such as class, gender or ethnicity. Further, children should be understood not as 'passive subjects of social structures and processes', but rather as active agents who participate in constructing their own social lives, as well as the lives of those around them. Yet, notwithstanding the recognition of children as active social beings, 'it remains true that their lives are almost always determined and/or constrained in large measure by adults' (Prout and James 1990: 30). In Canada this means that the politics of childhood continue to revolve around the labelling and management of interactions between adults, children and institutions under the rubric of 'socialization'.

Critics of socialization theory note that while adults are notionally granted status as full and complete social actors within this schema, children are correspondingly envisioned as 'incomplete', as 'adults-in-the-making' (Thorne 1993: 3). The emphasis placed on the 'futurity' of children serves to define childhood as 'the period in the life-course when, through the socialization of children, the future shape of society itself is set out' (James 1998: 140). In consequence, not only is an inherent plasticity on the part of children presumed, but so too are the tutelary responsibilities of parents for their children underscored. Children's defined malleability is anchored by a sense of risk and a need for caring, parental control 'lest children's potential for change run wild and their adulthood, and hence future adult society, be endangered' (Thorne 1993: 141). Since 'a plurality of models of "the child" may be articulated for and on behalf of children' (James 1995: 61) the task of specifying which models of childhood are utilized by which adults, where, and when becomes a matter of particular concern for critics of socialization theory. In the meantime, children are obliged to embody the sets of ideas about 'the child' preferred in various institutional settings such as the school, the family and the state (Thorne 1993: 61-2). By the same token, parents are obliged to take appropriate account of disciplinary expectations concerning the 'normal development' of 'the child' if they are to fulfil their assigned duties (James 1998: 141). In short

> traditional socialization theory, in arguing for the vulnerability of the child's present being, continually emphasizes the need to nurture, constrain and protect the child lest its future prospects as an adult be thwarted or damaged. In this way, the social institution of 'childhood' – that complex of material, social, moral and economic constraints that shapes children's everyday lives – is held to place an important steadying hand upon a child's demands for access to the adult social world. (James 1998: 141)

The dependence of children (and especially middle-class children)[9] fosters the conceptual and practical interdependence of childhood, the family and the home in countries such as Canada. Indeed, parenting is what transforms a couple into a family, making it not only the site for reproduction but also the primary locus for socialization (James 1998: 144). But the conceptual embedding of 'the child' within 'the family' has been accompanied by surveillance and regimentation of childrearing and other facets of domestic life through the use of authoritative expertise wielded directly and indirectly by teachers, therapists, social workers and other representatives of the state (Knowles 1996; Wigman, 1990). This arrangement makes childhood and child rearing a highly contested domain (Wolfe 1991) and the family a complex sociopolitical product (Knowles 1996: 35-6). A clear tendency in the Western world towards a 'professionalization' of parenting (Fine and Mechling 1991: 65) has, not surprisingly, been accompanied by an augmentation of parental insecurity concerning the adequacy and appropriateness of family childrearing efforts (Wolfe 1991: 72-3).

Parental insecurity is also fuelled by the economic restructuring that has swept across Canada and the world in recent decades. Increasing economic and social unpredictability has set reality at odds with traditional expectations (Newman 1991: 130). The shrinking of the middle classes[10] in North America has been precipitated by a decline in the average standard of living and the escalating disappearance of what were once seen as being 'good' (and continuing) jobs (Newman 1991: 132). It has become difficult for many children to reproduce their parents' class status in terms of projected employment and income. While it was once possible for many Canadian teenagers and young adults to earn enough through summer employment and term-time, part-time jobs to finance most, if not all, of the costs of a college or university education, this is no longer the case. The competition not only for 'student' jobs but also for full-time employment among graduates has become fierce.

An increase in the numbers of two-career families and single-parent families in both the US and Canada has, for differing reasons, seriously undermined the capacity of parents to satisfy the expectations of family life generated during the early postwar period (Stacey 1991; Wolfe 1991). This shattering of 'modern' family life (Stacey 1991: 27) has incurred domestic tumult and contestation, forcing families to discover for themselves what actually works for them (Wolfe 1991: 5). Most working parents have also been beset by an acute shortage of time to spend with their children for the purposes of informal education (Persell 1991: 284). Parents born in Canada during the 'baby boom' have, therefore, entered into their responsibilities as parents at a time when expectations of childrearing have been growing. Suffice it to say that mothers, in particular, but fathers also find themselves increasingly held accountable for the eventual outcome of their children. Parents have been subjected to exacting theories of child development that emphasize the malleability of children and, thus, the responsibilities of parents for creating suitable conditions and resources for appropriate child development.

In a context where parents tend to be held responsible both by themselves and others for the future success of their children when they become adults, it is scarcely surprising that activities such as community sports for children and youth, which make extravagant claims about their ability to prepare children to become competent and even highly competent adults, hold a seductive attraction for parents. In effect, sport organizations and the sport industry as a whole present their activities or 'products' as a means by which children can be equipped with attitudes, skills and habits that would furnish them with a 'competitive edge' to face the challenges and uncertainties that lie ahead of them. The principal, though by no means only, benefit that sport organizations and the sport industry hold out to parents is that of enhancing their children's 'self-esteem'.

The growth of the concept of self-esteem during the past century parallels the emergence of psychology as an academic discipline and form of therapeutic practice. Developing as one of a number of self concepts[11] that refer to the manner in which one perceives oneself, one's behaviour and one's opinion of how others view one, self-esteem generally refers to an individual's satisfaction with the self concept (Calhoun and Morse 1977). In fact, it is only since the early part of the twentieth century that the concept of self-esteem has been 'employed as a tool for unlocking the inherent secrets of human behavior' (Ward 1996: 8).

> Since this time, self-esteem, or such corollaries as self-efficacy, self-concept, self-evaluation or self-ideal congruency have come to be viewed as something that everyone possesses in varying degrees. By determining the degree of self-esteem possessed by an individual, it becomes possible to access, predict, control or enhance an individual's life. (Ward 1996: 8)

Since the 1960s North American society has been engulfed by a professional and popular discourse on self-esteem that has effectively transformed this concept into something that is accepted as 'basic truth about human experience and motivation' (Ward 1996: 1). Once established as part of the working knowledge of experimental and clinical psychology,[12] the currency of the notion of self-esteem rapidly spread to education, social work and various manifestations of the self-help movement. By the early 1970s parenting manuals were providing step-by-step instruction about how mothers and fathers should go about building a solid sense of self-worth in their sons and daughters. Indeed

> [s]ome manuals went so far as to warn parents that if they did not work on building their child's self-esteem, particularly that of young girls, the child was at risk of becoming an insecure, unhappy teenager ... Girls with low self-esteem were said to be at danger of developing depression, eating disorders, being a victim of crime, becoming involved in destructive relationships, practicing

unsafe sex and being unable to compete in the high-tech job market. (Ward 1996: 13)

The alliance between self-esteem and self-help and parenting literature allowed the concept to move into new areas and develop a larger, more encompassing, network of support. As the self-esteem literature became more popular and was integrated into TV discourse and everyday talk, the concept became much stronger than before. In this phase, the network of self-esteem had recruited an entirely new set of allies, including TV talkshows, teenagers, those seeking help, policy makers, drug addicts and parents. Its network of support was now so encompassing that it had become a truth. (Ward 1996: 14)

Today the putative possession of positive self-esteem is linked not only to a general notion of personal well-being, but also to one's chances of material attainment (Ward 1996: 12). Programmes for the enhancement of both children's and adults' self-esteem have been advocated by the women's movement, social policy analysts and business consultants. While the construction of self-esteem has become a lifelong assignment for North Americans, and although the notion is founded on the supposition that 'the only one who is responsible for how you feel is yourself', nonetheless, parents are held firmly responsible for nurturing their children's self-esteem (Ward 1996: 12@3).

Clearly, a society that wholeheartedly subscribes to the concept of self-esteem is fundamentally different from one that does not; moreover, the factors and actants 'which were mobilized to build the concept of self-esteem into truth are also responsible for building a particular social order or arrangement' (Ward 1996: 16). This is exemplified by the manner in which the concept of self-esteem parallels and articulates with other features of contemporary North American culture. In an anthropological study of the experience of downward class mobility in the American middle class Newman (1988) asks why so many Americans who are being subjected to large-scale postindustrial economic processes of decline that ordinary people cannot control tend to see themselves as being responsible for the situation that has befallen them. She explains this behaviour in terms of the workings of the ideology of meritocratic individualism, a doctrine rooted in Calvinistic theology, which has at its centre the notion that individuals are responsible for their own destinies:

One's occupation, or more precisely one's career or trajectory within an occupation, are viewed as a test of commitment, and the product of hard work and self-sacrifice. Cast this way, success is not a matter of luck, good contacts, credentials or technical skill, but is a measure of one's moral worth, one's willingness and ability to drive beyond the limitations of self-indulgence and sloth. It is this equation of occupational success and inner or moral qualities that rebounds on the unemployed manager's self-image, making him or her feel not just unsuccessful but worthless. (Newman 1998: 76)

[M]eritocratic individualism provides a system of meaning through which individual experience is understood and evaluated. It shapes life by imposing expla-

nations and moral tales; it creates a received wisdom. The main motifs of managerial culture involve the legitimacy of competition and hierarchy; the myths
and heroes of the managerial world provide explanations for the prosperity and
success of the few and the downfall of the many. Meritocratic individualism is
more than an abstract philosophical doctrine. It is a culture which has the
power to reach inside displaced managers and devastate their sense of self-
worth. (Newman 1998: 80)

Newman observes that downwardly mobile managers in America tend
to fall victim to beliefs they hold dear: that one's occupation is a measure
of one's moral worth; that success comes to those who are really deserving;
and, that 'people are the masters of their own destiny' (Newman 1998: 94).
It is the rare individual 'who can hold these features of managerial middle-class culture at bay, who can shield him- or herself from the disorien-
tation of downward mobility. Only through culture can one gain a sense
of identity, and only through culture can it be taken away' (Newman 1998:
94).

The similarities and points of articulation between the concept of self-
esteem and the ideology of meritocratic individualism are striking. Each
of these cultural doctrines comprises a system of meaning through which
individual experience is interpreted and evaluated. Although positive self-
esteem promises to deliver self-satisfaction and competence, whereas mer-
itocractic individualism focuses upon self-sacrifice and the determination
to overcome self-indulgence, there is a complementarity between these
objectives. What is more, the concept of self-esteem is backgrounded by
the supposition that 'the only one who is responsible for how you feel is
yourself', while the 'received wisdom' of meritocratic individualism is
premised on a belief that equates occupational success with inner qualities. Thus, each of these cultural constructions place the onus for individual life success on the qualities of the individual rather than the structural
properties of the economic, political and social context within which he
or she exists. In North America both formulations have achieved such a
high level of popular acceptance that they have come to constitute essential and taken-for-granted 'truths' that have the power to reach into peoples' lives and mediate their self-consciousness.

What self-esteem and meritocratic individualism also have in common
is that both hold adults responsible for achieving the ideals that they
espouse. In consequence, the cultural predicament confronted by
Canadian parents is twofold. As adults, they are obliged to earn a liveli-
hood and, in so doing, to demonstrate their commitment to realizing
their talents and responsibilities as fully competent and morally worthy
individuals. As parents, they are expected not only to provide for the material needs of their sons and daughters but also to attend to the nurturing
and shaping of their children's self-esteem.[13] Of course, parents are not
left entirely to their own devices to accomplish these tasks of childrearing
and socialization. Teachers, child-care workers, social workers and a host
of other community and state officials are mandated to take leading parts

in various socialization projects. These figures are also empowered to scrutinize and assess the behaviour of children, to intervene in more or less intrusive ways into family life and to hold parents accountable for acting (or, at least, being seen to act) in ways that correspond with institutional definitions of 'the child' and what may be said to be in 'the best interests of the child'. In Canada this list of socialization functionaries has also been expanded to include coaches and officials of organized community sport for children and youth.

Constructing and Contesting Children's Sports

In Canada community sports for children and youth are designed and controlled by adults and are typically highly regulated. They are premised on an explicit socialization agenda that is articulated in terms of a number of related purposes. First and foremost, children's sport is touted as a powerful vehicle for fostering the self-esteem and healthy development of children, thereby enabling them to obtain a sense of self that will equip them to become complete and competent adults. Adult-supervised community sports are commonly represented as a safe and wholesome way for children to spend time and are regularly contrasted with the alarming alternative of the 'street' where it is feared that children will encounter unsupervised social spaces and potentially delinquent attitudes and activities. In addition to the health benefits popularly associated with physical exercise, sport is viewed as an arena where children can be introduced to the competitive dynamics deemed to be characteristic of the adult world(s) that they will eventually join. The capacity of sport to instill discipline into children is much mooted, and coaches often declare at the beginning of a season their commitment to promote and monitor children's adherence to one or more of a set of moral precepts that may include 'hard work', 'team play', 'responsibility to the team', acceptance of the authority of competition officials, respect for opponents and 'playing by the rules'. And as child and youth athletes move from lower levels of sport that accentuate 'participation' to levels which place greater stress upon competition, sport officials embrace the principle of 'excellence', encouraging and even insisting that each child or youth athlete should strive 'to be the best that you can be'.

To sustain themselves community sports require continuing, large-scale participation by thousands of children and the support of parents who will finance the enrolment of their sons and daughters in teams and clubs and furnish them with necessary sport equipment. Parents are usually also expected to provide transportation and, ideally, to take an active part in the ubiquitous fund-raising activities associated with this sector.[14] Why and how so many Canadian parents are initially attracted to children's sport has already been established.[15] Moreover, findings from the US that indicate that 96 per cent of Americans believe that sport teaches good citizenship and appropriate social values[16] (McCormack and Chalip 1988)

Figure 6 After the hockey game [Sam Beitel]

corroborate the overwhelmingly positive cultural status enjoyed by children's sport in North America.[17]

The rationale that 'sport is good for kids' is characteristically transformed by adults involved in child and youth sport into an all-purpose explanation of their own activities in this large and varied sector: namely, 'we do it for the kids'. This credo is used to justify all manner of actions, to make explicit the extent of one's contributions to children's sports and to disclaim any interest beyond that of altruism. It is a claim that can be and regularly is marshalled to legitimate virtually any given practice or decision, or their opposites. The explicit manifestation and vigorous contestation of conflicting interests is, indeed, an aspect of children's sport that is readily acknowledged by coaches, parents and even child and youth athletes. That organized sport is more often than not riven by smaller and larger disagreements and disputes (which in Canada tend to be ethnographically classified and subsumed under the generic term 'politics') is viewed as a most unfortunate but inescapable circumstance. Since

Canadians nonetheless commonly contend that politics ought not to be a part of sport, it is important to identify the sources of some of the inherent tensions and divisive purposes that 'inappropriately' but frequently serve to generate 'political' contestation in children's sport.

Parents and child athletes seldom have the opportunity to view the operations of provincial, let alone national, sport organizations at close hand or, if they do, for a lengthy period. Yet it is at these levels that crucial decisions about the rules that govern community sports are made year after year. Veteran sport volunteers and a smaller number of paid officials and administrators in provincial and national sport bodies decide whether amateur sports will mirror some of the competitive characteristics of professional sports or whether different rules of competition and modes of organization might be better suited to children and youth and to encouraging greater levels of participation or higher levels of competition. The selection of teams and team members who will represent provincial and national sport organizations in national and international competitions is decided here. The appointment of coaches and selection committees to oversee these matters frequently generates a substantial amount of work for those chosen to perform these tasks, not to mention disappointment for willing candidates not selected to participate in such teams or competitions.

The operations of local sport organizations are, to a certain extent, more accessible and visible than the organization of children's sport at higher levels. At the local level the presence of 'politics' in children's sport may be downright difficult to ignore. Contentious dealings between opposing coaches during little league baseball games, for example, make patent the existence of differing interpretations of the rules and conventions of competition and diverse tactics that may be employed to promote one side's interests over those of the other. Coaches doing 'whatever it takes' to gain an advantage for their athletes or teams are commonly seen in action at these venues and/or reported by those who have attended such events. What may be less obvious are the 'behind the scenes' manoeuvrings by coaches and officials to recruit superior athletes to their teams or clubs and to seek advantage in submissions made to league officials.

Interactions between coaches and other officials with the parents of child and youth athletes can be seen and overheard at practices and competitions, although the telephone communications and occasional letters of protest that are initiated by perturbed parents may only be heard of at second or third hand. The enforcement by coaches of athletes' regular attendance at practices and competitions comprises another form of organizational power, as does the frequent requirement of active participation by athletes and their parents in fund-raising for teams and clubs. Families may even be requested to organize their Christmas or summer holiday plans in order to ensure that teams will be able to field full teams for tournaments and championships that may be scheduled without prior consultation by coaches or league officials. A family's failure to comply with these demands may result in child and youth athletes being penalized by receiving diminished playing time or even being dropped from a team.

Relations between coaches and officials, on the one hand, and children and youth, on the other, may also reveal more-or-less obvious tensions. The sometimes controversial manner in which certain coaches seek to reward or punish certain types of behaviour by athletes,[18] to lead athletes and teams to higher levels of performance and to achieve victory becomes discernible when one observes children's sport over a period of time. Coaches and officials often manage these situations with remarkable diplomacy and good judgement, but this is not invariably the case. One teenaged girl whom I interviewed shortly after she had been picked to join a highly competitive synchronized swimming club expressed to me that she was thrilled to be able to participate in a sport that she loved. When her mother advised me a year later that I might like to speak with her daughter again, the 'before and after' contrast was palpable. Possessed of a body that, in the view of her coach, was less than ideal for this particular sport, this athlete had sought to reduce her weight and had contracted a serious eating disorder. Although her bulimia was initially kept from her mother, eventually the stress that it imposed led the girl to withdraw from not only the club but also from school. Both the athlete and her mother – when she finally learned what had transpired – were distressed by the coach's behaviour.

Another aspect of children's sport that may be less apparent unfolds within families, between parents and children. As noted previously, there are many factors that incline parents to enrol their children in organized community sport activities and to do what is required to support their participation. To do so is, for many parents, to exhibit publicly their commitment to being 'good' parents by affording their sons and daughters access to activities that are commonly defined as being 'good' for children. In doing so, they not only publicly display a laudable and ostensibly selfless form of parenting but may also make use of their child's involvement in sport to create their own sport identities and relationships with other parents (Dyck 1995). Children's athletic performances are a medium through which parenting may be observed and interpreted.[19] As Ken Dryden, a former professional athlete who has since become a parent of child and youth athletes, has noted, there is a sense of vulnerability amongst parents who sit in the stands at a hockey match and have their child's character opened to scrutiny and debate by other parents on the basis of his or her play on the ice (MacGregor 1995: 246-71). Does a player move out of the way to avoid being body checked by an opponent, or does the child demonstrate the courage and self-discipline associated with cultural definitions of 'good' play? Notwithstanding the commonly encountered claim that many parents take vicarious credit for winning performances by their children, I would also note that, even in the absence of superior performance by child and youth athletes, displays of unceasing and self-sacrificing support on the part of parents can comprise a claim for the virtue of their abilities and inclinations as mothers or fathers. Thus, parents' interests in children's sports may, in certain respects, be not entirely coincident with those of their children.

And what are children's interests in community sports? My experience in interviewing child and youth athletes over a number of years in different parts of Canada confirms a common finding that, when asked, children will typically (although not invariably) reply that they play sports to have 'fun'. The fact that levels of participation in community sports for children and youth begin to decline rapidly in most sports as children reach their teenaged years suggests that when the management of these activities by adults – coaches, league officials and parents alike – begins to render these activities no longer the source of fun that they once were, or promised to be, they drop out of them. Nevertheless, my fieldwork with child and youth athletes also suggests that the reasons for their departure from community sports are often more complicated and less innocent than the commonly expressed 'fun' thesis may indicate. Children are, as Prout and James (1990) suggest, capable of exercising agency, not least in the context of community sports. Coaching regimes can be influenced by athletes' active or passive resistance to measures with which they do not agree, whatever the age of the athlete. Moreover, dealings between athletes on the same team or in the same club may feature manoeuvring and contestation, alliances and competition, that can be pursued just as vigorously as any adult politicking and sometimes with deceptive subtlety. In verbally 'rehashing' games or competitions, child and youth athletes can be no less aggressive in promoting their own achievements and drawing attention to the perceived shortcomings of their team mates and opponents as can be mothers, fathers or coaches. In short, the 'politics' that pervade children's sport potentially involve children and youth to just as great an extent as adults, albeit not necessarily in the same manner.

When a child or youth athlete for whatever reason(s) not longer wishes to belong to a particular team or club or to continue with sport in general, this decision is usually respected by parents, if not always immediately. One mother related to me her dismay at the prospect of losing familiar and valued relationships that she had formed with other parents in her daughter's swimming club when her daughter opted to stop swimming. The initial relief that the mother experienced when her daughter relented and opted to return for another year of competitive swimming was mixed with discomfort about the basis upon which her daughter's decision had been rescinded. Yet the ability of child or youth athletes to enter and continue to participate in organized sport remains dependent upon the willingness of parents to support this financially and logistically. This again returns us to the question of why parents continue to support organized sport even when they are exposed to the many and various disagreements and shortcomings encountered in these activities?

Whatever they may demand of and supply to children and youth, community sports also offer parents a theatre for addressing deep cultural concerns and for seeking to honour parental obligations. Seen from this perspective, children's sports also comprise a field of competition where parents vie to demonstrate to themselves and others their relative competence as parents through the level of achievement won (or not won) by their sons and daughters. To suggest that the degree of success realized by children and youth in various sport activities may be interpreted by their parents as reflecting positively upon their performances as mothers and fathers is not simply to invoke the image of parents celebrating their genetic contribution to a child's physical capacities. It is, instead, to note the extent to which parental co-operation and support is essential to sustaining these activities.

In Canadian society, where a child's presumed chances of success or failure in making the transition to adulthood is increasingly attributed not to the vagaries of shifting economic structures, the shortcomings of state policy or even old-fashioned notions that certain children might be inherently possessed of a 'bad' character, the onus of responsibility for a child's outcome falls squarely on parents' shoulders. Organized sport has appropriated key elements of the doctrine of self-esteem in order to 'sell' their activities to parents. Parents can demonstrate to themselves and others that they are, indeed, 'doing the best that we can' by exhibiting their willingness to sacrifice their time and money to sustain their children's participation in sport, even when these activities may be less than satisfactory in certain respects to either parents or to their children.

How parents construct and interact with sport organizations tells us much about how they envision the wider world. The 'zero-sum' orientation of sport tends to correlate with abiding cultural notions held in Canada about the competitive nature of contemporary life. If sport contributes not only to nurturing children's self-esteem but also to preparing them for the competitive aspects of adult life, then it can be construed as not an optional but an essential resource for child rearing. This line of thinking is recognized by the sport industry and community sport organizations and readily accords with the institutional rhetoric of character building that is extolled as a rationale for fostering participation in sport by children and youth.

Although parents may sooner or later encounter what they regard as serious disjunctions between these claims and the actual experience encountered in a given club or sport, they may fear the possibility that, were they to press their complaints, they and their children might even be asked to withdraw from the game. Just as the behavioural shortcomings of children can be attributed to parents, so too can a lack of acquiescence from parents be revisited upon child athletes by offended coaches. If a number of parents were to band together and insist that their complaints be dealt with, there is always the possibility that coaches and league officials might simply decline to continue to volunteer their time and efforts to a given team or sport. Thus, parents are inclined to overlook the fact that coaches and officials, teams and leagues depend upon the continued participation of children and parents to sustain these sports. The demands of time and effort that parents would incur in attempting to organize themselves to exercise the possible influence that they might exert over community sports are usually sufficiently exacting to prevent this from being attempted by any but the most determined of parent activists. Yet to engage in confrontational activism in children's sport is to court disapproval for one's 'political' behaviour. Even worse, it might elicit a difficult-to-refuse invitation to take on a time-consuming role within the club or league.

For all of these reasons parents are for longer and shorter periods inclined to acquiesce with the arrangements proffered by community sport. The values that sport organizations claim to furnish to children through participation in sport are, in effect, 'sold back' to parents by organizations and a sport industry that is eager to maintain and enlarge its own operations. Thus, parental responsibilities and concerns, as articulated in contemporary ideologies of child development and socialization, are used instrumentally by sport officials to obtain continuing participation by both children and parents. Although a certain number of dissatisfied child athletes and disgruntled parents can be expected to leave given teams and sports in any given year, their departure is in some ways logistically less significant than the contribution that their participation has made to sustaining the team or sport in previous years. As long as leagues and clubs somehow survive from one year to the next, there is always the prospect of attracting new athletes and their parents in the coming season.

Conclusion

The elucidation of certain problematic features of organized sport for children should be read neither as a blanket dismissal of the people and activities that comprise this field nor as a denial of the capacity of children's sport to provide meaning, fun and other forms of enjoyment and satisfaction to many people. Indeed, I hold fond memories of days and seasons spent in the distant and more recent past, initially as an aspiring hockey and football player, subsequently as a parent of child and youth athletes, as a coach in two sports and as a sport official.[20] I look forward to future seasons in a field that has become both a space for personal engagement as well as one of anthropological interest.

The larger issue raised in this chapter concerns the capacity of bureaucratic entities, such as organized sport, to employ cultural ideologies in ways that render precarious taken-for-granted assumptions about the nature of relations between ostensibly voluntary organizations and their clients. Here we are venturing into territory that has been examined by Herzfeld (1992) in terms of the notion of secular theodicy. What this entails is 'the idiom of grumbling against the state through which people seek to excuse their humiliation at its hands' (Herzfeld 1992: 127). This grumbling invokes stereotypes of bureaucratic aloofness and indifference used as a means of coping with disappointment when state bureaucrats disappoint. Nevertheless, whenever citizens resort to using these stereotypes to account for their lack of success in seeking bureaucratic redress, they reinforce the expectation that bureaucracies are inherently unresponsive and that probably nothing can be done about this. This expectation can, in turn, be systematically transformed into a self-fulfilling prophecy by tactically astute officials. Thus, when citizens contemplate disputing bureaucratic decisions, says Herzfeld, they must prepare to fight on two fronts (Herzfeld 1992: 46). The first entails delving into the often obscure and overlapping rules and organizational minutiae that surround bureaucratic operations. Concessions can occasionally be won in this arena by citizens who have the determination and requisite cultural skills to persevere with their requests. Yet even limited success may demand a disproportionate investment of time and energy on the part of the petitioner, but from the outset dissatisfied citizens must also contemplate the possibility and ramifications of encountering culturally predicted failure that may even serve to jeopardize their standing in their communities. For anthropologists to examine bureaucratic practice as something separable from the popular response – more often than not, grumbling acquiescence – that it begets, is to overlook a key aspect of bureaucratic power.

In the case of children's sport the answer to why parents tend to put up with a system that disappoints many of them in fundamental ways takes two parts. First, sport offers a culturally attractive product, notwithstanding disjunctions between what is promised and what may be delivered. Second, parents are, by and large, fearful of the costs of disputing and resisting the arrangements that are offered to them and the conditions of participation required of them by sport organizations. In children's sport, secular theodicy involves labelling disputes and disagreements as instances of 'politics'. The received popular wisdom that 'politics don't belong in children's sport' embodies not only an idiom for questioning the legitimacy of complaints or disputes that have been or might potentially be pursued by parents, but also a means for instructing parents that participation in children's sport does not entitle them to resist preferred organizational practices. The stereotype of the 'meddling' parent can be readily applied to troublesome, 'interfering' parents not only by coaches, but also by other mothers and fathers who may wish to distinguish themselves as 'good' parents. The children of 'complaining' parents may be given less playing time, overlooked in the selection of future teams or even threatened with immediate expulsion. Those parents who are prepared to pay the social costs attached to challenging the status quo may – even if they are successful – no longer have a child involved in the sport by the time even relatively modest changes are effected. In the meantime, 'troublesome' parents can anticipate being excluded from whatever forms of camaraderie are enjoyed by other parents, the coach and sport officials. For a parent to become 'political' is almost invariably to court disapproval.

The cultural emphasis placed upon individual needs and responsibilities in children's sport provides little basis for initiating collective parental opposition to existing sport practices. Parents are encouraged to interact with each other, but only through channels and in accordance with guidelines established by coaches and officials. Notwithstanding the lip service that is commonly given to co-operation and 'teamwork', organized community sport frowns upon forms of parental mobilization that operate outside the confines of coach or official control. Even child and youth athletes are discouraged from analysing their own or teammates' performances independently of the coach. Ironically, it is those who doggedly work their way into and up the hierarchical managerial structures of sport organizations who appreciate the value of co-operation and the advantages of maintaining careful limits upon parental participation. They are the representatives who end up speaking on behalf of children's sport in Canada, explaining that 'we do it for the kids'. Perhaps the most incisive illustration of the cultural power conceded to sport organizations and the sport industry through cultivated parental acquiescence was provided by the response to the Ben Johnson scandal. The ability of the Canadian sport industry and sport bureaucrats to transform its response to an instance of utter corruption in elite professional sport into a rationale for extending the role of organized sport further into the lives of Canadian children cannot help but attract the attention of anthropologists interested in the cultural dynamics of power in social life.

Notes

1. I wish to thank Vered Amit for her careful reading of an earlier draft of this chapter and for her perceptive suggestions for revision.
2. Some important exceptions to this general neglect of the organizational dynamics of organized sport for children and youth include Andrews, Pitter, Zwick and Ambrose (1997) Fine (1987) McCormack and Chalip (1988) and Seppanen (1982).
3. See, for example, Amit-Talai, 1994; Amit-Talai and Wulff, 1995; James, 1986, 1993; Stephens, 1995; Wulff, 1988.
4. Ben Johnson, the winner of the men's 100 m competition at the 1988 Olympic Games was disqualified from the competition and forced to return his gold medal when post-race testing revealed that he had used steroids, a banned substance, to achieve his victory. See MacAloon (1990) for an analysis of the subsequent inquiry into the scandal.
5. Each club offered one sport, with the exception of the local chapter of the Special Olympics, which co-ordinated a number of sport activities for its child and adult members.
6. It is worth noting that the median household income of the parents surveyed was between $50,000-$75,000 annually, while almost a third reported household incomes of over $75,000 per annum, incomes

that would have placed most of these parents in a middle to relatively high income range. This raises questions not so much about which parents were surveyed, but rather about which children from which families can afford to participate in children's sport activities in British Columbia. In view of the relatively high incomes of the parents surveyed, attention needs to be given to the constraints placed by class and income upon participation in children's sport.

7. Identifying parents as 'customers' of sport services, the survey found that most parents agreed that coaches involved in children's sports needed training to perform their duties efficiently and reported that most parents were prepared to contribute additional funds for this purpose. Whether this line of inquiry represented an attempt by consultants who conducted the survey and who themselves are part of the sport industry to advance the claim that extra funding of the sport system is required is a matter of interpretation.

8. The driving time to each of these towns from New Westminster would be approximately an hour each way.

9. Löfgren (1987: 84) notes that the economic dependency extended to middle-class children in Sweden in the nineteenth century effectively cost these children their freedom. The same could be said of their Canadian counterparts in the late twentieth century.

10. Newman (1991: 121) identifies the ability to own a house as a benchmark of middle-class status in the US.

11. This set of 'self' concepts includes self-esteem, self-actualization, self identity, self worth, self-satisfaction and self-love, all of which pertain to notions of pride, satisfaction and happiness. The difficulties encountered in differentiating the precise purposes to which these associated terms have been put both in academic psychology and clinical practice is noted by Calhoun and Morse (1977).

12. Ward (1996: 10) notes that by the 1950s '[s]elf-esteem was fast becoming a central concept for psychologists without the cultural and reputational capital to be called theorists. It now was becoming important for those doing the manual labour of psychology.'

13. Woodhead (1990) makes a powerful point about how the conceptualizing of childhood in terms of 'needs' serves to attach both authority and emotive force to otherwise debatable cultural constructions championed by professional practitioners.

14. Seppanen (1982) depicts the club structure for children's sport in Finland, one that is similar to that which exists in Canada, as a situation where active, supportive parents become virtual 'servants' of their child and youth athletes.

15. Higgitt's (1994) study of low-income parents in Winnipeg, Manitoba, reports a frequently expressed regret on the part of parents about their inability to enable their children to participate in community sport activities.

16. McCormack and Chalip (1988) also remark upon the extent to which

the ideal of competitive achievement is, thereby, promoted as a pervasive element of the world of American adolescents.

17. Sport environments are, however, by no means unitary nor undifferentiated. Andrews, Pitter, Swick and Ambrose (1997) characterize children's soccer in the US as an activity that celebrates cultural values and ideals prized by white, middle-class, suburban mores. In their view, the overwhelmingly racially segregated nature of children's soccer in the US constitutes a 'compelling popular euphemism for class and racial superiority' (Andrews et al. 1997: 280).

18. Stephen's (1995: 11) observation of the anger that may be expressed at children who are not observing and reproducing 'traditional' cultural values is pertinent here.

19. The extent to which children's behaviour can be can be read, as Knowles (1996: 100) puts it, as 'telling a story' about family life needs to be recognized. James (1998: 147) also reports the manner in which elementary school teachers in England construct narratives of schoolchildren that incorporate information about their parents, family and home. James also notes the manner in which schoolteachers tend to attribute children's failures in school to their home lives while taking credit for whatever accomplishments may be registered. Although there is not space here to discuss similar dynamics at work in children's sport, suffice it to say that similar processes are to be found in sport activities.

20. I even have fond recollections of several (otherwise normally dreaded) fund-raising events that were rendered most enjoyable by the children and parents with whom I shared these occasions.

References

Amit-Talai, Vered (1994), 'Urban Pathways: The Logistics of Youth Peer Relations', in V. Amit-Talai and H. Lustiger-Thaler (eds), *Urban Lives: Fragmentation and Resistance*, Toronto: McClelland & Stewart, pp. 183-205.

Amit-Talai, Vered and Helena Wulff (eds) (1995), *Youth Cultures: A Cross-Cultural Perspective*, London/New York: Routledge.

Andrews, D.L., R. Pitter, D. Zwick, and D. Ambrose (1997), 'Soccer's Racial Frontier: Sport and the Suburbanization of Contemporary America', in Gary Armstrong and Richard Giulianotti (eds), *Entering the Field: New Perspectives on World Football*, Oxford/New York: Berg, pp. 261-81.

Calhoun, George Jr., and William C. Morse (1977), 'Self-Concept and Self-Esteem: Another Perspective', *Psychology in the Schools*, 14(1): 318-22.

Dyck, Noel (1995), 'Parents, Consociates and the Social Construction of Children's Athletics', *Anthropological Forum*, 7(2): 215-29.

— (2000), 'Home Field Advantage? Exploring the Social Construction of Children's Sport', in Vered Amit (ed.), *Constructing the 'Field': Fieldwork at the Turn of the Century*, London/New York: Routledge, pp. 32-53.

Dyck, Noel and Grant Wildi (1993), *Creating Community Sport for Kids: A Survey of Community Sport Clubs and Associations for Children and Youth in Coquitlam, Port Coquitlam, and Port Moody, British Columbia, During the 1992-3 Season*, Burnaby, British Columbia: Department of Sociology and Anthropology, Simon Fraser University.

Fine, Gary Alan (1987), *With the Boys: Little League Baseball and Preadolescent Culture*, Chicago: University of Chicago Press.

Fine, Gary Alan and Jay Mechling (1991), 'Minor Difficulties: Changing Children in the Late Twentieth Century', in Alan Wolfe (ed.), *America at Century's End*, Berkeley/Los Angeles/London: University of California Press, pp. 58-78.

Herzfeld, Michael (1992), *The Social Production of Indifference: Exploring the Symbolic Roots of Western Bureaucracy*, New York/Oxford: Berg.

Higgitt, Nancy C. (1994), *Factors Influencing Residential Mobility Among Families With Children Living in a Low-Income Area of Winnipeg, Manitoba*, Ottawa: Central Mortgage and Housing Corporation.

James, Allison (1986), 'Learning to Belong: The Boundaries of Adolescence', in Anthony P. Cohen (ed.), *Symbolising Boundaries: Identity and Diversity in British Cultures*, Manchester: University of Manchester Press, pp. 155-70.

— (1993), *Childhood Identities: Self and Social Relationships in the Experience of the Child*, Edinburgh: Edinburgh University Press.

— (1995), 'On being a child: The self, the group and the category', in A.P. Cohen and N. Rapport (eds), *Questions of Consciousness*, New York/London: Routledge, pp. 60-76.

— (1998), 'Imaging Children 'At Home', 'In the Family' and 'At School': Movement Between the Spatial and Temporal Markers of Childhood Identity in Britain', in N. Rapport and A. Dawson (eds), *Migrants of Identity: Perceptions of Home in a World of Movement*, Oxford/New York: Berg, pp. 139-60.

Knowles, Caroline (1996), *Family Boundaries: The Invention of Normality and Dangerousness*, Peterborough, Ontario: Broadview Press.

Löfgren, Orvar (1987), 'Deconstructing Swedishness: Culture and Class in Modern Sweden', in A. Jackson (ed.), *Anthropology at Home*, ASA Monographs 25, London/New York: Tavistock, pp. 74-93.

MacAloon, John J. (1990), 'Steroids and the Stade: Dubin, Melodrama and the Accomplishment of Innocence', *Public Culture*, 2(2): 41-64.

MacGregor, Roy (1995), *The Home Team: Fathers, Sons and Hockey*, Toronto: Viking.

McCormack, J.B., and L. Chalip (1988), 'Sport as Socialization: A Critique of Methodological Premises', *The Social Science Journal* 25,(1): 83-92.

Minister's Task Force on Federal Sport Policy (1992), *Sport: The Way Ahead. An Overview of the Task Force Report*, Ottawa: Minister of State Fitness and Amateur Sport and Minister of Supply and Services Canada.

Morss, J.R. (1990), *The Biologising of Childhood: Developmental Psychology and the Darwinian Myth*, Hillsdale USA: Lawrence Erlbaum Associates.

Newman, Katherine S. (1988), *Falling From Grace: The Experience of Downward Mobility in the American Middle Class*, New York: Free Press.

— (1991), 'Uncertain Seas: Cultural Turmoil and the Domestic Economy', in Alan Wolfe (ed.), *America at Century's End*, Berkeley/Los Angeles/London: University of California Press, pp. 112-30.

Persell, Caroline Hodges (1991), 'Schools Under Pressure', in Alan Wolfe (ed.), *America at Century's End*, Berkeley/Los Angeles/London: University of California Press, pp. 283-97.

Prout, Alan and Allison James (1990), 'A New Paradigm for the Sociology of Childhood? Provenance, Promise and Problems', in A. James and A. Prout (eds), *Constructing and Reconstructing Childhood: Contemporary Issues in the Sociological Study of Childhood*, Basingstoke/New York: Falmer Press, pp. 7-34.

Seppanen, P. (1982), 'Sports Clubs and Parents as Socializing Agents in Sports', *International Review of Sport Sociology*, 17(1): 79-90.

SOAR International (1994), *Sport Parent Survey*, Victoria: prepared for the British Columbia Ministry of Government Services, Sports and Commonwealth Games Division.

Stacey, Judith (1991), 'Backward Toward the Postmodern Family: Reflections on Gender, Kinship, and Class in the Silicon Valley', in Alan Wolfe (ed.), *America at Century's End*, Berkeley/Los Angeles/London: University of California Press, pp. 17-34.

Stainton Rogers, Rex and Wendy Stainton Rogers (1992), *Stories of Childhood: Shifting Agendas of Child Concern*, New York: Harvester Wheatsheaf.

Stephens, Sharon (1995), 'Children and the Politics of Culture in Late Capitalism', in S. Stephens (ed.), *Children and the Politics of Culture*, Princeton, New Jersey: Princeton University Press, pp. 3-48.

Thorne, Barrie (1993), *Gender Play: Girls and Boys in School*, New Brunswick, New Jersey: Rutgers University Press.

Ward, Steven (1996), 'Filling the World With Self-Esteem: A Social History of Truth-Making', *Canadian Journal of Sociology*, 21(1): 1-23.

Wigman, Bert (1990), 'The Incitement to Self-Interest: Donzelot, His Critics, and the Case of the 'New Education' in South Australia', *Anthropological Forum*, 6(2): 257-75.

Wolfe, Alan (1991), 'Change From the Bottom Up', in Alan Wolfe (ed.), *America at Century's End*, Berkeley/Los Angeles/London: University of California Press, pp. 1-13.

Woodhead, Martin (1990), 'Psychology and the Cultural Construction of Children's Needs', in Allison James and Alan Prout (eds), *Constructing and Reconstructing Childhood: Contemporary Issues in the Social Study of Childhood*, London: Falmer Press, pp. 60-77.

Wulff, Helena (1988), *Twenty Girls: Growing Up, Ethnicity and Excitement in a South London Microculture*, Stockholm: Department of Social Anthropology, University of Stockholm.

7

Reflections on the Social and Cultural Dimensions of Children's Elite Sport in Sweden

Yngve Georg Lithman

The concept of 'children's sport' is loaded with a number of positive connotations in our societies: healthy children who in friendly ways play ball, soccer or ice hockey, are engaged in gymnastics, track and field, wrestling or whatever the case may be.[1] They learn what it means to cooperate, have sensible 'leisure habits', develop their talents, set a goal and work toward its realization, and keep out of bad company. Society as a whole is supportive and builds sport centres and arenas while the schools have also taken account of sport. The literature written for young people is replete with stories of how sports have saved young people from the streets and have provided them with alternative and successful careers. It may be added that by far the largest part of the social science literature about children's sport, regardless of how 'theoretical' or 'applied' it purports to be, is firmly committed to socialization and norm-learning perspectives. A child's participation in sport is seen as expressive of processes whereby the child is equipped mentally and morally for the society in which he or she lives.

The purpose of this chapter is not to contrast the popular view of children's sport with what it 'really' is, nor to advance arguments for certain reforms. Rather, the intention is to reflect upon children's sport as a cultural phenomenon, in particular how it manifests and actuates culturally given conceptualizations and symbolisms. One may go even further and claim that children's sport is a field of activity where the participants – children, parents, leaders – are engaged in a joint act of creating meaning. This can only be understood by acknowledging that children's sport is part of a wider societal context, although this is not intended to be a circular argument. Into children's sport as a field of activity thus flow cultural goods and culturally given questions, and in some measure there is a kneading of these into partially new goods and new questions. These, in turn, are of significance to the orientations of the participants, as well as to the society outside of children's sport. Although for analytical purposes it may be necessary to make a distinction between sport on the one hand, and that which is outside sport on the other, it would run counter to the argument to be presented here to stress that distinction. What is 'in sport', or what is created there, is as 'real', in all senses of the word, as what exists outside of sport.

With this perspective, one is led to a number of questions about what sport is, and what the 'cultural' in sport stands for. A comprehensive treatment of this requires answers to questions such as what sport is in a cultural perspective? How is one to understand how sport is embedded in and a part of the rest of society? But children's sport actuates not only what sport is, but also what a child is as a cultural category. Which notions about children are manifest in children's sport? To deal with how sports and children are culturally constituted in our societies is no easy task. These issues raise fundamental questions about the shape of our societies and the cultural logic upon which they are based: what is a 'person', what is the child supposed to become? And, concerning two common concepts used to divide time and spheres of activities, what is 'work' and what is 'leisure'? Nevertheless culture, understood in terms of shared cognitions, symbols and consciousness, does not exist in a vacuum but must be seen in relation to people's social life in a more general sense. To this realm belong social relationships, the organization of everyday lives, work-related anchorages in society and individuals' economic and temporal resources. So the 'cultural' has a reference in the 'social', and vice versa, and these two aspects of human life interact in a continuous dialectic.

If what has been said above reflects some of the complex background against which children's sport has to be understood, it also follows that each investigation of this field has to recognize its limitations. The purpose of this chapter is to present in outline form an analytical framework for examining this field.

Sport in Society

How is it to be understood that sport has become such a massive contemporary phenomenon? Why is the largest section of a daily newspaper devoted to sport? How can one explain the jogging craze? Why the Heysel tragedy? Why are competitive sports played? Why do hundreds of thousands of parents, once or several times a week drive their children to sport practices? How do we explain children's sport?

The sociological and anthropological literature about sport, often exciting (perhaps because so many of its authors have had a personal relationship to sport and have thought hard about the nature of this experience) often has its starting point in the analysis of how sport is tied into society. Some issues have received considerable attention, such as how sport is related to national(istic)/ethnic concerns, how it reflects or is made a part of ideological or other conflicts in society, how it involves gender relations, and how behaviour at sport events may pertain to issues of social control (for example Dunning 1993; Guttmann 1991; Hargreaves 1994; Hoberman 1984,1997; MacAloon 1981; MacClancy1996). Cultural historians and developmentally oriented anthropologists such as Mandel (1984) and Blanchard and Cheska (1985) regard sport as a specific part of society with a developmental history of its own. However some of the most significant inspirations for analysis in this article have been drawn from the (rightly or wrongly) so-called neo-Marxist tradition.

Rigauer's (1979) attempt to demonstrate the parallels between sport and work results in a claim that the two are basically identical and thus co-support each other in the maintenance of society. This relates to a tradition where sport is seen as one vehicle through which the labour force is reproduced and socialized. Sport is thus not an 'alternative' to everyday living. Prokop (1971: 21) makes an even stronger statement, suggesting that sport is 'the capitalistically distorted form of play through which' – to paraphrase Guttman's (1978: 69) characterization of this neo-Marxist argument – 'sport does not offer compensation for the frustrations of alienated labour in capitalist society, it seduces the luckless athlete and the spectator into a second world of work more authoritarian and repressive and less meaningful than the economic sphere itself.' Another twist to the neo-Marxist argument, with a broad sociological grounding, is represented by Gruneau's (1983) treatment of how the organization of sport betrays class conflicts and the international position of the Canadian state. Somewhat similar, at least in its ambitions, is the approach taken by John Hargreaves (1986) in an attempt to transplant Foucaultian- and Gramscian-inspired analyses to sport. Hargreaves's discussion of the commercialization process, body control as expressive of power, and the role of the state in sport are themes that have become central to many authors.

A more pronounced cultural analytical perspective in a more anthropological vein is also exemplified in the sport literature. One of its most prominent exponents is Guttmann (actually not an anthropologist as far as academic specialization is concerned), whose starting point is that sport has its roots in the spontaneous expression of physical energy (1978: 89) but that its expression must be seen as the rationalization of the romantic. To this same category, according to Guttmann, belong such things as the Apollo moon voyages. Even if Guttman has a firm launching pad in Weber and shows a considerable grasp of general sociology in his criticism of the neo-Marxists, his basic stance on what sport 'is' remains unclear, but certainly his analysis of how baseball, through its embracing and expression of certain core values of American culture has become a national sport, is firmly rooted in a persuasive cultural analysis – although there are some who would not accept this statement (such as Wills 1992). One foundation of Guttman's thinking is that sport is both a reflection of and an alternative to everyday social and cultural life. In contrast to the scientific worldview arises a romanticism that drapes itself in the idiom of the scientific worldview: 8.84 is something quite different than 9.94 – at least if you are a 100 m runner. The scientific worldview's division of seconds into hundredths of seconds is expressed in the valorization of the athlete, and the romanticism surrounding the human body and its efforts receives increased nourishment. This approach is also helpful in understanding the cultural logic behind, for instance, the disqualification of Ben Johnson at the Seoul Olympics, as it translates itself into notions of what the body should be, proclaiming ideals of bodily purity and 'fairness'. By not 'being himself', by virtue of using performance-enhancing drugs, he cheated the spectator – the spectator did not see what the spectator thought he or she did.

A stroll through the sport literature undoubtedly shows that sport is an intimate part of the surrounding society and culture and expressive of these. Sport does not exist, nor is it possible to analyse it, outside of an understanding of the society in which it is generated. That general social and cultural processes and phenomena are manifested in sport is indisputable. But which? And how? What an anthropological analysis can contribute to this field must be an understanding of the relationship between immediate social organization, the social relations of sport and the management of meaning that takes place in sport – the understanding of what takes place between co-actors in concrete social situations. This was the premise of the project on children's sport from which this chapter stems.

Towards a Cultural Analytical Perspective

To make sense of observations gleaned over several years of intermittent fieldwork related to children and youth engaged in elite ice hockey and gymnastics in Sweden forbids simple explanations. What follows is not an attempt to 'deduce' from the empirical material. Instead, the argument advanced here presupposes that the researcher has to suggest interpretations, and show how these interpretations make sense in terms of accounting for the field material. This model, of course, emerges in a continuous dialectic between data and theorizing, but it cannot be solely deduced from data.

A general starting point is that our societies are what Weber, perhaps, would have called 'non-transparent'. For the individual citizen, society is difficult to grasp and handle and in a sense remains disguised. Not least is this demonstrated in the fact that contemporary Western society and culture does not provide a 'thick' symbolism concerning fundamental existential questions. The person does not experience him- or herself as a part of a cosmic plan of the kind provided by Christianity or Islam during certain times. Instead, the 'individualist revolution' (Dumont 1986) has led to an individualistic ideology where the individual is made the focal point, the central value in society and culture. The single person is no longer seen as someone subordinated to a religious or secular plan – someone whose existence is there for the joy of God or the larger social good. Life and death, love, birth, creation, passion, ageing – this is all in an ideological sense contained within the individual life course and made into the attributes of the individual.[2] The individual becomes the existential.

This process of ideological individualization has permeated Occidental thinking during several centuries rooted in the Enlightenment era as well as the capitalist mode of production, and is related to how 'the economic' establishes itself as a specific sphere in society, disembedded from webs of social relationships (Polany 1971; Dumont 1977; Oesterreich 1979). The person is established as an individual and vested with and made individually responsible for morals, life course and actions.

The singular body also becomes an individual body, and the body is in large measure seen as a moral expression. Until fairly recently, 'good posture' was one of the concepts through which youngsters learned to demonstrate their submission to authorities. Through 'good posture' the individual demonstrated – at least in the north European Lutheran context – that he or she was a morally well-equipped person. Bodily posture, interpreted as a sign of individual moral worth, became an expression of social order. Social order became, in a sense, individually moral.

But in what ways is this non-transparency constituted today? In a society built on an individualistic ideology, there is a lack of given, codified and religiously or secularly legitimated answers to fundamental existential questions. Of fundamental importance is also that the very organization of society makes transparency impossible. This observation applies both on a more aggregate level as well as in interpersonal relations. How, then, can we integrate our daily activities with existential questions? How is our life, death, love and creativity coupled to what we spend the better part of our time on? How are the products of our working lives – a mended elevator, a scientific paper, a construction blueprint, a payment in a super-market – related to our lives in a more existentialist sense?

This line of reasoning comes close to what some authors have discussed under the label of alienation, involving how a person is alienated from the products of his or her efforts (Fromm 1955). For two reasons, one might wish to shun this perspective, although it is easy to have considerable sympathy for some of its developments. First, there is in the alienation concept the inherent assumption that the non-alienated exists. But to find this one would (if not subscribing to a radical socialist utopia) be forced to compare one's circumstances with traditional societies so fundamentally different from our own that the value of the comparison becomes fairly futile. Second, and perhaps even more important, the discussion of the non-transparency of our societies should be coupled to a discussion of the 'meeting' of peoples in our societies. What opportunities are there in our societies for people to manifest themselves to each other in interaction?

The human 'meeting', as discussed here, rests on Mead's (1967) classic discussion of the relationship between 'self' and 'other', and the subsequent development of these concepts provided by other authors. The starting premise is that Self has both the status of object, Me, and the status of subject, I. I can see both Me and Others, but Self can only be produced in relations with Other. Thus, man (or woman) is a social product resulting from social interaction. The relationship between I and Me is shaped through how Others react to the Self. In Sartre's (1956) existentialism, this reasoning is extended to the claim that I can only see my Self through how Others see Me, but (and this is an important point for the following discussion) as Sörhaug (1984) puts it, the Self is always at least in some measure defined by Others. But Self can never be Others. Self can therefore never quite be itself.

For Mead, the tension between Me and I represented a dynamic force in social life; for Sartre, the gap between I and Me represents a kind of ontological loss attaching to being human, but the interesting thing in the context of this chapter is how this gap is constituted in different societal conditions and then managed. That these issues receive particular attention after the 'death of God' and the advent of the individualism revolution, prior to which religious and other large-scale symbolic systems defined man and the individual, is obvious.

If the individual Self is constructed in an interchange with Others, what can be said about the shape of this interchange in view of what has been said above about society becoming less transparent? Has the individual, so to speak, become less transparent to him- or herself? And to others? The answer suggested in this essay is in the affirmative, and is built on the premise that the Self in some sense may be seen as the result of a learning process – that is, in the social interchange, one learns who one is, what that which is Me comprises. Such learning presupposes, however, a relatively stable and integrated end result, a certain consistency in how Others react to a person. Equally important, it presupposes a certain knowledge about who the Other is. All Others are not equally significant to person's notions about who he or she is.[3]

It can be assumed that the changes that our societies have seen in an individualizing direction, both ideologically but also in certain other regards, affect both an individual's transparency to him- or herself, and also the knowledge that an individual has about Others. Each individual's life course, it can be argued, has become more unique, not least in comparison with that of members of earlier and coming generations. Each parent is also aware of the fact that his or her children will, only to a very limited extent, reproduce their parents' life courses, culturally, socially and professionally. Youth culture, geographical mobility, day care centres and a wealth of 'large-scale' social factors all point to this prospect, that the possibilities to be significant others across generational boundaries has decreased. Also, not least over the last fifty years, we have witnessed a development away from a whole set of 'communities' that had as one feature that the individual's life in large measure could be interpreted as representative of a modality rather than as an individual idiosyncrasy. Both in rural agricultural society, in company towns and in the workplaces and neighbourhood 'communities' in cities, it may be assumed that the knowledge individuals had about each other, and the identity one then presumed between Self and Other, made the individual into something that was experienced as a shared modality rather than a Sartrian ontological loss. Daily interaction or 'rubbing shoulders with' the same set of people within a community life of this kind, it is hypothesized, may have had the significance of substituting to some extent for a dying or dead God.

So we are faced with an increasingly non-transparent society in which people in an ongoing individualization process experience ontological loss. In what ways does this lead us to an understanding of sport? The hypothesis advanced here is that in the sportive expression, the bodily management intrinsic to sport provides a comprehensive symbolic expression for fundamental questions concerning what the individual is, the nature of relationships between people and peoples' place and movements in society, thereby making non-transparency situationally and symbolically transparent. Fundamental existential questions are coupled with issues about the individual in society and given a comprehensive symbolic expression. The aesthetic dimension, the 'perfect' execution of a play in hockey or a superb execution in the roman rings in gymnastics, provides a ritualized seal of confirmation, immediately available for the emotional infusion anthropologists have described in rituals that engage existential and social fundaments.

The Body as Boundary and Sign, and the Emergence of an One-Dimensional Ideology

The relationship between Self and Others has been discussed above in terms of seeing oneself in others. But one may also direct attention to the media through which communication between Self and Others take place. Between Self and Others there is a boundary constituted of the symbolism that is expressive of the presentation of Self to Others (Mead's 'significant symbols' partly belong in this discussion), but a thought-provoking hypothesis presents itself: that the body is no longer perceived as a sign for other things, as a sign for who one actually is, but instead has come to be regarded as who one actually is. There is no longer a 'body' and a 'person' in the sense that a problematization of a distance between them is possible. This seems to be an essential ingredient of the ideological fundament for the present surge in children's sport.

This ideology is also heavily promoted in the market place and reaches effectively into children's sport. An illustration to this is provided for example by items like the widely circulated catalogue from the sports equipment dealer 'Gymkraft' (roughly translated as Gymnastics power).[4] The section on pages 26 and 27 declares that, 'With an exercise corner at home, the exercise will get done', and that all this happens when you exercise:

> You develop strong muscles in the whole body – your physical shape and stamina improve, you can take more, both physically and mentally – your motivation, joy of life and self-confidence increase and you feel better. Your ability to achieve improves. You lose weight – your arm strength improves.

And so on. The illustrations show beautiful people, not least sexy women, utilizing the Gymkraft equipment. What does all this tell us?

A first observation is how the lack of exercise is coupled to bad consciousness and morals – with Gymkraft's gadgets, the exercise will finally get done. Further, exercise is not only intended to provide some general bodily well-being, but is also tied to motivation, joy of life, self-confidence, mental stamina, reduced tension and stress, clearer thinking and increased creativity. In the catalogue there are also numerous references to symbolically heavily laden concepts such as the heart and the blood system, and sexual connotations are evident in numerous instances. However, it is not just a correlation or, rather, an identity between body and person that is demonstrated. A desirable condition, 'feeling well', is also defined, as well as a way of getting there – through subjecting the body to the discipline offered by the exercise technology. This bodily suffering is self induced and joyous, desirable in order that an esteemed condition will emerge; the identity between body and person demonstrates that the individual has the will power, including a self-flagellating ability, which is required in order to realize the notions about the good life formulated in (parts) of our culture.

So the body has ceased to be a sign of something. Instead, an identity has arisen between the 'bodily' and the 'spiritual' aspects of the individual through an ideological-cultural development. The conceptualization of the person has become homogenized into a single whole. The bodily is fused with the non bodily, and the non bodily with the bodily. The person, both as a boundary against others, entailing the visible (the body), but also as a self concept, including the notions about who one is, has became fused into a single entity.

This development represents an aspect of the 'individualism revolution', the valorization of the individual in Occidental thinking, but the individualistic ideology has been extended to signify that a person's moral/ intellectual qualities have become firmly a part of the body (and vice versa). The individual's moral-intellectual qualities are no longer to be perceived as an attachment to thought systems outside the individual. An ideological inversion has occurred – the individual becomes sovereign, but not (only) to choose among the moral/intellectual baggage around him or her. Instead, the moral/intellectual qualities encompassed within the individual are viewed as derived from within the individual. We may, therefore, talk of the emergence of a one-dimensional ideology within which a person's bodily and mental aspects are understood to be fused beyond any possibility of disengagement from one another. This also means that one of these aspects cannot be considered or handled in isolation from the other.

In such a perspective, one's own body is a permanent reference, and the ideology takes its starting point in those concepts that couple the moral/intellectual with bodily/physical aspects of the individual: motivation, feeling well, health, self realization, well-being, being in shape, being 'naturally and beautifully tanned', possessing willpower, 'stronger life', relaxation, 'peace of body and mind' and so on , to refer again to Gymkraft's catalogue.

The One-Dimensional Ideology

The view of what a person is, which has been outlined above and which is today distributed through many channels, is widely accepted within the sport movement. In children's sport, particularly in the elite competitive brackets, the conception of the child as a one-dimensional being where the intellectual/moral and the bodily/physical is seen as a fused and given entity, receives perhaps its clearest expression. This can be studied in a number of circumstances within children's sport: how the child's athletic achievements are coupled to the total evaluation of the child as a person; how the parents of sporting children are internally ranked with regard to their children's abilities; and, how children's sporting activities have a determining impact on all aspects of family organization, including both financial and time budgets. Indeed, one may well argue that in many families with athletically active children, there is no factor that has such a pervasive influence over the organization of daily life, including even the parents' working lives. The success of a child in sport is not the success of the child 'in sport'; it is, with just slight exaggeration, a statement about the total worth of the child.

It should be added that the one-dimensional view of a person also furnishes the opportunity for establishing a precise ranking between individuals. As the intellectual/moral and the bodily/physical has fused and received an unequivocal expression in the bodily achievement, athletic achievement provides a singular and comprehensive clarity for judging who the individual is and, as far as children's sport is concerned, the evaluation of the children is also extended to their parents.

The Seriousness of Children's Sport

What has been said above can be summarized as an argument about a non-transparent society, which features difficulty in constituting the Self through interaction with Other(s), since the mirror Other has become blurred. Therefore, an orientation towards boundary symbolism has occurred involving specifically the body. The structure of the one-dimensional ideology demands an ideological universe referenced for one entity in the body and its expressions. So how does all this come together in the world of children's sport?

To avoid misunderstandings, it should be stated that the world of children's sport comprises many things. What is presented here from elite level children's sport, however, appears to anticipate the direction in which large segments of children's sport are moving. In clubs which used to have what were explicitly called 'social aims', the situation is also changing. So the Aelvsjoe soccer club in a Stockholm suburb still claims to have 'social aims' but this is now concatenated with the pragmatically based consideration that a too-early 'separation of the wheat from the chaff' may result in the loss of good players who just happen not to be 'stars' in their

Figure 7 Ice hockey players [Yngve Georg Lithman]

preteen childhood. Social aims, while ostensibly still there, are now more an expression for prevailing thinking about how to achieve a good first team in the future.

The first thing which strikes anyone who comes into contact with children's sport is how seriously participation in this whole sphere of activity is taken to be. Counting in the calendar for the month of January for a ten-year old boy who was engaged in ice hockey and gymnastics, one finds that he was expected to be with his ice hockey team nineteen days, including two full days for a tournament, six other games and eleven practices. His gymnastics schedule embraced fourteen practices, one one-day competition and three days of training camp. It was a given that he would attempt to be present at each practice and competitive event. He saw his future in terms of applying for a place in an athletically oriented highschool (a Swedish school form organized in collaboration with the various sport federations) and thereafter as a professional hockey player. In a discussion with a schoolmate, they agreed that they would probably not see much of each other as grown ups since one would become a hockey 'pro' in Canada, the other a soccer 'pro' in Italy.

On the hockey team the notion shared by the kids themselves that winning was the important thing, was fully and unreservedly embraced. During the particular season that is reflected in the calendar page mentioned above, the coach started to use only two 'line-ups' out of three towards the end of important and uncertain games. The club's objective was that the team would win a place in the top division of the St Erik's tournament (a Stockholm-wide, age- and division-structured tournament for ice hockey teams, now renamed Aftonbladet Cup, after the new sponsor). Among the players, the use of only some of the players in important and critical situations led to internal distinctions within the team based on skill. After one game, one of the ten-year-old players discussed with a team mate whether the team should start games against difficult teams with two line-ups and three centre forwards instead of the usual three line-ups. To make a long story short, among the players there were no sentiments that there was something inherently wrong in reducing the number of players used, only arguments about who should be benched.

What can be said about coaches and parents? Why, for instance, does a forty-year-old electrician work as a coach and devote some ten to twenty hours a week to a hockey team of ten-year-old boys? One explanation, in itself not invalid, is that this raises his social standing in a variety of circles. Friends in the sport club, workmates and others, will accord him a higher rank due to his athletic activities. Nevertheless, this explanation, it may be argued, misses the main point: why does participation in sports do this, and does it not trivialize this electrician's massive input of time into coaching if it is interpreted solely as a vehicle for achieving social prestige?

The demands made upon the parents can be understood when contemplating the family schedule. A thousand dollars is easily spent in equipment, gas money, training camps and club fees. The parents' working days will, if possible, have to be adjusted. Vacations will have to be placed so that they fit with training camps, meets or competitions. One mother who worked as a hospital attendant, described a hockey training camp for her son as 'three extra nights at the hospital', in order to earn the fee.

So what is it that induces coaches and parents to make these efforts? What is it that provides sport and children's sport with its popularity and emotional engagement? The answer relates to the capacity of sport to provide a comprehensive, miniaturized and manifest image of human beings, of society and of basic existential questions. Through its miniaturization and embodiment, this image also becomes possible to manage and manipulate. It is also available for and amenable to being appropriated by the individual as a thinking, feeling and acting subject.

The Manifest Individual

Sport operates, as has been argued above, with a condensed, one-dimensional image of man or woman. The individual is seen in terms of his or her immediately available presentations and prestations. The value, as expressed in a coach's selection of skaters during a hockey power play (when the opposing team has fewer players due to an assessed penalty) or of some players having to sit when only two line-ups are used, is immediately demonstrated. It is also significant that one of the recurring conflicts that emerges in children's sport is when a parent of a low-ranking child athlete argues that too much emphasis is placed upon current achievement and insufficient consideration is accorded to players' athletic potential. The underlying rule that the best players are to be rewarded (rather than affording every member of the team an equal opportunity to play) is not questioned, only such things as at what age the child is able to show 'what stuff he or she is really made of'.

The condensed concept of man and the resulting simplicity with which individuals can be ranked also has significance for the social ranking of the parents. Parents whose child is performing competently or rapidly improving will be asked to take on important tasks such as serving as the team's parent representative or equipment manager. The parents of sporting children are thus accorded a social standing indirectly, through their children's achievement. To have a successful child athlete means, in the world of competitive children's sport, that one is regarded as someone who more than other parents symbolizes what a human being should be. So, children's achievements are a kind of proxy achievement for their parents. Whoever has watched some parents' ritualized scolding and rejection of their children when they perform poorly or, alternatively, parents' enthusiasm when their sons and daughters are successful will have vivid images with which to illustrate this statement.

The Manifest Society

Not only the person becomes manifest in sport, but also what society is all about. This can be illustrated most readily by examining issues related to careers and material rewards. In the non-transparent society, it becomes a question why one ended up where one did. Why did one become an electrician, an academic or an industrial worker? Yet, to interpret one's situation in terms of voluntarism and an open society does not feel completely meaningful. What was it that one actually did choose? Certainly not more than some aspects of the circumstances in which one finds oneself. And looking around, one does not think that society particularly distinguishes itself by its transparency, or that social life is easy to grasp. Society is, perhaps, not chaotic, but also not very easy to comprehend.

Into this non-transparency comes sport, not simply or only as a miniaturized version of society, but rather as a type of activity whose content in certain regards is not predetermined. In this vacillating model of sport as an immediate reproduction of society or as an 'empty' activity, open to interpretation, lies the power of sport to provide explanatory images of society. This duality can be illustrated in terms of two different parents and their approaches to sport, but is also common to a single individual's sense of what sport comprises.

One father of two of hockey-playing sons explained on one occasion that 'when the oldest son started to play hockey, he was for a few years among the best in the team. He was always given lots of ice time, and played power plays and so on. The others started to catch up with him, and sometimes he now has to sit when the coach only uses two line-ups. And that's one of the fine things with sport, because that's the way it is in society too. If you don't work hard and fight and exhaust yourself during practice hours, nothing will happen. And he's starting to realize that now.' This father perceives a direct parallel between athletic endeavours and social life, and the lessons from one field of activity are directly transportable to the other.

Another father, an immigrant to Sweden and industrial worker, never fashioned this particular type of linkage. Instead, his view was that sport represented a kind of repudiation of the organizing principles in existing society. In his eyes, it was a given that what ought to be rewarded in society were the persons who best manifested the one-dimensional ideology outlined above. His son's athletic achievements as a sprinter, soccer-, hockey- and bandy- (another team sport on ice) player was the foundation for the father's realm of interests. He was a faithful watcher during each practice session. It may be added that his son 'had to quit playing bandy' because – to the father's mind – he developed skating strides in bandy that would be inappropriate as far as his hockey career was concerned. The son's future, the father firmly believed, lay with professional hockey. For this father, the world of sport – built on the one-dimensional ideology about persons and with its specific variety of a vitalistic ideology – was the kind of reality around which he thought society should be constructed.

Both these examples show how different connections are made between sport and society. They have in common, however, that sport is used in a discourse about how society is or ought to be constructed. This statement is true not only on an ideological and intellectual level, for sport also provides fathers and mothers of athletic children with the tools to operate upon these notions in an everyday praxis. The first father, a computer technician, can in his relations with his children sustain his images of the surrounding society using sport as a medium. The immigrant father, wielding his stop watch on forest trails during the summers supervising his son's training, demonstrates that there is a reality which is as real as any other and which has to do with bodily-individual expression. In both of these examples, one may note how images of society as it is or how it should be, are appropriated into a manageable praxis where a parent operates upon those social and cultural principles that he or she finds valid. The non-transparency is made transparent, manageable and expressible. This also provides that parties to the interaction, such as father and son, are made manifest to each other.

To this should be added the observation that the professionalization of sport, as the saying goes, contributes to the impression of 'authenticity' that increasingly surrounds sport. Playing with an elite children's hockey team can, in fact, in a few years time be transformed into top professional contracts and the realization of dreams of playing in the National Hockey League. Whoever suggests this is a marginal phenomenon has not seen the number of Gretzky or Forsberg posters displayed in their bedrooms by hockey-playing youngsters. That only a handful will get the chance even to try out as professionals would not be immediately evident from the manner in which hockey parents may talk or jest about it.

It would be misleading to leave the issue of material rewards for bodily expressions in sport merely with a comment on professionalization. Instead, one must also appreciate how the world of sport and athletes, even including the games of ten year olds, becomes part of a general commoditization process, the significance of which is, paradoxically, to further increase the belief in the authenticity of sport. On the hockey helmets of ten year olds one reads 'Philips – the thinking office', because this company supports the team with roughly $1,000 per season. If the team wins the St Erik's tournament, the participants will receive a number of gifts at a public ceremony while the announcer recounts which companies have donated what. The value of the prizes that each player receives is not large, totalling perhaps $100, but the symbolism is unavoidable: the individual athlete, seen through the one-dimensional ideology, receives these goods as a reward for achievement expressed through the management of his body.

Manifest Relations

One of the most characteristic features of modern sport is that each achievement is accorded a value. It is measured, weighed, timed and judged. An individual is accorded a worth related to how much he or she can achieve compared to others. The value of a team is judged according to how it manages compared to other teams. The ranking is based on clear and easily defined principles and is expressed in how individual players are used in a team, particularly in a competition such as he St Erik's ice hockey tournament, a stratified competition that includes teams of nine year olds.

So how are notions about the individual related to the notions about the team? The dictum here is that the fate of the team reflects the abilities of its individual players, as well as the coaches' ability to 'use the material'. In this, there is a paradox, for to use the material correctly means letting every individual achieve to their maximum, showing the true level of his ability. But in order to do this, the player must subordinate himself to the coaches' directives. The hierarchy between coaches and players thus receives its justification in that it is seen as allowing each player to perform at his maximum. Simply but correctly expressed, the patterns of social relationships exhibited in sport are built upon the practice that each individual is accorded a place in a structure, such as a team, depending upon achievement, and that the hierarchy is there to let individuality achieve its highest expression.

But what about 'communitas' – doesn't the belonging that transcends individuality and which manifests unity in non-structure exist in sports?

Surely, but it may well be argued that it exists in sport in spite of a wealth of factors pressing in the opposite direction. In the daily monotony of practising individual sports, as in gymnastics, one sees genuine expressions of comradeship and community between the participants. In training camps, one may well see similar things (at least when the dread of a pre-season 'cut' from the team does not exist), but the extent to which sport activities themselves contribute to communitas, if at all, is highly debatable. There is not much in the organization of elite level children's sport that nurtures this state of relations.

This also translates into a denial of the significance of 'team spirit'. This no doubt existed in situations where teams symbolized regional identities or were emblematic of high schools, and it is certainly to be found in some nooks and crannies of children's sport. However, in my fieldwork notes, there is little to suggest its importance. Ten-year-old players are recruited from teams in lower divisions, with the attractions for 'moving up' being primarily the provision of a free helmet, a promise of better coaching so the child can better develop his skills, and the opportunity to belong to a 'real' organization with sponsors and an indoor hockey arena. The children were firmly steeped in an ethos of being individuals, and the team was there to help them achieve their own individual best performances. The discussion referred to above between the players who wanted the team to start with a reduced lineup in important games should also be kept in mind here. Some teams carried the reduced lineup principle to the extreme and only carried some twelve players on the bench for important games.[5]

The Manifest Technology

The manifestation of these principles occurs not only in interaction but also through negotiation of ostensibly technical matters. For example, to buy a skate is not an easy thing. It may easily engage several parents in lengthy discussions about which blades and which shoes have which advantages and disadvantages. In addition, there is also a whole science about where the 'curve', the actual skating surface of the blade, is to be put, and what length it should have. Should speed be maximized? Then there should be a somewhat longer 'curve'. Should, instead, the ability to turn be maximized? Then a short 'curve' is in order. Where different top players have their surfaces located on the blade is introduced in the discussions. The 'curve' is thus a recurrent theme in discussions among hockey parents. Moreover, when the skate has been bought, it has to be sharpened and the ability of various persons to produce a good blade is fiercely debated. The digitally directed computerized sharpener that has been introduced into many arenas greatly simplifies the grinder's work, but it also provides numerous occasions to discuss computers, skills and the relationship between people and technology – not in the abstract but in terms of how it enables ten year olds to render true expressions of themselves.

What is all of this about? Of course there is an element of instrumentality in all this: some skates have certain qualities, and many grinders cannot produce a good blade. Much more interesting, however, is how one can see the ways in which sport is linked to contemporary technology as these relate to other dimensions of the non-transparent society. Sport, so to speak, brings technology down to a level where it is put at the disposal of the individual in a graspable manner. Technology is appropriated into the technology of the body and made contextually manageable, manipulable and operational. That an anthropologist would detect a whiff of 'magical thinking' in, for example, the shaping of the blade of a ten-year-old hockey player into a presumed copy of how Wayne Gretzky prefers his skates only adds salience to this observation.

When Everything Comes Together

The manifestation of the individual, of society, of social relationships and of contemporary technology has been examined above. Much of the fascination of sport has been attributed to issues of these kinds. There is, however, one more essential item to note – an item that has the character of being something of a condensed expression of all the things presented above: that is, what happens when someone gets a perfect stride on newly made ice and the passed puck is 'glued to the blade' while the recipient moves past an opposing defenceman? This refers to those moments in games when everything goes right. This, then, has to do with the aesthetic dimension in sport.

Briefly put, in these moments everything that has been said above about what sport is to its practitioners – players, coaches, parents and spectators – receives its confirmation. The particular athlete is totally confirmed in the perfect execution as are those notions that carry the athlete in his or her athletic endeavours. Those manifestations and appropriations that are expressed in sport are confirmed in the aesthetics of sport. The existential issues – of who one is, who one's father or mother or son is, what society is, the nature of those relationships between generations – are all confirmed through the achievement of the 'absolute', the perfect. The aesthetic dimension, often glossed over in the sport literature, is firmly part of the line of reasoning advanced in this examination of the crucible of elite sport. Without the notion of perfection lodged in aesthetics, sport would not have the ability to engage us on such a fundamental level.

Children, Children's Sport and Society - a Final Comment

In our society we live within an ideology of individualism. The individual is seen in terms of intentionality, agency and opportunities for choice. Society is seen in terms of openness and ability to change, and many of our everyday experiences seem to confirm this. If Members of Parliament raise old age pensions and increase the allowance contributed to the national sport federation, there will be cheques arriving at the appropriate addresses with the decided amounts.

The basis for this whole view, however, is that we believe that our everyday notions give accurate depictions of the forces and powers that guide our lives and organize our societies. In this chapter an attempt has been made to demonstrate that our everyday notions about these things do not do justice to the cultural and social complexity that exists within our societies.

To some extent, this observation is another case of the fish-in-water problem. The fish only lives in water, and that it would be possible to live anywhere else is, to the fish, an impossibility. That there are two-legged beings living in air is nothing but a joke, and that they would devote themselves to running a hundred meters in less than nine seconds is, to the fish, an absolute absurdity. Transposed to my own preoccupation with understanding sport, we must move out of our everyday understandings about these things. As far as it is possible for us to obtain a reasonable understanding of these matters through contextualizing them in analyses of cultural and social significance, we may be able to arrive at a more insightful understanding of these phenomena – as well as a more considered sense of what we want our participation in such activities to accomplish .

Notes

1. As with most things I write, this chapter also relies on many discussions with my wife, Eva Lithman. As parents of athletically active children, we have for several years had a running dialogue about these issues. What is presented here is a part of a larger project on sport, in which Bruce Kapferer is an intensive intellectual sparring partner. The Swedish Research Council for the Humanities and Social Sciences and the Swedish Sports Research Council have generously supported the project.

   There are, of course, significant differences in children's sport between countries, and the literature testifies to this. The arguments put forth in this chapter are based upon fieldwork conducted in Sweden, but I suspect that the analysis has broader applicability. It should also be pointed out that the fieldwork was conducted into elite-level sport activities.
2. This argument has some affinity with, but is also different from that presented by, Novak (1976).
3. It is important to point out, that when writing about 'stable and integrated' results in identity formation, this is done from a perspective radically different from the developmental one associated with the works of Erikson. That approach, in my view, ties together descriptive and normative connotations in their conceptualization, thereby advancing a reified image of what 'identity' is. 'Stable' and 'integrated' in my usage

is meant as nothing more than a descriptive statement, having nothing to do with what should make people happy. I should also add, that when I use the term significant 'Others' I am inspired by, rather than faithful to, Mead's deliberate use of the term in a much wider sense, or, perhaps better, in a less absolute sense. The line of reasoning I am pursuing can be substantially elaborated without affecting the basic thrust of the argument: namely, that in relations between men and women, the kneading and confirmation of the Self in some measure is based upon the very non-identity between Self and Other.

4. The whole input into 'sport culture' by various media, from items such as Gymkraft's catalogue or newspapers, as well as much of the input from the corporate world generally, has been glossed somewhat rhapsodically in this chapter.

5. Some years ago, the Swedish hockey federation tried to institute a system for children's hockey in parts of Sweden where each lineup had a large digit from one to three (or four), and each lineup was to be given equal ice time. The referee was to call new lines onto the ice every two minutes. The experiment had to be abandoned, supposedly because of cheating on the part of the coaches, some of whom shifted the digits between players during games.

References

Blanchard, K. and Cheska, A. (1985), *The Anthropology of Sport: An Introduction*, South Hadley, MA: Bergin & Garvey Publishers, Inc.

Dahrendorff, R. (1979), *Life Chances: Approaches to Social and Political Theory*, Chicago: University of Chicago Press.

Dumont, L. (1977), *From Mandeville to Marx: The Genesis and Triumph of Economic Ideology*, Chicago: University of Chicago Press.

— (1986), *Essays on Individualism: Modern Ideology in Anthropological Perspective*, Chicago: University of Chicago Press.

Dunning, E. (ed.) (1993), *Sports Process: a Comparative and Developmental Approach*, Champaign, IL: Human Kinetics Press.

Erikson, Erik (1965), *Childhood and Society*, Harmondsworth: Penguin Books

Fromm, E. (1955), *The Sane Society*. New York: Rinehart's.

Guttman, A. (1978), *From Ritual to Record: The Nature of Modern Sports*, New York: Columbia University Press.

Hargreaves, Jennifer (1994), *Sporting Females: Critical Issues in the History and Sociology of Women's Sports*, London: Routledge.

Hargreaves, John (1986), *Sport, Power and Culture*, Cambridge: Polity Press.

Hoberman, J. (1984), *Sport and Political Ideology*, Austin: University of Texas Press.

— (1997), *Darwin's Athletes: How Sport has Damaged Black America and Preserved the Myth of Race*, Boston & New York: Mariner Books.

Lithman, Y.G. (1988), *Kämpande kroppar, moraliska kroppar: retorik och social kontroll i den tidiga gymnastiken. Svensk idrottshistorisk årsbok,* Stockholm: SVIHF.

MacClancy J. (ed.) (1966), *Sport, Identity and Ethnicity,* Oxford: Berg.

MacAloon, John J. (1981), *This Great Symbol: Pierre de Coubertain and the Origins of the Modern Olympic Games,* Chicago/London: University of Chicago Press.

Mandell, R.D. (1984), *Sport: A Cultural History,* New York: Columbia University Press.

Mead, G.H. (1967), *Mind, Self and Society,* Chicago: University of Chicago Press.

Novak, M. (1976), *The Joy of Sports,* New York: Basic Books.

Oesterreich, E. (1979), 'The Privatization of Self in Modern Society', *Social Research* 46(3): 600-15.

Polanyi, K. (1971), *The Great Transformation: The Political and Economic Origins of Our Time,* Boston: Beacon Press. (1st printing 1944).

Prokop, U. (1971), *Soziologie der Olympische Spiele: Sport und Kapitalismus,* München: Hanser Verlag.

Rigauer, B. (1979), *Sport und Arbeit. Sociologische Zusammenhänge und ideologische Implikationen,* Münster: Rowohl.

Sartre, J.-P. (1956), *Being and Nothingness,* New York: Philosophical Library. Ström, L.-I.

Ström, L.-I. (1987), *Idrott och politik: Idrottsrörelsens politiska roll I Tredje riket, DDR och Förbundsrepubliken,* Östersund: Raben & Sjögren.

Sörhaug, H. C. (1984), *Identitet, grenser, autonomi och avhengighet: stoffmissbruk som exempel,* Uppsatser till nordiska etnografmötet. Oslo: Socialantropologiska institutionen.

Will, George F. (1992), *Men at Work: The Craft of Baseball,* New York: Macmillan.

8

Culture, Context and Content Analysis: An Exploration of Elite Women Gymnasts in the High-School World

Melford S. Weiss

The key to anthropological insight is found in the culture concept, a critical construct that allows people to define their human experiences. Simply put, all folk subscribe to a more-or-less bounded set of explanatory models that underlie, explain and govern their lives, often distinguishing their group from others. It is culture, then, that best reveals how Americans are different from Russians or Trobriand Islanders.

Furthermore, the cultural guidelines that allow us to better understand all Americans can also be applied to help us explain pertinent differences among American musicians, politicians and athletes, and, within the athletic arena, discover the distinct cultural identities of NFL football players, US Open tennis stars and elite gymnasts.

To be sure, all athletes share some ideologies about competition, socialization, training and body image but the dramatic and often revealing cultural experiences tend to be sports specific. While the term 'subculture' is often applied to participants in a particular sport, Crosset and Beal (1997: 82) prefer the term 'sub-world' as more accurate. Nonetheless, should you wish to grasp the reality and fantasies of an elite gymnast's lifestyle, you must understand the cultural codes that shape it. This study is about their world view, the behaviours, values, symbols, and dilemmas of American competitive elite women gymnasts.

A second key concept that shapes this study is context because cultural events always occur in specific contexts. Moreover, the context of an event often shapes its interpretation. Are men made up to look like Native Americans caught in the act of destroying government property hoodlums or gangsters, or are they patriots if the event is the infamous Boston Tea Party and the reader of the event is an American rather than an Englishman? Skills are also learned and practised in specific contexts. Paratroopers, for example, learn how to jump at Fort Benning, GA, not at the beaches of Malibu. Understanding paratrooper rituals, then, depends upon an intense and intimate knowledge of life on a military base (Weiss 1971: 163-8). In the same sense, petite gymnasts learn their skills within the gym, an enclave with specific and often unspoken cultural rules.

While we will address the realities of that 'gym world', our study will emphasize another context quite familiar to elite gymnasts – that of the high-school – for our gymnastic superstars are also adolescent girls who must attune their athletic goals to the frequently confusing demands of teenage life, and it is in this context that we must comprehend some of the basic cultural rules that shape the adolescent school world.

The Analysis of 'Content'

Life and case histories, network serials and daily routine interviews chronicle significant details that circumscribe an event or a series of related events (Agar 1996: 155-60). The focus is upon the informant's organization of cultural facts and the interplay between the culture and the individual (Langness 1965). The format is often that of a structured or unstructured interview, a narrative or an observation. Content analysis adds insight to unique events and uncovers the expressive domains of ordinary happenings. By contrasting pertinent academic and social experiences (student/teacher relationships, the work ethic, identity, socialization, role models) for 'Suzy Student' and 'Jane Gymnast', content analysis is used to illustrate some of the dilemmas of adolescent US women gymnasts as they attempt to decipher the cultural codes and behavioural intricacies of the high-school world. A second set of contrasts will discuss elite gymnasts and high-school star athletes focusing upon socialization dynamics within the gym and at school, the persuasive influence of the peer group and the role of the athletic mentor – the coach.

Methodology

Participant observation defines fieldwork (Freilich 1970: 2). These intimate experiences are necessary, nay sacrosanct, for all cultural anthropologists because it is the basis of ethnography, the essential element of research. Just as important, participant observation often functions as a rite of passage to the anthropological profession.

Traditionally, anthropologists operate in unfamiliar cultural settings, thus they must first learn the appropriate cognitive categories and learn them well enough so that they become normative and natural. Only then should the anthropologists apply more rigorous research strategies.

Although I was a scholar-athlete in high school and college, I knew little about the lives of gymnasts or the gymnastics world, nor was my knowledge much better when I became an anthropologist. My serious interest commenced with my elder daughter's involvement, and continued as she changed from a fun-loving novice into a dedicated elite competitor. Thus began my immersion in the world of gymnastics folk, the gymnasts, coaches, judges, parents and the joyous agonies of training and competitions. Fortunately my daughter acted as one of my key informants and made my entry into her 'world' a bit less difficult. Through participant observation,

I became privy to the instrumental and expressive cacophony of gymnastics life, and when I was comfortable with my knowledge, started serious research. I was to remain, as Michael Agar (1966: 1-2) would put it, a 'professional stranger' but a sympathetic and thoughtful one.

My most successful research techniques were learning about network serials (encounters in daily life) and the life and case histories of my adolescent and adult informants. As an anthropologist, I exercised the methodological techniques of my profession, linked behaviour to cultural constructs and presented the data in terms of meaningful native categories.

A Modified Case History: An Elite Gymnast in the High School World

Because anthropologists study manifest and latent complexities of culture, their efforts are often enhanced by including anecdotal, personal and intimate experiences of those they observe. This addition adds a more poignant understanding to ethnographic description. It has always been that flavour, those vivid emotional and surprising human examples that convey a more sensitive and empathetic meaning, what we like to think of as an insider's worldview.

One such illustration is the modified case history, its purpose to describe important synchronic or diachronic behaviours and incidents that surround a particular event or a series of related events. Consider my own work with US Elite women gymnasts. How could I best portray the dilemmas they face by pursuing a short lived yet extraordinarily demanding career as a professional athlete, while concurrently trying to resolve the difficulties inherent in also being a high-school teenager? One process I decided to employ was contrast; that is, to depict part of that high-school experience from the perspectives of 'Suzy Student' and 'Jane Gymnast', two young women who are attending a local high school. We will allow their growing-up 'stories' to tell us about their lives.

Entering high school is both immensely satisfying yet frustrating. Cautious at first, new students desperately try to decipher the pertinent and perplexing social and academic codes. It isn't always easy. Being 'part of', or 'fitting in', is critical and most students are able to devise an identity that allows them to belong someplace as leaders, followers or wannabes (Hurrelmann and Hamilton 1996: 39-62). How well they fit in is often a matter of experience – what confuses a frosh may hardly bother a senior.

Suzy Student typically entered her Freshman year as bewildered as anyone else so it was easy and comfortable to socialize with the friends she knew she could count on from her junior high years. Having played little league soccer, she went out for the Junior Varsity soccer team and soon added her teammates to her list of new 'buds'.

We shouldn't be surprised that Suzy soon discovered pep rallies, football and basketball games, parties and dances, and that cute guy in algebra who always sat next to her on the school bus. Perhaps the most challenging part was learning about other people and about herself. She quickly identified who the most and more popular students were, and more importantly, why they were so attractive. Similarly she spotted the 'geeks', nerds and losers. She found that some of her classmates were eager to become her friends and others were just trying to use her friendship.

During the week her world was filled with classes, but after school and on the weekends it was your peers that really mattered. You might go with them to a movie, share a birthday party, kill a lazy afternoon studying for that big chapter test and later go strolling at the mall. You could group-date together, or just spend endless hours enjoying each other's company, listening to tapes and CDs, monopolizing the family phone and sharing daydreams and fantasies. Suzy learned which designer labels were acceptable and which were 'really rad', and what new hairstyles were popular. She would continuously compare the fictitious and real stories she heard about boys and girls with her own fledgling experiences. It took Suzy one semester to think she had found her niche.

While soccer practice somewhat occupied her during the season, her schedule was flexible enough to complete her homework assignments, do extra credit work to bring up her history grade and occasionally plan ahead so that academic responsibilities would not clash with social life. Once in a while she would miss a school day for something special like skiing with her mom or leaving early for the family's Christmas vacation. She once missed 48 hours fighting the 'flu. Still, Suzy managed to always make up her missed work and her grades were good. She knew they had to be because she was going to the university and her parents and friends had told her that the admissions people looked carefully at your GPA.

Suzy didn't think too much about her teachers. She liked or respected some more than others. But teachers, well, they were teachers; you did what you had to do, not more and no less. Next year she thought she would drop soccer – no one came to the games anyway – and maybe try out for cheerleading. And then there was this football player, a 'babe' with totally blue eyes who was always looking at her.

Suzy's parents are delighted that their daughter is growing up although they worry more now about drugs, drinking and the wrong friends. Like many parents of teenagers, they seem to understand less of Suzy's world and Suzy asks for their wisdom less often. Financially they support their daughter's wardrobe, allowance and ski trips but they expect Suzy to contribute when she can. And she does by working as a weekend babysitter and as a lifeguard at a swim club in the summer months.

If Suzy seems like an airhead and seems to favour some superficial qualities, she really isn't and doesn't. She's a Freshman, just learning about new ways to think about it all. Throughout her school years her interests will continuously change. She'll become serious about some other courses and despise others. She'll be maybe more, or maybe less, selective about boys, learn to trust her own judgement and become more confident about her abilities. Of course, when she graduates and begins her college career, she'll go through the process all over again.

Jane Gymnast shared many of Suzy's apprehensions about high school. She also wanted to belong, to make friends and succeed socially and in her classes, but she wasn't searching for a new identity. She was a gymnast, an Elite, a member of the US National Team and an aspiring Olympian. She had been serious about being a gymnast since her first competition when she was six years old. To put it another way, she was a gymnast who happened to be attending high school.

Jane didn't belong to any junior high clique. How could she? She never had the time and the girls she did know were more like friendly acquaintances. Her real 'buds' were, of course, her teammates, yet even at the gym, the transient nature of gym groups could isolate her from making and maintaining many long-term attachments (Weiss 1982: 60-1). To tell the truth, she had always felt a little like a stranger at school but by now she was so used to it she didn't think of that as a problem. Sure, she liked meeting new people, but realistically, those time-consuming after-school activities were out as was babysitting to earn some extra money. Maybe there would be an occasional free evening, or perhaps a Saturday night dance. Maybe.

Typically pleasant and on her best behaviour in public, Jane had long since learned how to please others, She also knew not to boast about her gymnastic accomplishments; normal people never really understood. At first, Suzy seemed different, at least Jane thought she was, and Jane was delighted when she was invited to Suzy's birthday party. Darn! It was a Friday night sleepover and workout began promptly at 7 a.m. Saturday morning. Jane was embarrassed, apologizing for leaving the party early and although Suzy never mentioned it, they kind of drifted apart.

Jane frequently tried to spend lunch period with the 'totally' popular cheerleaders, assuming that they represented the cream of high-school society. She eagerly listened to their stories about the game and the boys. The seemed to like her and were always asking about gymnastics, but she wished they wouldn't make it seem like such a big deal. On the other hand, it did make her feel special, and Jane often admitted to herself that without her gymnastics she would just be ordinary, like everyone else, and she wasn't sure she had the social skills to compete with the other girls. She thought they knew so much more about popularity and boys.

So she remained a gymnast, didn't brag, but in English class when the essay topic was about conquering fear, she told about her ordeal at the Elite trials, competing with a 102 degree fever. When her geography teacher asked her about travelling, she recounted her experiences at a competition in Caracas. Somehow gymnastics always managed to fit somewhere but it wasn't always to her advantage. Jane grew tired of all the 'Gee, do you know Marylou, or Dominique or Mitch' questions, or , 'Hey, my eight year old sister does gymnastics too.' Jane desperately wanted the

Figure 8 Christie Pozsar's Gym, April 1997 [Melford S. Weiss]

other students to recognize her as a person and not a performing acrobat – especially the guys. She grew tired of, 'Can you do a flip', and 'Let me see your muscles' comments. Oh well, at least they noticed her.

Exams and homework were a different matter. Competitive and a compulsive organizer, Jane had no choice but to plan her schedule which usually included six hours of workout each day. Then there were competitions, which always meant travelling and missing classes. She studiously arranged with each teacher to be excused from class and to make up assignments, and it wasn't always easy, like when the big midterm and USA Championships fell on the same day. As a student, Jane was 'decent', having already learned how to routinely cope with emotional stress and an exhausted body, but she felt that if she had more time to study she would have done even better. Once when a report was due on Wednesday, Jane pushed herself and stayed up half the night to finish it. But when half the class complained that they needed more time, the teacher relented and gave them two more days. Jane was furious. 'How dare they! I did it and I don't have all their freedom.'

While Jane struggled to keep her grades up, she stayed away from the Honors courses and wished she had time for those extra-credit assignments. Grades were important, but only as another competitive arena rather than a ticket to the university. Oh, Jane knew she was college bound and probably with a full-ride scholarship; her coach would see to that. She did impress her teachers though; taking orders and doing what you were told with no backtalk was what life at the gym was all about anyway. She preferred men, they were so much like her coach and it was easy to become a teacher's pet.

What Jane knew she was missing was the practical and esoteric knowledge that becomes the cultural basis for high-school social sophistication, the kind of know-how that only comes from hands-on experiences. While Jane might evaluate the choreography of a new floor routine with practised expertise, that skill had little to do with helping her understand testosterone and teenage boys or increasing her popularity with cheerleaders. And while they were always talking about those things at the gym, Jane suspected it was based more on wishful thinking and lacked streetwise smarts. Someday, she would have to deal with all that stuff, but not now.

What Jane did know about was international travel, television and sports magazine interviews and how to pack her bags better than her parents. She had learned to be quite self-sufficient. And while that competence might be meaningful for a gymnast, it didn't teach you much about being a triumphant high-school teenager (Weiss 1983: 38-9).

While Suzy had decided to forgo soccer in favour of cheerleading, Jane had neither options nor choices if she wished to remain a competitive gymnast. Next year would be the same as all the others – finish classes, get an early dismissal and spend your life at the gym.

Once in a while, Jane envied Suzy; it would be so nice to be just a student, go to parties and football games and all that. But fantasies do not get you to the Olympics. Jane's been a gymnast since she was four, doing things other girls don't even dream about. She had made too much of an investment to give it up. Still . . . it doesn't hurt to daydream now and then.

Jane's parents are involved emotionally and financially in her gymnastics career. They too have made sacrifices, and when asked, say it was worth it all. We know they will be delighted and relieved when Jane graduates and goes on to the university with the athletic scholarship she is sure to receive (Weiss 1984: 44-5).

Some day, Jane will have some catching up to do. Her athletic isolation from the social scene may have kept her away from drugs, alcohol, bad company and other intimacies, but it also kept her from confronting them.

As the years pass, both Jane and Suzy will become adults, their teenage persona will give way to other concerns, new relationships and adult identities. I suspect that their high-school experiences may play a consequential part in how they choose to live the rest of their lives.[1]

Summary

The high-school world is as replete with guidelines for making friends, being popular and gaining status as they are for pleasing teachers and earning grades (Brake 1985). These guidelines are based upon complex cultural assumptions about right and wrong, what fits, what doesn't and the symbolic meaning of 'rad' and 'nerdy'. These assumptions are about behaviours, attitudes, the ability to manipulate symbols, verbal and non-verbal cues, dress, hairstyle and the like. And these assumptions are part and parcel of the contextual framework of adolescent high-school life.

As Jane Gymnast navigates the corridors and classrooms of her high school, she is concerned about being accepted by her schoolmates and, to a lesser degree, her teachers. Critical for her success is mastering the cultural intricacies of friendship, popularity, status and of teachers, classes and grades. She is also aware that being a gymnast prevents her from more satisfying social opportunities. While she appears to have successfully adjusted to academic demands by selectively using the knowledge gained through her gymnastic experiences, she realizes she will remain a tangential member of her school's social scene.

The Elite Gymnast and the Star Athlete: A Tale of Two Talents

An elite female gymnast is also a teenager whose rise to glory often coincides with her right to earn a driver's license. She can be a memorable heroine at sweet sixteen, and forgotten thereafter.

We are particularly interested in how her lifestyle differs from those of other high-school age athletes, and how her special experiences as a gymnast influence her choices. Finally, because our teenage gymnast ordinarily spends a good portion of her day in school, we ought to learn more about how she adjusts to the often confusing regularities of the high-school world.

Socialization is that illusive process where a people's young are supposed to learn the pertinent complexities of life. Certainly by the time a child has grown into a teenager, she has inherited a working knowledge and perhaps a reluctant curiosity about adult living, though her more immediate joys and agonies receive most of her attention. Moreover, those adolescent years are considered a critical developmental stage – often, we are reminded by psychologists, an indicator of future potential (Coleman 1961). Most teenagers also live ordinary lives. That is, they adopt lifestyle activities statistically appropriate to their age, gender, social economic status, geographic region and ethnic group (Adams and Gulotta 1983). While some adolescents seem to excel in sports, in drama class or auto shop, their exploits are rarely extraordinary. They are usually only a bit better than their best local competitors. There are, of course, young men and women with truly exceptional talent; the math whiz, violin prodigy and the petite nationally ranked Elite gymnast.

High-School Athletes

Gymnasts are athletes, so perhaps it's proper to start our story there. That the high-school world honours its star athletes is common knowledge. Not only do top performers gain immediate notoriety with their schoolmates but from the adult world as well. For some communities, the winning reputation of their competitive teams may be their only claim to fame (Miracle and Rees 1994: 158).

High school, however, is where you often begin your athletic calendar. It's a start, hopefully followed by collegiate scholarships, and, only for the most proficient, the dream of a professional career (Miracle and Rees 1994: 130). No one would seriously think about comparing your all-conference basketball whizbang to Michael or Shaq, not yet anyway. Second, the most noticeable athletic and social recognition goes to boys rather than girls (Goldberg and Chandler 1989: 238). If feminine stars wish for instant popularity, they will have to combine their sports prowess with other attributes as looks, personality, brilliance and social skills to achieve similar recognition (Thirer and Wright 1985: 164). Finally, because athletic endeavours are a part of their school identity, success in the sports arena can easily carry over to other activities. What this allows an athlete to do is maximize a prestigious reputation within the school setting.

An accomplished gymnast is very different. First, she has already achieved acclaim at the highest level of her sport while she is still enrolled in high school. She is, so to speak, Emmit, Brett, Jerry, or one of the lesser lights of the National Football League right now. And it's quite possible her career will peak before she begins her senior year.

By the time *John Senior*, the All-State wide receiver, has led his team to the regional championships, little Jane Gymnast, two years younger, has displayed *her* talents for the USA in Tokyo and Paris. In fact, when John was first learning how to catch a pass on the seventh grade playground, Jane was busy winning medals at the Junior Olympic National Championships. She had already won her state title when she was only ten.

Naturally, these differences in their winning experiences are related to the number of top competitors and when they started serious training. Jane began at five, first competed at nine, qualified as a Junior Elite at twelve and was an Olympian at fifteen. When 18 year-old John receives his high-school diploma, he'll first be testing himself at Notre Dame. But when Jane graduates, she's probably ended her US Gymnastics Federation career. Her athletic scholarship to UCLA may be a final award for her excellence, not a beginning.

Perhaps, most important for her socialization, Jane never competed for her high school; all of her training took place at private clubs. Thus Jane's workouts and competitions always took her away from school. For John, a homecoming game in the packed stadium was a prelude to the Friday night victory dance and the football awards banquet. Parties inevitably followed each game, so John's football life easily tied him to his school's social scenes, to his first date with that cute cheerleader, to a supposedly impromptu gathering with his teammates down by the river.

Jane managed to get to the homecoming game (it was a rare treat) and she screamed as loud as anyone else when John caught the winning touchdown pass. But no one had asked her to the dance and she didn't know where any of the 'rad' parties she happened to hear about were held. She convinced herself it was probably just as well; workout was at 8 a.m. the next day and on Monday she was leaving for a meet in the nation's capital. Jane is excused from the physical education requirement and leaves school early for her 2 p.m. to 7 p.m. weekday workout. To be sure, Jane also participates in a series of multiplex activities but with other gymnasts instead of her high-school compatriots. It is Jane's gymnastic schedule that keeps her from more intimate school socializing.

Jane may be a promising Olympic hopeful, a Pan-Am Games champion, but the chances are that most of her classmates don't know it. Jane hardly ever talks about her gold medals and, at the one swim party she did attend, kept her T-shirt on all night worrying what the other kids might say about her 'buff' shoulders. Even if her gymnastics exploits were recognized it still might not help her social life. The 'totally' popular girls, Jane truly believes, are Homecoming Princesses and Cheerleaders.

The Peer Group

Of course our gymnast is not only an athlete – she's also a high-school student, subjected to the same pressures and passions commonly shared with her classmates.

High-school years are difficult ones because change rather than stability is the rule. Students are expected to experiment with newly acquired knowledge and feelings – some of them counter to parental approval – while their teachers demand new competencies and perspective. They are treated at times like children, at other times as adults and the shift in expectations doesn't always seem reasonable. During these years, sexual awareness is heightened when bodies sporadically sprout and blossom (Ianni 1989: 22-54).

Perhaps the confusion is understandable, for American youth have no definitive rites of passage from child to adult status, leaving teenagers structurally in limbo. To help offset individual uncertainties and puzzling adult behaviour, adolescents turn to the peer group for support.

During the high-school years peer groups can include both males and females, though there is still strong same-sex bonding. Peer affiliation is usually based on common interests, allowing both full and partial membership in loosely constructed groups. Some groupings are based on 'style' (preppies, punks, cowboys), other centre upon 'activities' (cheerleading , drama club, student government, even 'doing drugs'). Within each group there are the movers and doers, followers and 'wannabes'. To make matters more confusing, there is constant shifting making for overlapping identities and some students do not participate in school-based activities at all. Most adults (including school personnel) find it rather difficult to really comprehend the peer group/status system though most students intuitively know who belongs where and who doesn't (Bishop 1995: 476-89).

Realizing that a youngster's interests, desires, maturity levels, commitments and best 'buds' change, high-school society allows much movement across interest, popularity and activity systems. While some athletes may comfortably identify themselves as 'jocks' for all four years, some do not. John entered as a barely popular preppie, discovered the drama club as a sophomore and only became a 'serious' football player as a junior. When he became a senior, he became involved with environmental issues, an interest that did not seem to threaten his athletic popularity. Apparently the role of athlete and scholar are not necessarily contradictory in high-school social structure (Snyder and Spreitzer 1992: 521). Though his interests have shifted, his social, athletic and intellectual life still remained tied to his school, his explorations a result of new high-school friends and activities.

Although Jane and John attended the same school, Jane was never really part of it. She had neither the time nor the energy to be a full participant. Her world was at the gym where there was only one concern – gymnastics. Prestige ranking and popularity there is based upon a single criterion – competitive excellence. There is no time or place for alternative interests. So significant is that single goal that other interests are considered threatening. How could Jane even think of trying out for cheerleader? What if cheerleading and gymnastic demands conflicted?

For Jane, the gym peer group is, to paraphrase the late Vince Lombardi, the 'only thing'. Locked into physically exhausting and emotionally draining daily workouts and competitions, Jane cannot help but share her triumphs and tragedies with her team mates. Who else could understand it all? A gymnast's learning environment is a rather austere place where all activities are deliberately regimented. In some ways it has more in common with military academies and even prisons than public high schools. Surely it is the centre of the gymnast's life and a focal point for their social life. Although it represents a time shared with friends, one to be treasured, it is also gruelling, more often than not responsible for ambivalent feelings. The athletes claim they hate having to go to the gym as much as they hate being away from it.

Ambivalence also characterizes interpersonal relationships. For while you may train as a team, the best accolades are given for individual performance. Team spirit aside, you will inevitably end up competing against your best friends. Thus camaraderie is tempered by jealousy; harmony and tension co-exist side by side. Like those in high school, special friendships are based upon personalities and shared experiences. But because the girls are taught to view themselves as gymnasts first, the usual ethnic and class divisions so noticeable in high-schools are submerged. A gymnast from a wealthy Anglo family may share room, board, hair ribbons and dreams of glory with a Korean-American girl whose immigrant parents are struggling with the English language. Jane may squeeze into Guess jeans, while Kim shops at K-Mart, but at competitions their team leotards are identical as are their valiant attempts to master a reverse hecht on the uneven bars. Invariably it will be their level of gymnastic expertise and dedication that will largely determine friendship patterns (Weiss 1987: 38-9).

The peer groups that dominate ordinary and ritual aspects of meaningful life in high-school are almost always age graded. Peers are age mates, the chasm between fourteen and eighteen year olds too great to easily bridge. Moreover, freshman and seniors rarely share enough commonalties to appreciate each other's adventures. Finally, most high-school activities are structured to maximize class-level distinctions.

However, at the gym, those differences are not strong enough to overcome the fifty weeks a year that gymnasts spend involved in each other's intimacies. Even after workouts they may share living quarters and meal-times. Not surprisingly, their free-time activities (shopping, sightseeing, movies, birthdays, sleepovers and some pizza pig outs) become bonding experiences. Because the girls spend so much time together and so little time with anyone else, they soon develop a working friendship that transcends ordinary age differences. Older girls look out for their younger surrogate sisters and the competitive team often becomes a fictive family. As real as these bonds of 'sisterhood' are, they are also fragile, subject to real and imagined slights, jealous outbursts or smoldering envy. Other outlets for emotional expression and relief are rare so they too are channelled into multiplex dimensions with one's own kind.

Of course there is sibling-style rivalry where your teammates turn into your competitive enemies. Nevertheless, powerful consciousness of kind survives. Too few non-gymnasts can identify with or understand their intense and cloistered life. It's harder on the younger girls who must often make the effort to appear more mature than their years. That they seem to grow up faster is a worthy testament to the patience of their older teammates and the persuasive power of group norms. Thus unlike the high-school world, where students may belong to overlapping groups, where they may shift their affiliations as new interests develop and where grade distinctions help to determine groupings, the gym world offers few, if any, alternatives. The reach of their sport is so pervasive that other dynamics remain subservient to the group and its single goal, competitive excellence (Weiss 1986a: 58-9).

That 'Significant Other' Adult

Sociologists frequently refer to adults outside of the family who are important for a growing teenager or child as a 'significant other'. Often, this person is responsible for instrumental or expressive guidance; helping an adolescent reach goals, providing social or moral advice and acting as a role model. The relationship is usually personal and can be quite intense (Coleman 1961). Nowhere is this more evident than in the gymnastics world where that significant other is almost always the coach – a male coach.

While top-level clubs employ women as coaches, choreographers and dance/beam specialists, women rarely hold the titular status of 'head coach', nor do they command the dominant position in the gym. That does not mean that the gymnasts do not mimic their behaviour and attitudes; it does mean however, that women are ordinarily responsible for their specific expertise rather than their control of a winning competitive tradition – and even the youngest gymnast is well aware of status differences. We are not saying that women can't . . . But gymnastics has long been a sport where male coaches assume overall responsibility for training teenage girls (and boys) as Elite level gymnasts (Sands 1984: 9-15).

This arrangement creates a unique dilemma. Male coaches, generally speaking, tend to view their gymnasts as athletes without gender. Because both their formal and practical out-of-gym experiences with adolescent women is limited, they may ignore gender-related concerns with growing up and downplay problems of feminine hygiene and personality, making the gymnasts unlikely confidants in these matters.

Male coaches are also the unwilling victims of the 'touch' but 'don't touch' syndrome. Whereas they must spot, manipulate, stretch and handle the girls during workout, they must never suggest improper intimacy. Perhaps one way to relieve both tension and mistaken intention is to joke about matters more serious and to engage in verbal-joking duels. The girls, well aware of the 'unwritten rules', may tease their coach with risqué innuendo.

Still, despite this potentially uneasy element in their daily encounters, the coach and gymnast enjoy a close and emotionally tight partnership, each one dependent upon the other for their success and reputation. The coach is often characterized as both a friendly 'big-brother' and an evil 'step-brother', as both a 'Scrooge ' and a 'Santa', a tease, a pal, a villain and hero, a friend and enemy. It is virtually impossible, given daily workouts and numerous competitions, for the gymnast and coach to spend so much time together without learning each other's intimate life history and personal psychodramas. This knowledge may allow both coach and gymnast to attempt to manipulate their respective social 'styles'. Indeed, if the parents permit the coach to act *in loco parentis*, he may suggest 'proper' leisure activities, course of school study, diet and even hairstyle. He is therefore a very 'significant' person in his gymnasts' lives (Weiss 1986b: 42-4).

The athletic coach at a high school is a less intense figure. It is not uncommon for a high-school coach to do double duty as a teacher. Moreover, a high-school coach's timetable is usually restricted to a particular sport's season. And while the athlete/coach relationship can become close, it is ordinarily not overwhelming. High-school teams are much larger than the normal gymnastics training group and the coaches are not as intimately involved with all of their players all of the time. Finally, a high-school coach's employment and future does not always depend upon a winning season or producing top-level individual competitors. A school coach is more apt to be thought of by student-athletes as a teacher whose bond with students is similar to that of other teachers.

The gymnastics coach is both athletic mentor and teacher, the distinction structurally unimportant so that coach/teacher roles easily overlap. In junior and senior high school, teachers and coaches are specialists, seeing their charges one or maybe two periods a day; their focus is a single subject rather than all-around development. Their concerns are ordinarily more academic than personal and an intense relationship is unlikely to last longer than a student's school career.

Gymnastics, on the other hand, is a one-on-one sport with a ferocious bond between performer and coach; a bond that will endure much longer than the four years of high school. That bond is as emotionally draining and satisfying as any adolescent-adult dyad could be. Perhaps its intensely personal dimensions are best revealed in their terms of address used by the athlete. In high school, the sports mentor is usually called 'Mr' or 'Mrs', and more likely 'Coach . . .' For gymnasts, the coach is *always* Bela, Steve, Mary or Mel.

Conclusion

While there are many cultural assumptions that influence all high-school teenagers, there are identities within the school society that follow particular subcultural guidelines. One such group consists of star athletes, ordinarily a prestigious status, especially for high-school males. While Elite female gymnasts are nominally classified as athletes, their lifestyle experiences may be quite different from those of other school athletes. Some pertinent differences relate to socialization dynamics, peer group pressures and the role of that 'significant other' adult in their lives – the male coach.

High-school star athletes and elite gymnasts are known for their exceptional sports prowess, yet within the high school, the gymnast receives less social recognition for her achievements. And even when she is acclaimed, her talent may not bind her to that high-school world. Because her training and competitions take place outside the confines of the school, it actually prevents her from a fuller participation in school social activities.

Note

1. We are assuming that the elite gymnastics experience ought to substantially shape the gymnast's adult life. Unfortunately there are no quantitative longitudinal studies to back this assumption.

   A brief follow-up on 'Suzy' and 'Jane' reveals that Suzy received her BA in English from a private college. After graduation, she moved in with her boyfriend, an engineer she first met at a fraternity party. Suzy works for an advertising agency but is not overly excited about her employment opportunities. She plays tennis at a racquet club on Wednesday evenings and Sunday mornings.

   It took Jane five years to complete her communications studies BA at a major university. She was recruited as a sales representative by a well-known sports conglomerate. Jane is single, lives at home and works out regularly at a health club.

References

Adams, Gerald and Thomas Gulotta (1983), *Adolescent Life Experiences*, Monterey: Brooks Cole Publishing Co.

Agar, Michael H. (1996), *The Professional Stranger*, San Diego: Academic Press Inc.

Bishop, Julie A. (1995), 'Peer Acceptance and Friendship: An Investigation of Their Relationship to Self-Esteem', *Journal of Early Adolescence*, 15(5): 476-89.

Brake, Michael (1985), *Youth Culture*, London: Routledge & Kegan Paul.

Coleman, James S. (1961), *The Adolescent Society: The Social Life of Teenagers and its Impact on Education*, New York: The Free Press.

Crosset, Todd, and Becky Beal (1997), 'The Use of Sub-Culture and Sub-World in Ethnographic Works on Sport: a Discussion of Definitional Distinctions', *Sociology of Sports Journal*, 14(1): 73-85.

Freilich, Morris (1970), 'Fieldwork: An Introduction', in M. Freilich (ed.), *Marginal Natives: Anthropologists at Work*, New York, Harper & Row.

Goldberg, Alan P. and Timothy Chandler (1989), 'The Role of Athletics: The Social World of High-school Adolescents', *Youth and Society*, 21(2): 238-50.

Hurrelman, Klaus and Hamilton, Stephen (1996), *The Social World of Adolescence: A Sociological Perspective*, New York: Aldine DeGruyter.

Ianni, Francis A.J. (1989), *The Search for Structure: American Youth Today*, New York: The Free Press.

Langness, L.L. (1965), *The Life History in Anthropological Science*, New York: Holt, Rinehart & Winston Inc.

Miracle, Andrew W. Jr. and C. Roger Rees (1994), *Lessons of the Locker Room: The Myth of School Sports*, New York: Prometheus Books.

Sands, Bill (1984), *Coaching Women's Gymnastics*, Champaign: Human Kinetics Pub. Inc.

Snyder, Eldon, and Elmer Spreitzer (1992), 'Social-Psychological Concomitants of Adolescent Role Identity as Scholar and Athlete', *Youth and Society*, 23(4): 507-22.

Thirer, J. and S.P. Wright (1985), 'Sports and Social Status for Adolescent Males and Females', *Sociology of Sports Journal*, 2(2): 164-71.

Weiss, Melford S. (1971), 'Rebirth in the Airborne' in James T. Spradley and David McCurdy (eds), *Conflict and Conformity: Readings in Cultural Anthropology*, Boston: Little Brown & Co., pp. 163-8.

— (1982) 'What Happens as Little Gymnasts Grow Up: Teen-age Women in a Competition Sport', *International Gymnast*, 29(2): 60-1.

— (1983), 'Nicole and Joy: Two Gymnasts on the Road to Glory', *Sacramento Sports*, 2(9): 38-9.

— (1984), 'Parent Burnout: Mom and Dad have Given Up', *International Gymnast*, 26(7): 44-5.

— (1986a), 'Burnout: A Social Perspective', *International Gymnast*, 28(1): 58-9.

— (1986b), 'The Coach Burns Out: A Gymnastics Dilemma', *International Gymnast*, 28(4): 42-4

— (1987), 'Teen Gymnasts: Aliens in the High-school World', *International Gymnast*, 29(5): 38-9, 59-62.

Part IV

Sport as Cultural Performance

9

'America' in Takamiya: Transforming Japanese Rice Paddies into Corn Stalks, Bleachers, and Basepaths[1]

Charles Fruehling Springwood

Sunday evening, 20 July 1997, I sat cross-legged, facing Kentaro Saito,[2] a Zen Buddhist philosopher who had travelled all day by rail from Saga prefecture to meet me here in Takamiya, a small town some 45 miles north of Hiroshima. The sun had gone down, but sitting outside on a wooden deck, our faces were illuminated by a few lanterns as well as the coals from a nearby barbecue pit. Saito, wearing an austere brown robe, peering through rimmed spectacles that gripped a clean-shaven scalp, smiled warmly, 'I am most pleased to be able to meet you tonight, Dr. Springwood.' In shorts and T-shirt, exhausted from having played both games of a baseball doubleheader earlier that afternoon, I listened carefully to Saito sensei's story, which included fragments of his life history and a sense of his motivation for coming over 200 miles to speak to me.

I pause first, however, to contextualize this encounter between a cultural anthropologist from Illinois and a Zen Buddhist by clarifying precisely why I had arrived in this particular place. I had written a 'multi-locale' ethnography (Springwood 1996) analysing two nostalgia sites in the US: the National Baseball Hall of Fame in bucolic Cooperstown, New York and the Dyersville, Iowa baseball diamond featured in Hollywood's 1989 *Field of Dreams*, which served as the film's main stage. The film's protagonist, Iowa farmer Kinsella, is guided by mysterious voices to destroy his cornfield and replace it with a baseball field. He obeys this voice, and as a result, a surreal world of magical events unfolds, and ultimately, Kinsella's baseball hero, Shoeless Joe Jackson,[3] and his deceased father are brought back to life. The real-life owners of the farm where the scenes were shot decided to maintain the ball diamond as a backyard souvenir of sorts. And then, as the much hackneyed phrase goes, life imitated art when – just as character Terence Mann predicted that if Kinsella kept his field in the face of growing financial pressures *People Would Come* – visitors from around the US and later international tourists came to see this field (see Mosher 1991; Springwood 1996).

Having keen research interests also in Japanese society, naturally I was intrigued to learn that in 1993, a forty-three-year-old Japanese freelance copywriter living in Hiroshima, Hori Haruyoshi, decided to build his very own baseball field. The field he wanted to build would be a replica of the one in Dyersville, Iowa. Now a secular tourist Mecca of sorts for baseball aficionados, movie buffs and enthusiasts of commercialized pastoral landscapes, this Iowa site became an object of fascination for Hori who had grown up playing baseball, Japan's most-loved team sport. When the movie was released in Japan in 1990 in conjunction with a visit by the Iowa governor and state business leaders to solicit Japanese investment, Hori saw it along with millions of other Japanese, quickly making it at that time, the highest grossing foreign film. Fascinated by the film's mythopoetic bricolage of emotion, pastoralism, baseball, spiritualism and nostalgia, united by an odd narrative of Americana, and indeed, impressed further by the story of an Iowa farmer who dared to keep a Hollywood *Field of Dreams* in his own backyard, Hori became committed to – obsessed with – building his own version of this pastoral diamond in land-scarce Japan.

And so, in the summer of 1997, I ventured to Hiroshima to personally investigate this Eastern version of the midwestern American baseball diamond that had so occupied my attention for years. Hori was quite excited to receive as a guest someone who had actually written a book about the Iowa field. In fact, he was somewhat intimidated by the thought of it. I was the special guest of Hori and his baseball team, the Corns, during the holiday weekend of 18-22 July. A party was thrown in my honour on Sunday evening, and to highlight the occasion, Hori invited Saito sensei, who had his own agenda for coming. The Corns, who invited the anthropologist to play first base, competed in two games that afternoon against a semi-pro team from Hiroshima. After the Corns lost 'both ends of the twin-bill', members of each team settled down to a keg of beer, bottles of sake and grilled vegetables and chicken on a wooden platform in foul territory along the third base line.

Left fielder, architect Seichi Kawabata, met Saito sensei at the rail station and drove him to the field in his Nissan Pathfinder. Upon his arrival, others scurried to erect a movie projector and screen on the deck in order to show a special film that was tucked snugly under Saito sensei's arm. The Zen master is something of a renaissance person and the film he brought for me to view at the field was one he produced. Of course, it was a baseball movie – an historical drama – titled *Ningen no Tsubasa* [*Wings of a Man*]. Shot in black and white to affect a rustic veneer, the film is about the life and career of a famous 1940s baseball star, Shinichi Ichimaru, who played for Nagoya. He left baseball to fight in the Second World War as a kamikaze pilot. The story situates the only professional baseball player to serve as a kamikaze fighter as a man hopelessly in love with baseball who experiences great internal conflict about the role both he and his nation played in the war. Two hours long, the film ended with Ichimaru's death when his plane completes a mission, and we all rubbed our eyes – scratching our numerous mosquito bites – as the lanterns were relit.

Saito sensei quizzed me, 'What did you think of the film?' I replied that it was well made and interesting and that I was most impressed to learn that it was his first film project. Saito sensei's English was quite fluent, with a near-native American accent. Along with a Zen school, he runs both a karate school and an English academy. He learned his English, along with impeccable French, in France where he studied philosophy and history at the Sorbonne. In fact, it was in France where he was first introduced to Zen. He is a peace activist who travels frequently to Third World nations promoting international aid projects. 'I do not actually like baseball', he offered. 'I was asked to become part of the *Wings of a Man* project when the original producer had to quit for financial reasons, and because I was impressed by Ichimaru's life and passion for baseball and for peace, I thought I could embrace the story's message.' As we ate and drank, Saito sensei began to suggest various ways I might become part of the movie's promotional vehicle. Hori was nearby, wearing a smile of satisfaction, listening and from time to time adding a word of agreement or acknowledgment.

In this paper I seek to outline in greater detail the brief history of Hori's baseball diamond, understanding it to be a most informative illustration of the contemporary relationship between sport, cultural performance and the global economy. Sport is ever more characterized by fuzzier – even dissolving – boundaries between the field, the court, the turf, the backyard, the restaurant, the living room, the bar, the Internet, the spectator and the athlete (see Rinehart, forthcoming). These various sites of experience form a corpus of sporting practices, signs and economies in which anything and everything is commodified. Sport, I believe, has emerged within the present transnational global economy as the predominant social field where meaning, pleasure, power and resistance flourish. Indeed, images such as that revealed in a *National Geographic* photograph (Tomaszewski 1996:126) as a female Zapatista commander marches out of the Mexican Lacandon jungle adorned in a blue and pink house dress, black mask obscuring her features and her black hair tamed by a Chicago Bulls cap, force us to reconsider the novel ways in which consumers produce ranges of meanings, unanticipated, by the way they watch, play, read, dress and cheer. It cannot be known for certain from the picture alone whether this revolutionary actually follows Michael Jordan and his team mates. But in any case it requires the development of a new appreciation for the contours of flow of sporting images. Haruyoshi Hori seeks to locate his self meaningfully within a transnational circulation of the signs, symbols and experiences of this 1989 film. His project reveals the pivotal role that the commodity of advanced capitalism – more than ever now image and simulacrum – plays in creating novel cultural fields for new consumer classes.

As such, this ethnographic research offers a glimpse of what people actually do with popular televisual commodities produced by transnational interests such as Universal Studios. I argue that the circulation of the *Field of Dreams* narrative effects the dispersion of 'America'. But the dispersion of sign commodities is a radically uncontrollable, unpredictable process. Indeed, what starts out as a dispersion of America often becomes the displacement of America.[4] Mr Hori authors his materialized landscape from a privileged position of class as well and his project is read as a practice of leisure, a playful form of self emplacement. Cultural geographer Stacey Warren noted:

> [Cultural technology's] role in creating the landscape is indisputable, but analysis cannot stop there. Half of the hegemonic process is missing; we must still ask how people incorporate these places into the cultural practices of their everyday lives, and how these places form part of the 'moving equilibrium' of an always contested, always changing popular culture. (1993: 183)

Hori's engagement with the *Field of Dreams* narrative reveals a fetish for the televisual commodity that allows him to engage prior ways of imagining 'America', as he has come to imagine this nation through the eyes of a postwar, middle-class Japanese man. Within the spaces that emerge from the dialectic between the practices of consumption and the activities of production, the consumer reconfigures *through practice* a range of possible meanings of texts and signs. This particular spatial image of America's bucolic heartland has been utilized in idiomatically Japanese ways. In fact, ultimately, Hori's consumption of the *Field of Dreams* allows him, as well as those who also participate in his dream, to creatively *Other* 'America' and Americans.

Agrarian Mythopoetics and 'Pure' Motivation

Hori formed a financial group in 1993, *Tomorokoshi no Kai* (The Corn Association) to raise money for the field. Ultimately, with the help of Kazuyoshi Masuda, Hori secured rights to a 1.5 hectare rice-paddy located in the isolated village of Takamiya, about 60 kilometres north of Hiroshima. Just as the movie had parlayed the pastoral aesthetics of corn into a central symbol as luscious, Technicolor green stalks of the plant traced the outfield arc of Kinsella's field, Hori insisted on recuperating this icon of America's heartland. In staging his landscape, he planted specially ordered corn seed, a crop rarely seen in Japan, in his outfield. He named his team, for whom the field would be hometurf, the Corns, and he designed their green and white jerseys. Each season, the players ceremoniously 'harvest' the corn in the outfield, captured by home video and snapshots, then grill the 'ears' along with chicken over coals in foul territory along the third base line. The performance is suggestive of a suburban 'fourth of July' celebration in the US.

A rice paddy was transformed into a corn-laced baseball diamond. The displacement of rice – a plant used repeatedly throughout Japanese history to fashion and refashion the Japanese self (Ohnuki-Tierney 1993) – by corn, the ostensible metonym of American pastoralism in the film, was ironic. Hori hesitated when I asked him to articulate why and how rice might signify *Yamato damashii*, the Japanese spirit, but he spoke enthusiastically about the articulation of corn (maize) with America; indeed, he referred to Joseph Campbell's writings in discussing the centrality of the plant to the mythos of native American peoples. Initially, as a researcher, I struggled to unpack this curious celebration of corn as a quintessentially American sign, and I attempted to tease from Hori and his teammates a more thorough articulation of some deeper significance to this peculiar symbolism. Locating corn as essential to the national persona of America by tracing its history to native American societies seemed to me a provocative move by Hori.[5] Ultimately, however, these players merely identified and enacted an existing metonymic corpus of American heritage signs, one already including corn, fashioned previously through centuries of discursive work in the US. Because the movie had already encoded it as such, a corn stalk proved to be a crucial if flattened and overdetermined sign in order to completely fashion an authentic American baseball field.

The *Field of Dreams* narrative predominant in the US turns on the articulation of nation, sport and agrarianism, and thus, it compares favourably with a set of Japanese discursive practices to locate the contemporary national identity in terms of traditional, rural villages of a Japan seemingly vanished. Indeed, it is the articulation of particular themes from the *Field of Dreams* and similar nostalgia heritage movements in the US with the historical imaginaries of the Japanese people that suggest the possible reasons for the film's remarkable success in Japan. In Japan, as with so many other industrial nations, a nearly complete transition among the polity from farmer to urbanite was accomplished between the 1850s and the 1970s. As Japan has become one of the most urban nations, its sentimentality for a rural past has flourished. Not unique to Japan, a discourse has emerged, constructing the countryside as the authentic space of the national spirit, and the material consequences of this nostalgia include a 1980s government programme – spearheaded by then prime-minister Nobuko Takeshita – to fund the making and re-making in the hinterland of 'old hometown villages', or *furusato zukuri* (Robertson 1991; Smith 1997: 167-71).

Japan, like many nations, returns variously and repeatedly to these constructed notions of agrarian utopia, and it has again since the early 1980s when the *furusato* has become a common tourist space. Several members of Hori's Corns baseball team mentioned that their fascination with the *Field of Dreams* film centred on the persona of protagonist, Ray Kinsella, who, throughout the story, resists the pressures of bankers seeking to foreclose on the farm, even though he is losing money by keeping the baseball field rather than planting corn. Kinsella's actions are hardly the stuff of a quintessential agrarian revolt. Of course, in the end, he keeps the field, magically people from all over come to visit and – effecting a genuine capitalist utopia – without even thinking about it, they each hand over twenty dollars. But Japanese audiences are drawn to his dilemma.

Nearly every Japanese who spoke to me about the film said that the actions of Ray Kinsella revealed a truly remarkable essence. The word used

Figure 9 Visitors to the field participate in the ritual corn
harvest[Charles Fruehling Springwood]

most often was *makoto*, which indicated a great admiration for the
resilience of this character who, despite great pressure to do otherwise, listened to the film's magical voice and followed his own intuitions.
According to David Plath

> If any single idiom can be taken as central to the many Japanese vocabularies of
> growth it is the notion of reaching out for 'sincerity' (*makoto*), of striving to act
> from motives that are totally pure . . . Whatever its form, however, pure action
> is totally absorbing. It is human 'peak' experience in its Japanese guise. In such
> moments you are no longer hampered by awareness. (1980: 47)

Clearly, the *Field of Dreams* is not representative of a classic Japanese film
of any genre, but what emerges is a sense of several features of the narrative that suggest a context for the film's overwhelming reception in Japan.
From the economic tensions surrounding ownership of agricultural real
estate to the actions of certain characters to its melodramatic veneer, the
story contains themes that seem to resonate well with Japanese audiences.
In a society preoccupied by its own national debates about the significance
of the farmer, the 'traditional' rural village, and new ideas about personal
freedom and space, the story of an Iowa farmer's ability to incorporate his

love of baseball (the most popular team sport in Japan) and his agrarian existence into a highly manicured, bonsai-like, utopic baseball field struck a popular cord.

Time, Space, and Freedom in Contemporary Japanese Identity

I read Hori's enactment of the *Field of Dreams* narrative and his reproduction of the Dyersville landscape as a practice in/of late capitalism in which the global social order has been informed by 'the transformation of reality into images' (Jameson 1983: 125). But Hori's particular engagement with this American baseball diamond is nuanced by a Japanese cultural idiom that turns on the relationship of an individual with certain objects or spaces in her everyday life. I believe that, for Hori, the prevailing significance of the field is that it is his very own space where he can imagine his very own world and manage his very own baseball games.

In recent years, a remarkable sociolinguistic phenomenon has emerged in Japan that highlights a new, contemporary set of attitudes and structures of feeling about individualism and personal, private freedom. A new idiom of selfhood thrives through personal relationships with material objects that seemingly extend individual freedom. This is illustrated by examining an array of English words that have been adapted to the Japanese lexicon. These borrowed English morphemes are seldom recognizable once adopted into Japanese. For example, *sarariiman*, from salary and man, refers to the stereotypical lifetime employee of a Japanese company. The newer understanding of Japanese individuality and personal mobility is conveyed by a series of *mai*, or my words. Specifically, the phonetic pronunciation of the English 'my' has been transport into contemporary Japanese, glossed in romanization as *mai*. Examples include *maikaa* (my car), *maikon* (my computer), and *maihomu* (my home). These coinages emphasize the novel meaning that such contemporary objects or spaces have for a new generation of Japanese, and they reflect new options for the individual such as the opportunity to travel at one's own pace (*mai pesu*), and the luxury of personal, private space (see Passin 1980). David Plath explains:

> These mai words suggest the individuating potential of owner-user mass technology, of machines that empower the mundane self to expand into new domains of action and imagination. By their linguistic form the mai words imply that this self-machine linkage is so novel that it cannot be adequately communicated by conventional Japanese terms for personhood . . . [Such material symbols as the automobile and the modern private home have] become a master metaphor for personal freedom within an industrial order. (1990: 231)

Hori, indeed, seems to have procured for himself an attachment to space and the freedom it promises in a fashion clearly informed by the *mai*-generation.

Hori was convinced from the outset that by building this baseball field he would be doing something significant. Hori and his supporters were quite conscious of the emerging narrative about their actions and they sought to control, indeed author, this story. Before ever meeting Hori in 1997, I viewed a 100 minute video that he sent to me titled *Ore tachi no hiirudo obu doriimsu* (*Our Field of Dreams*). It is a fairly high-quality documentary directed by Hori himself chronicling the evolution of the field's construction beginning with the initial ground breaking. Ultimately, it was made available for purchase for 5000 yen ($40) at the field and in a few regional stores. Hori and his friends are seen struggling to transform what had been, in reality, a nearly flooded uneven, and inhospitable landscape into a Hollywood diorama.

They are seen driving borrowed construction equipment, using arms and wheelbarrows to remove boulders, digging trenches to lay a large drainage pipe among many other tasks. In one scene, they offer a brief, Japanese-style prayer before hoisting a large log to form a bridge. The struggle to smooth and drain the once-terraced rice paddy would take about two years. The narrative foregrounds the physical labour required to construct the site even more clearly than the movie highlighted Kinsella's efforts. The group nature of these efforts is emphasized, and the documentary inscribes Hori's story with the notion of hard work and work as moral form, very much in the tradition of a Japanese ethos of *samu* or disciplined work as a pathway to Buddhist salvation. Usually, work on the site occurred on weekends and holidays and members of the Corn Association would stay in the farmhouse adjoining the emerging baseball diamond. In the evenings, viewers see them eating, drinking beer and sake and even sleeping in futons. All of these scenes of work and play are punctuated by short, on-site interviews with Hori, who discusses how it feels to see his dream taking shape. And there is no doubt that it is his dream and that he is the 'visionary', even though the documentary foregrounds collective effort. Groups, especially in Japan, have leaders and Hori appears to demonstrate for the Corn Association members an understated spiritual will. However, the building of the field was a deeply emotional event for many in the group as two Corns teammates fight back tears in the video as they stand, along with Hori on a stage at the opening. Having drawn upon their own funds and having organized several fundraising activities including concerts and flea markets, to date the group has raised over $40,000 for maintenance of the field.

Hori grew up playing and loving baseball as a child in Tokyo having moved there from Nagano with his family. He played sandlot baseball, never playing in high school or college. His persona is striking. A conspicuous facial tic punctuates his speech, which is soft, articulate, and distinguished by philosophical musings. Both in person and in the video, he commands the perhaps self-motivated presence of an artist – seemingly *avant garde*. At the end of my research as I was leaving he handed me a copy of a 110-page manuscript, titled *Washira No Hiirudo obu Doriimsu* (Our

Own *Field of Dreams*)[6] which he eventually published (Hori: 1998). It, too, chronicles his love affair with baseball, the movie and the construction of his field.

Writing advertising and public relations copy in Hiroshima, he lives a comfortably middle-class life in Japan, married, with one son. Unlike the Hollywood narrative that so inspired him, family is not a significant part of his involvement with this site. While in the US, the movie and the Iowa tourist spectacle have been engaged as celebrations of American 'family values' and nostalgic reunions between sons and their fathers, Hori's many weekends spent building the site represented time away from family. This is the case for all of the men who join Hori to work and play at the site, a group including several business executives, engineers, a travel agent, a teacher, an advertising executive, a car salesman and a shopkeeper. One woman has been part of the group from the beginning. Single, Fuji is a furniture maker who lives and works in a small room attached to the farm house next to the site. She is the team's pitching ace. With the exception of Fuji's presence, the Corn Association approaches their play in a fashion generally typical of the masculinely gendered social relations of leisure. Specifically, Japanese men commonly pursue leisure activities in groups, away from their families. In urban locales, sons often see little of their fathers (Allison 1994) and neither Hori's son nor father figure prominently in his relationship to the field. One way in which the Corns' social relations diverge from common masculine leisure practices in Japan is that they do not reflect Hori's work-a-day relations. Males-at-play typically are males who work together, but since Hori's work is solitary, no such corporate social formations exist.

***

Before arriving to meet Hori's group, based on prior knowledge of Japan, I was expecting a slick, highly produced site. Perhaps, I thought, Hori's field might surpass the one in Iowa for beauty, precision and symmetry. I envisioned a site embodying a vast array of commercial interests and corporate sponsors, Japanese style. On the contrary, Hori's field is modest, and the corn he took great pains to grow is short, the grass in his outfield is sparse and the playing surface remains bumpy. Still, with the homemade bleachers and scoreboard and the gorgeous rural surroundings, the field has charm. From the bleachers, one can see beyond centrefield, across the highway, a series of colourful building tops poking through trees several hundred yards up the side of a small mountain. It is an amusement park, a New Zealand theme park (see Yoshimoto 1994: 193). Hori's story was written up in several newspapers in 1995 when the site was completed. And over 1,000 tourists purchased tickets to appear at the grand opening on September 3, marked by a three-game inaugural tournament including the Corns and the Tokyo Cooperstown Fouls, followed by a rock concert.

Each summer, Hori and friends return to sow corn and prepare the field. The Corns invite several teams to compete with them on the field. Late each July, as noted previously, the corn is harvested followed by a barbecue. There are no grand efforts to advertise and in contrast to the Dyersville counterpart – which continues to receive over twenty thousand tourists each summer – no more than 1,000 visitors came in 1996 and 1997 combined. This does not disturb Hori for whom the site seems to function now primarily as a mythopoetic playground, a spacious 'get away' nestled in the mountainous agrarian landscape sufficiently far from Hiroshima. It is a place of refuge where he can bring his own baseball team to spend weekends and holidays. To be sure, the public sign-value of his exploits remain a part of his pleasure and desire; but the significance of the site as a private space (albeit one framed as Hollywood simulacra) has emerged as paramount. In Japan where open land is scarce, and where the cost of real estate is prohibitive, Hori has authored a space seemingly available only to millionaires. Yet this middle-class intellectual has crafted what many must dream for – a rural, 'American' baseball field he can call his very own.

Consuming America and Performing *Kokusaika*

During a critical scene near the end of the film, the avuncular character Terence Mann offers the following words in claiming baseball to be the spiritual glue of the American ethos: 'The one constant through all of the years . . . has been baseball. America has rolled by like an army of steamrollers. It's been erased like a blackboard – rebuilt and erased again. But baseball has marked the time. This field – this game – it's part of our past . . . It reminds us of all that was once good, and it could be again.' This prose is representative of a much larger discursive corpus conflating baseball and America, and such discourse has also penetrated Japan where baseball is hailed, simultaneously, as a metonym for both America and Japan (see Springwood 1992).

Japanese society has developed a highly nuanced fascination with America and its commodity images. In particular, the popularity of visits to and images of rural America has marked recent years as US tour agents catering to Japan book tours of anything from the Iowa home of Little House on the Prairie author Laura Ingalls Wilder to the *Field of Dreams* site in Dyersville. My fieldwork at the Dyersville site was complemented by examination of another baseball nostalgia site in the US, the baseball Hall of Fame in Cooperstown New York (see Springwood 1996). This site has also been extremely popular among Japanese and a description of one such engagement allows for a broader understanding of what, precisely, Hori's place making signified.

On 29 September 1990, a dream that had been conceived by Kunihiro Kurata in December 1989 was consummated when an amateur baseball team – the Osaka Old Kids – played a game on Doubleday Field. Then fifty-year-old Kurata, employed by an Osaka advertising firm, decided to visit Cooperstown and the Baseball Hall of Fame as he happened to be in the US on business. He trekked to this upstate locale in the middle of winter after the crowds had vanished. Although its once green, manicured outfield was by then snow-covered, Doubleday Field – with its large sign reading 'Birthplace of Baseball' – is what impressed Kurata most. The 'historic' mystique of the place called to him, and Kurata decided to return to Cooperstown in the summer to play a game of baseball with his recreational team, the Old Kids. In an interview with a Japanese journalist, Kurata said:

> I only understood after visiting. Apparently, when the baseball sanctuary was first established, there was quite a bit of resistance to locating the Holy Land of baseball in a remote town 400 kilometers from New York City . . . However, once they visited this place, like I did, they were struck by the power and the beauty of the natural surroundings, and realized that as times and the generations change, this spot will always remain the same, thus making it the perfect spot to preserve the past. (Yatsuki 1990: 14)

His discourse is barely distinguishable from public relations copy about Cooperstown's bucolic essence.

Kurata and his colleagues play *kusayakyuu*, literally 'grass baseball', a recreational genre whose participants are said to play with youthful enthusiasm. Specifically, they play *nanshiki*, which is very similar to softball in the US in which a softer, rubberized ball is used. Several of Kurata's *kusayakyuu* teammates joined him in a pilgrimage to Cooperstown where they hoped to play a special match against the people of the New York village. Finally, with the help of officials from the Hall of Fame, a match was arranged against the Leatherstocking Base Ball Club, a group of locals who perform a version of 1840s baseball at the Farmer's Museum. One of the Osaka Old Kids, Michiro Kizaki, was accompanied by his fiancée so that they could be married on the historic field. A celebratory goodwill summit emerged with the Old Kids staying at Tunnicliff Inn on Main Street where they hosted several drinking parties for their hosts. The Old Kids presented to their hosts a commemorative designer towel embossed with the Japanese characters meaning 'every ball has a soul'.

The teams faced off for two games, one according to the rules of *nanshiki*, and one played following the 1858 Massachusetts rules. Among the various thank you notes the Leatherstocking Club received, a letter with the following passage incorporates the pastoral allegory central to baseball nostalgia in both the US and Japan. It is printed as written and the conspicuous second-language errors remain:

> Reminding beautiful Cooperstown that was surrounded by woods and lake, my heart was filled with emotion. I can picture one scene by one scene of the best day – beautiful contrast between street trees and the row of houses, vivid green lawn in Doubleday Field, splendid Hall of Fame and Museum, people's gentle eyes, contact with heart, and your warm reception.

More poetry than prose, this sentiment embodies the affective component of the touristic gaze and consumption of place.

Japanese people who travel to the US and incorporate 'American' cultural texts and spaces of leisure into their worlds underscore James Clifford's argument as he seeks to illuminate the 'global world of intercultural import-export in which the ethnographic encounter is already enmeshed' (1991: 100). According to Clifford, 'If we rethink culture and its science, anthropology, in terms of travel, then the organic, naturalizing bias of the term culture – seen as a rooted body that grows, lives, dies, etc. – is questioned. Constructed and disputed historicities, sites of displacement, interference, and interaction, come more sharply into view' (1991: 101). From the Osaka Old Kids travels to Hori's field, we can see one aspect of a much larger process of Japan consuming America. Mitsuhiro Yoshimoto argues that:

> In postmodern Japan, everything is commodified, including the sense of nationhood. America is, therefore, just another brandname, like Chanel, Armani, and so on. We can, of course, read a sign of colonial mentality in the Japanese craving for 'America' as a brand name; however, we can also cynically say that it is only part of the system of differences which needs to be reproduced perpetually for the survival of the Japanese capitalist economy. (1994: 195)

The emergence of this fetish for 'America' articulated with a national movement of the 1980s and 1990s known as *kokusaika*, or internationalism. Japan has become preoccupied in recent years with its position vis-à-vis the global process of internationalization. What began as a sort of political slogan became the ubiquitous, fashionable rhetoric of politicians, universities, corporations and even home economics clubs: we desire to 'internationalize' Japan (see Goodman 1993: 221-6). Participation in this novel ethos of pursuing the foreign as a way to signify one's cosmopolitan, international attitude is viewed sceptically by some as representing merely a lifestyle choice, from the outset emptied of possibility. Yoshimoto wrote:

> this new logic of postmodern nationalism – or what Frederic Jameson refers to as neo-ethnicity – is euphemistically called *kokusaika* or internationalization. While domestically it means the presence of more imported goods and image-formation, externally it refers to the phenomenon of more Japanese going abroad . . . What kokusaika does not include is precisely one of the most fundamental ways of internationalizing Japan: the genuine acceptance of foreigners and those Japanese who are too 'contaminated' by foreign cultures. (1994: 198)

Indeed, the authors of several papers in Mannari and Befu's *The Challenge of Japanese Internationlization* (1983) also read *kokusaika* as a novel form of Japanese nationalism wherein the engagement with the foreign, especially the American, as a mode of consumer taste serves to reproduce the Japanese identity as quintessentially different and essentially not international.

The *Field of Dreams* in Takamiya is one instance of this effort to sustain cultural engagements with Western commodities and the global flow of Western cultural capital. We see the subtle convergence of variety of transnational interests around the production of this *Field of Dreams* site. For example, Wendol Jarvis is in charge of the Iowa film board and has worked with the Iowa Department of Commerce to enhance Japanese investment in his state using the popularity of the film as a economic promotional tool. He was invited to come to Takamiya with the Ghost Players. An Iowa investor, Al Vigil, who recently purchased an interest in the Dyersville site, read about Hori's project in the *Washington Post* (Togo 1995). He and the Ghost Players, a group of Dyersville area farmers – mostly ex-collegiate baseball players – who formed a team in the image of the returned-from-the-dead players in the movie, made plans to visit the Takamiya site and play the Corns. The Ghost Players, several of whom actually appeared in the film as extras, have become somewhat well known having appeared at various state and county fairs, in television commercials and even in a Japanese rock video.

Arrangements completed, the Ghost Players, Al Vigil and Wendol Jarvis all arrived in Takamiya on 11 May 1996 to meet and play the Corns. It was the consummate moment of Hori's life as well as that of many other Corns players. The appearance was publicized, and several hundred spectators arrived to photograph and to shake hands with the Ghost Players who represented a living embodiment of the televisual realm. These men were, in essence, Hollywood, America and Iowa. The all-white, all midwestern team defeated the awe-struck Corns 12-5. In a fashion typically Japanese, Hori was preoccupied, anticipating the Ghost Players' disdain for his less than Technicolor replica. To his relief, they approved of his efforts saying that he had done a 'good job'. To this day, with a pleased grin, Hori often recites that compliment, in English. Indeed, he uses the phrase to thank the Corn Association members at the end of his 110-page manuscript. The *Field of Dreams*, then, is at the centre of a transnational (trans-Pacific) space of cultural exchange which builds on pastoral nostalgia and popular images of the midwestern US.

I agree with David Mathews (1997: 90) that 'the mere consumption of American commodity-signs cannot be equated with the Americanization of local cultures.' The readings of the *Field of Dreams* narrative in Takamiya contrast with those found in the US where the predominant themes are conservatism, masculinity and the nostalgia for a lost bond between fathers and sons. In Japan, involvement with the story turns on a fascination with America, and much more so than in the US, the *Field of Dreams* is about baseball. The intensity with which the Corns approach their baseball is unmatched in Dyersville. And Hori expressed surprise that Americans read the significance of the film in terms of fathers and sons; his father has never even visited the site.

'Although the essential hyperreality of contemporary culture has meant that America is everywhere but nowhere at one and the same time, the popular signification of America, and hence that of American cultural products and practices, is necessarily contingent upon the unique complexities of national cultural conjunctures' (Andrews 1997: 91). The Hiroshima production with the all-white Ghost Players, and Hori's field more generally, might be an attempt to construct a Japanese version of America in which the US is viewed as white, spacious, bucolic and as a nostalgic utopia. These readings of America would be, of course, imaginary, but evidence suggests that, in fact, Iowa, pastoral baseball fields and abundant rows of corn are images with which Japanese society constructs stereotypes of America. In a sense, then, when Japanese people visit this field, they may indeed be practising a form of 'Othering' that takes America as its object much in the same fashion perhaps that White America 'Others' Native America with productions of commercialized Indian Villages. Of course, this is not the only image of America prevailing in Japan; the bucolic America is an America Japan longs for and the *Field of Dreams* stereotype competes with visions of America as filled with guns, drugs and violence – an America in this latter instance that represents Japanese society's worst fears about its Western ally.

If You Build It, the Anthropologist Will Come . . .

That July evening, after meeting Saito sensei and seeing his film, I heard a most interesting explanation for my presence and Saito's involvement with *Wings of a Man*. The sensei admitted that he was a follower of Zen mysticism, and as such, believed that he could communicate with deceased people:

> With the help of a medium I contacted Ichimaru twice while doing the movie, so that I could confirm some of the historical events which we weren't sure of...such as the ending of the movie, when he tosses a baseball out of the cockpit, but he said that was accurate. The second time I contacted his spirit, the medium told me that Ichimaru was next to me, although I couldn't see him. He instructed me to write his name on a baseball, and then to draw a wavy, blue-green line connecting the two seams on the other side.

At this point, he handed me the ball with the ghost-inspired markings. He explained that he tried in vain to understand what the ball was supposed to mean:

> Next to Ichimaru, in the background, was a fat *gaijin* [non-Japanese] baseball player, in pinstripes, and another baseball figure, whose face was unclear. We decided that the heavy guy was Babe Ruth, but we didn't know who the third person was. Later, I met the trainer of the Orix Blue Wave [pro baseball team in Kobe],[7] who began helping me promote the [*Wings of a Man*] film. He then introduced me to Hori Haruyoshi, who told me all about his field and the ghost players. Suddenly, I realized that the third person was Shoeless Joe Jackson! The significance of my meeting up with Hori san became clear . . . [The trainer], Hori, and I struggled to figure out the meaning of the ball, though. Suddenly,

I realized it! Ichimaru spoke Japanese when he told me to draw the blue-green wave, using *aonami*, so I hadn't made the connection. Blue Wave! The name of the Orix baseball team! The green streak in the wave stood for the name of the Orix stadium: Green Field.

Saito sensei explained that the link between the two 'arcing' seams represented a bridge between Japan and the US. He suggested I had come to Japan in order to help him take back the message of the film – peace – and get people in the US interested in *Wings of a Man*. He and Hori then began to construct an argument that some cosmic guiding influence had orchestrated their (and my) actions. For example, the Ghost Players from the US came to Hori's field on 11 May, the date on which Ichimaru was killed. The date the field opened was on 3 September, which, they realized only later, when pronounced in Japanese becomes a homonym (*kusa*) for grass and the brand of baseball they play, *kusayakyuu*. Finally, they felt that the clinching piece of evidence was my surname: Springwood. Saito sensei pointed out that Hori's personal name, Haruyoshi, can be written with characters meaning, literally, 'springwood'.

I remain sceptical that my research in Takamiya was divinely guided but I respect the conviction of Hori and Saito that their involvement with this Hollywood film about Shoeless Joe Jackson and the Japanese production portraying Ichimaru's baseball and military careers was a matter of a mysterious 'forces'. Of course, readers familiar with the *Field of Dreams* will realize immediately that this emphasis on coincidences and having one's actions seemingly predetermined mirror the narrative and plot from the movie, whose story turns on a series of mysterious occurrences and characters whose impulses and motivations became clear only after the fact. Enacting this structure of feeling from the movie was a key aspect to the larger engagement with the story and the field. In fact, during a scene in the aforementioned documentary, as Hori and friends are laying a drainage pipe, someone explains to the camera, 'Nobody knows exactly what might happen as we are doing this, building this field. But, there must be a reason or purpose.'

***

Lash and Urry described the conditions of globalization that anticipated and informed a practice such as the Corn Association and its *Field of Dreams* as 'disorganized capital', with the sea of change in modern society in which large organizations, workplaces and cities are of diminishing significance for each individual, the processes of forming, fixing and reproducing 'subjects' is increasingly 'cultural', formed of available 'lifestyles' not at all based on where one lives or whom one knows, that is, on those who are immediately present (1987: 276). Haruyoshi Hori represents this new class of consumer, and this class is distinguished by 'the pivotal role that commodities may play in objectifying the life spaces of' individuals (Lee 1993: 175). Our understandings of sport must be reconfigured to account for the novel ways it constitutes social relations, cultural identities and experience. Intelligent and well educated, Hori is perceived by those around him as an artist and this image is also one embodied in his persona. His artistic visions and investments, however, are structured by, in this case, the global televisual commodity in whose flow he is intimately bound. These commodities have become the means through which identity, culture and difference are communicated. The problem Hori represents for the cultural analyst is how to read the prevailing, dialectical tension between the global market of the commodity sign and the consumer. Lash and Urry (1994: 133) argue that this late economy of signs and space implies a radical break with aesthetic modernism, which revealed an autonomous, reflexive subject characterized by expressive depth. The circulation of images in the current global culture, however, involves not aesthetic subjects, but rather flattened objects. Consider the cultural career of Hori in the context anticipated by Lash and Urry who claim that 'Here it is not the agents who decide, reflexively among the symbolic objects, but the objects which choose the agents' (1994: 134). Some will read Hori as a flattened subject, but his passion is not imaginary.

Perhaps Hori is best viewed as an artist in the tradition of the *avant garde*. But while *avant garde* has traditionally signified a modernist critique of the mass, the vernacular and the kitsch, a new practice of the *avant garde* might be helpful in clarifying the contemporary forms of sporting practice. Robert Rinehart (forthcoming) wrote: 'the avant-garde of postmodernity is fragmented, multivocal, and tinged with a sense of parody and irony which was not . . . a condition of . . . the *avant garde* of modernity. This postmodern *avant garde* is one that paradoxically rejects and embraces bureaucracy, its own seriousness, and commercialization.' Hori and the Corns are the perfect consumers (Lee 1993) and as authors of a novel culture of consumption and informed by a transnational flow of capital, they embody new forms of exchange and modes of locating self within the commodity. Clearly, in performing America, they construct a space where the flow of signs and pleasures complicates all prior distinctions between producers and consumers (Fiske 1987), highbrow and lowbrow, audience and performer and indeed, *avant garde* and kitsch.

Notes

1. Funding for this research was made available through the Artistic and Scholarly Development Grant, provided by the Mellon Centre at Illinois Wesleyan University. The author wishes to thank C. Richard King, Al Vigil, Teri Sato, Miki Sato, and Cris Thompson. This paper is dedicated to Josua Dayton Springwood.
2. In Japanese, family names are generally written and spoken first. However, I have written all names following the Western custom, personal name followed by surname. Further, all names that appear are pseudonyms, except for Hori and Kurata, whose practices and identities are common public knowledge.

3. Shoeless Joe Jackson – a central character in the movie – played for the Chicago White Sox until he was banned for life from the game for his involvement in a 1919 betting scandal. Some argue he was unfairly banished.

4. I am indebted to C. Richard King for insight regarding this notion of the 'displacement' of 'America'.

5. There exists a rich tradition of linking a contemporary American identity to an agrarian, maize-centred and Native American past. Indeed, the annual celebration of Thanksgiving ritually invokes a mythical reading of the social relations between European colonists and Native Americans, enacted over a shared meal that included, at its centre, corn.

6. *Washira* is translated here as 'our own'; it is a colloquial phrase common in the Hiroshima area. It implies an emotional, vernacular and even masculine attachment to the space or object in question.

7. It is common for professional teams in Japan to go by names with English words such as the Yomiuri Giants or the Hiroshima Carp. Orix is the name of the company owning the team.

References

Allison, Anne (1994), *Nightwork: Sexuality, Pleasure, and Corporate Masculinity in a Tokyo Hostess Club*, Chicago: University of Chicago Press.

Andrews, David (1997), 'The (Trans)National Basketball Association: American Commodity-Sign Culture and Global-Local Conjuncturalism', in Ann Cvetkovich and Douglas Kellner (eds), *Articulating the Global and the Local: Globalization and Cultural Studies*, Boulder, CO: Westview Press, pp. 72-101.

Appadurai, Arjun (1990), 'Disjuncture and Difference in the Global Cultural Economy', *Theory, Culture, and Society* 7(2-3): 295-310.

— (1991), 'Global Ethnoscapes: Notes and Queries for a Transnational Anthropology', in Richard Fox (ed.), *Recapturing Anthropology: Working in the Present*, Santa Fe, New Mexico: School of American Research Press, pp. 191-210.

Clifford, James (1991), 'Traveling Cultures', in Lawrence Grossberg, Cary Nelson and Paula Treichler (eds), *Cultural Studies*, New York: Routledge, pp. 96-116.

Fiske, John (1987), *Television Culture*, London: Routledge.

Goodman, Roger (1993), *Japan's 'International Youth': The Emergence of a New Class of Schoolchildren*, Oxford: Clarendon Press.

Hori, Haruki (1998), *Washira no Fiirudo obu Doriimusu* [Our Field of Dreams], Hiroshima: Media Factory.

Jameson, Frederic (1983), 'Postmodernism and Consumer Society', in Hal Foster (ed.), *The Anti-Aesthetic: Essays on Postmodern Culture*, Port Townsend, WA: Bay Press, pp. 111-25.

Lash, Scott and John Urry (1987), *The End of Organized Capitalism*, Madison: University of Wisconsin Press.

— (1994), *Ecomonies of Signs and Space*, London: Sage.

Lee, Martyn J. (1993), *Consumer Culture Reborn: The Cultural Politics of Consumption*, London: Routledge.

Mannari, Hiroshi and Harumi Befu (eds) (1983), *The Challenge of Japan's Internationalization: Organization and Culture*, Tokyo: Kwansei Gakuin University & Kodansha International Ltd.

Mosher, Stephen (1991), 'Fielding Our Dreams: Rounding Third in Dyersville', *Sociology of Sport Journal*, 8: 272-80.

Ohnuki-Tierney, Emiko (1993), *Rice as Self: Japanese Identities Through Time*, Princeton, NJ: Princeton University Press.

Palumbo-Liu, David (1997), 'Introduction: Unhabituated Habituses', in D. Palumbo-Liu and H.U.Gumbracht (eds), *Streams of Cultural Capital: Transnational Cultural Studies*, Stanford: Stanford University Press, pp. 1-21.

Passin, Herbert (1980), *Japanese and the Japanese: Language and Culture Change*, Tokyo: Kinseido.

Plath, David (1980), *Long Engagements: Maturity in Modern Japan*, Stanford, CA: Stanford University Press.

— (1990), 'My-car-isma: Motorizing the Showa Self', Daedalus 119(3): 229-43.

Rinehart, Robert E. (forthcoming), *Players All: Performances in Contemporary Sport*, Bloomington, IN: Indiana University Press.

Robertson, Jennifer (1991), *Native and Newcomer: Making and Remaking a Japanese City*, Berkeley: University of California Press.

Smith, Patrick (1997), *Japan: A Reinterpretation*, New York: Pantheon Books.

Springwood, Charles Fruehling (1992), 'Space, Time, and Hardware Individualism in Japanese Baseball: Non-Western Dimensions of Personhood', Play and Culture 5: 280-94.

— (1996), *Cooperstown to Dyersville: A Geography of Baseball Nostalgia*, Boulder, CO: Westview Press.

Togo, Shigehiko (1995, September 13), 'Hori Built It', *New York Times* 1A.

Tomaszewski, Tomasz (1996), Untitled photograph, accompanies Chiapas: Rough Road to Reality, written by Michael Parfit, *National Geographic*, 190(2): 126.

Warren, Stacey. (1993). '"This Heaven Gives Me Migraines": The Problems and Promise of Landscapes and Leisure', in James Duncan and David Ley (eds), *Place, Culture, and Representation*, London: Routledge, pp. 173-86.

Yatsuki, Junko. (1990). 'Osaka "Old Kids": Yakyuu no seichi de yume no enseishiai' ('A Dream Game in Baseball's Holy Land'), *Semba*, (September 1): 13-18.

Yoshimoto, Mitsuhiro (1994). 'Images of Empire: Tokyo Disneyland and Japanese Cultural Imperialism', in Eric Smoodin (ed.), *Disney*

Discourse: Producing the Magic Kingdom, New York: Routledge, pp. 181-99.

10

Sport, Celebrity and Liminality

Synthia Sydnor

- I surf to the QVC Shopping Network cable channel at 3 a.m. They are selling miniature football helmets for $49.95. In less than five minutes, 8,000 are sold. One phone-in viewer tells the hosts that she collects the helmets as an investment for her child's college education.
- Michael Jordan is golfing with friends in Florida, and a crowd has followed him to watch. He throws the core of an apple he has finished eating into the nearby stand of woods and a throng of onlookers run after his garbage.
- One of the happiest moments in my life occurred a few weeks ago, when my twelve-year-old daughter's cross country team won the Illinois State Championship.
- The 1994 Michael Jordan monument, Spirit, which stands in front of Chicago's United Center, is reputed to be the number one tourist destination in Chicago.

The above scenarios reveal that sport today – in whatever form – is distinct and special; these examples elucidate that a lot of 'things', such as apple cores discarded by Michael Jordan, are part of 'sport' because they inhabit the cultural spaces of sport. These passages unveil, to some degree, the notion of 'celebrity' and its link to things sport like; the examples also highlight that one doesn't have to be an athlete or on the contest field to be part of it all – to be part of sport culture. Even if for a fleeting imagined or illusory moment, at the end of this millennium, people gain power, cultural capital and thrill from being in the cultural spaces of sport and celebrity.

In this chapter, I conceptualize sport culture and celebrity culture to be liminal, everyday spaces of our times. I define these concepts (sport, celebrity, liminality, cultural/everyday spaces) in a particular way, which I believe can contribute to anthropological understanding of sport culture in many times and places. Juxtaposing anthropological interpretation of sport, celebrity and liminality with my deliberately mixed interpretations of a specific tourist site (the Michael Jordan *Spirit* monument in Chicago) I show by example how anthropologists of sport can combine classic anthropological themes (for example Victor Turner on liminality), with broadened, exploded definitions of 'sport', 'ethnography' and 'culture' in order to interpret the ubiquity of sport in our times. Postmodern peripherals of sport, the currencies of sport, the cultural capital of sport that decorates our everyday lives, intrigue me. I want to understand the every-thingness of sport (everything is for sale, everything can be had, every-thing is saved and collected or musealized) that saturates America and the developed world in an obsessive frenzied state.[1] I want to notice as an anthropologist how sport culture exotically permeates the developed world.

For example, my web search on HotBot reveals 25,408 'matches' for the basketball superstar 'Michael Jordan'. Ponder these words from a cross section of the Jordan web pages:

- I continued to pursue my dream of meeting Michael Jordan. (http://members.aol.com/jrcohan/homepage/index.htm)
- (Read THIS first). Recently I have received a lot of e-mails from people who think I am Michael Jordan. I would like to point out that I'm NOT Michael Jordan and I don't have any means of contacting him directly. I'm NOT associated with any organizations concerning the NBA or Michael Jordan. My name is Tomer Sagi and I just maintain this page as a hobby. I would like to apologize to all the people who thought I was someone else. (http://www.geocities.com/Colosseum/5058/)
- I strongly believe that Michael Jordan is the greatest basketball player of all-time. NO, I KNOW HE IS, and therefore I have set this page up to further glorify the man they call 'His Royal Airness'. (http://www.geocities.com/Colosseum/5058/)
- One of the quirks that goes with running a celebrity site is receiving messages from people believing you to be the star; as such, I receive a handful of messages addressed to Michael every week. Typically they are of the 'I love you, Michael' variety, so I usually don't pay much attention to these messages. But this past June I received a message from Mrs Carolina Santos from Honduras, who is currently in the States as her 10-year-old son, Andres, is being treated for cancer in Fort Lauderdale. The past few months, I have been corresponding regularly with Mrs Santos, and I have sent Andres a number of Michael-related materials I have received from Nike; while these little souvenirs, including an autopen-signed photo of Michael, have worked to lift Andres's spirits considerably (and his health – his tumour is almost gone, last I heard), deep within I knew that just sending Andres these items was not quite good enough. I had to reach Michael directly . . . (http://members.xoom.com/jordanhost/michael.html)
- Name: Michael Jordan, Position: God . . . oops . . . Guard, Height: 6-6, Age: 33. (http://ww1.sportsline.com/u/jordan/offcourt/index.html)
- Welcome to Christian's Michael Jordan Page. Hi, my name is Christian, and I live in Norway. Does anyone want to join me for pictures? How about a nice dunk to begin with? How about some videos? My first Michael Jordan movie. Michael winning the MVP award. (http://home.sol.no/~gunnarbu/airness.htm)

- This is a homepage centred around the Chicago Bulls and Michael Jordan. I am a real big fan of Mike's, and I have some interesting stuff you can check out. I'm eleven years old and live in New Jersey, and I don't get to see many Bulls games either on TV or live. I did see the Bulls against the Knicks at Madison Square Garden on January 23, 1996. The Bulls won.
  (http://members.aol.com/jrcohan/homepage/index.htm)
- At that moment it started to sink in – I was actually at a Bulls practice, and there on the hardwood right in front of me were Michael, Scottie, Dennis Rodman, Phil Jackson . . . everyone. It was truly unbelievable, and I still can't believe it right now . . . The images are so vivid yet otherworldly, as if it were all a dream – for once, things did work out for me, but in a way I had never thought was actually possible, as if I had just imagined it. Yet I can still feel Michael shaking my hand, and I can still see his eyes looking deep into mine. . . Which makes me wonder. . . why now? Why after all this time, all the disappointments and heartbreaks, did it come to pass at this time? Was it God's way of rewarding me after all I had done, His way to lift the burden that had been keeping me down and enable me to go on with my life?
  (http://members.xoom.com/jordanhost/michael.html)
- Otherwise, hanging from the arm of the Michael Jordan statue outside the United Center by the end of next season will be a noose with the strong likeness of one former Iowa State coach hanging from the end. All taxidermists, please get in line.
  (http://cbssportsline.com/u/page/covers/basketball/aug98/insider82598.htm)
- Michael Jordan Statue Series –557. 32 inches tall. Only 1250 made for special J.C. Penny's. Won at sports drawing. $1200.00.
  (http://www.icok.net/~jandgjoy/)
- The power of MJ: Take a trip to Chicago's United Center and you'll see basketball fans flocking to the Michael Jordan statue as if it's a mecca. It's a popular spot for photos and just plain hanging out before and after games.
  (http://wcco.com/partners/tv/talent/sportsbytes/partners-tv-talent-sportsbytes.-980310-223336.html)

These web sites represent the spaces of culture where history is being made in small, everyday ways.

I take culture to be an infinite, abstract, convoluted, unpredictable soup that humans live in, on, around and through.[2] Culture is a mystery with no need of solution, made up of metacommunications about a myriad of activities, representations and performances that humans engage in while on earth. *Sport culture* is anything and everything that carries a 'sport sign'; that is, that is somehow coded to have something to do with, or to signify, sport (to spectators, athletes, voyeurs, dreamers) including, in addition to 'real' sport, but not limited to: T-shirts with sport representations silk-screened upon them; autographed mass-produced baseballs; sports halls of fame; Bahktinian carnival; pilgrimages to games and festivals; sport souvenirs; the sport anthropology conference; a victory trophy; a baby rattle molded in the likeness of a soccer ball; sport instruction; virtual sport; memories of games; idolization of sport celebrities; music, smells, feels (see, for example Novak 1976; Csikszentmihalyi 1981: 14-26; Csikszentmihalyi 1990: 71-86; Cady 1986: 197-207), tastes (for example Spitz 1996: 81-4)[3] of sport; artifacts and fetishes associated with sport; dance, martial arts, physical therapies and religion (see also Prebish 1993) (if they want to be sport); ironic and performative sports, such as American Gladiators, Sumo-diving and dwarf bowling; and the implosion of superathletes into culture-at-large.

In his article about how the greatest player in basketball became the greatest brand in the history of sports, Henry Louis Gates Jr. takes a paragraph to list Jordan's implosion into transnational culture:

> Edible cake decorations, golf-club covers, shower curtains, pot holders, aprons, rulers, kitchen towels, sleeping bags, canteens, insulated travel mugs, napkins, tablecloths, popcorn tins, foam furniture, first-aid kits, gift wrap, memo pads, book bags, pencil sharpeners, erasers, buttons, key chains, wallet cards, magnets, ring binders, tissue holders, diaries, address books, envelopes, flashlights, kites, toothbrush holders, wastebaskets, Sony and Sega play stations, pinball games, soap dishes, walkie talkies, curtains, acrylic juice cups, gum, cookies, bandages and comforters; this isn't a list of all the commodities that Jordan has endorsed, but its the beginning of such a list. (1998: 48)

Consider also some of the changes in the scope and substance of sport culture in the past five years, a few of which are monumental historical and anthropological changes: the innovation of fantasy/role playing/virtual reality sport; the spawning of countless Internet sport sites such as online gambling, fantasy-team competitions, virtual participation in real sport events, exercise chat groups and celebrity-athlete 'stalker' sites; online exercise clothing and equipment shopping; and mass sport tourism to special sporting sites.

For millions of people, collecting (for example Fiske 1993, chapter 4) and shopping for sport-related items (baseball cards), or travelling to prestigious sporting events (the Olympic Games) to eat and socialize are more important than playing or watching the game. A team's colours or mascot, instead of its record, may attract fans and souvenir buyers. Exercise couture today is high-fashion, in turn filtering globally to streetwear and vice versa; and there is a rise of community members who blend drugs, pornography, alternative music and/or gang activity with sport and sport symbols. How we understand, watch and play sport has also changed through enhanced technologies in photography, super-slow-motion film and holography. Reality is no longer only experienced directly, but through filtered, enhanced, distorted mediation of editors, designers, artists. Sports culture of all sorts are the object of 'looking/gazing' and lens – at youth games, the stands are filled with parents adjoined to video cameras.

On US television, aside from broadcasts of sports events themselves, one can watch hours of sport commentary and spend days on-line viewing and purchasing sport culture items such as a polyester Joe Dimaggio blanket that comes with a gold baseball card that is 'authenticated' with a special magnifying glass that reveals a trademark hologram. The catalogues of mass middle-class consumption – one catalogue for example, offers for sale thousand-dollar basketballs signed by Michael Jordan, and bed linens in the sport motif of choice. It's not only catalogues, television or the Internet. Everywhere there are big and little sport motifs; the world converses, participates, watches and wears sport.

I grant that sport culture such as I have described inundates America and/or explicit cultures and communities more than others, but my task is not to provide a socio-economic-gender-race-transnational profile of sports immersion. Nor have I made it my task to fracture delineations between high and low sport culture. One idea that is crucial to my project is a theory of collecting, or musealization, as voiced by Jean Baudrillard, Umberto Eco, James Boon, Andreas Huyssean and others, which argues that 'our entire linear and accumulative culture would collapse if we could not stockpile our culture in plain view' (Fiske 1993, chapter 4). We collect to reassure us as to our ends, to be empowered, to feel good, as a form of closure (Stewart 1984; Sontag 1990). This musealization is seen by these writers as a 'simulation machine, which like television, sucks all meaning into a Baudrillardian black hole'(Huyssean 1995: 31).

I have briefly reviewed these concepts of musealization because my argument concerning sport, liminality and celebrity is dependent on agreeing that there is a cultural imperative to the collecting activities of humans and that epistemologically, most things that humans do can be abstractly conceived of as activities of collecting – when humans bracket, frame or formalize, they are engaging in collecting. We fret about our mortality, and to assuage ourselves, we collect. We collect peoples, such as Native Americans; we collect things to do on lists; we collect our community in sport stadia; and we collect pieces of sport culture – such as statuary of athletes – that serve as symbolic reminiscences of what the human body is capable of. In often abstract and distant ways, for example, by way of a T-shirt that proclaims 'PENN STATE UNIVERSITY', the wearer dabs sport celebrity upon himself at the same time as forming a collection and being himself part of a collection.

I disagree with the argument that practices of musealization such as the wearing of a college T-shirt are instruments of the existing order's mandate to keep us hypnotized and passive; or that they are orgiastic states 'of repletion and abundance where we are gorged with meaning and it is killing us' (Baudrillard 1988: 63, as quoted by Abbas 1990: 82). I read such sport culture (that is, the desiring and purchasing, travelling to, immersion into sport-related things), however obscurely related to sport (again, the apple core example is useful here), as terrain where, as we watch, buy, mimic or seek, we are whatever, where whatever can happen, be loved, be destroyed. Whatever is the term of Giorgio Agamben, from his The Coming Community (1994: 2.1; translator's notes 106.5-107.5). From Agamben '*whatever* refers precisely to that which is neither particular nor general, neither individual nor generic' (1994: translator's notes 1). A lot of our *whatevers* have to do with sport.

Whatever infers cultural spaces of timelessness, unmeaning, inbetween-ness; liminality. In liminal spaces there is a certain freedom to juggle with the factors of existence, to be famous for a few seconds, to speak the forbidden, to reverse social order, to tease societal taboos. Liminal spaces are becoming places where the old rules may no longer apply, where identities are fluid, where meanings are negotiated. Liminal spaces are aesthetic places, sometimes virtual or asynchronous – for instance liminal spaces like MTV Sports where artists create fragmented, gorgeously coloured and musically choreographed rushes of sport scenes on screens that provide opportunities for aesthetic experiences for watchers in living rooms, bars, prisons and malls. We see then, that photography, videography, literature, cinematography (in journalism, television, film, personal computing, music videos, advertising and the like) are as much sites of sport in post-modern times as are traditional sport sites, such as the biomechanics lab or the football field.

As we learned from classic anthropology, Victor Turner from Arnold van Gennep called the liminal betwixt and between (Turner 1967:106, 93-111; see also van Gennep 1960) or a borderlands, threshold. The liminal can apply not only to rites of passage of individuals or groups, but to the liminal spaces, the 'not here, not there', that are in culture at large. In liminal spaces, binary relations such as rich/poor, archaism/modernity, inside/outside, male/female, may disappear or be interrogated (Bhabha 1994: 245). Homi Bhabha says in his work, *The Location of Culture* that such liminal spaces are the 'inter' – the cutting edge of translation and negotiation, the in-between space – that carries the burden of the meaning of culture (Bhabha 1994: 38).

Bhabha[4] suggests in *The Location of Culture* that theory, being and history exist in a timeless space of unmeaning called the Third Space, a space that is beyond control:

> This is the space in which the question of modernity emerges as a form of inter-rogation: what do I belong to in this present? In what terms do I identify with the 'we', the intersubjective realm of society? This process cannot be represented in the binary relation of archaism/modernity, inside/outside, past/present, because these questions block off the forward drive or teleology modernity . . . What is crucial to [a vision of the future] is the belief that we must not merely change the narratives of our histories, but transform our sense of what it means to live, to be, in other times and different spaces, both human and historical. (1994: 245, 256)

I believe that examples of such liminal spaces are those that are connected to sport culture (as I have loosely defined it above) and to celebrity. By celebrity, I refer to fame, achieved recognition, notoriety, the act of being extolled, filmed or talked about by others – in real time or imagined, in the media or even in one's neighbourhood or small peer group. By the transposed label 'celebrity', I mean also to include the cultural activities associated with consumerism such as buying and selling pieces of celebrity, however distant that association to our usual notion of celebrity might be (for example requesting that one's hair be styled to look like a soap opera character on television; saving a ticket stub from a World Series Game; visiting the site of the *Field of Dreams*, a movie set for a fictional film (see Springwood 1996, 1999). I am also defining celebrity by those qualities normally associated with movie stars,5 sport heroes, television personalities, politicians, Hollywood, the tabloids, being in/on television, in the movies, in the public eye, a recognized maker of culture. I refer to the pervasive nature of celebrity and its pursuit – most of how we and those around us pursue it in little everyday ways.

Evidence our children – children everywhere – who want to be game-show hosts, famous athletes, fashion models, movie stars, Olympians. Evidence our acquaintances whose lives are defined around moments when they played guitar for a few seconds on stage with a famous band, saw a movie star in a restaurant, were interviewed on the news show, made a pilgrimage to the Olympic Games.

I point to the millions who fantasize that they are on the court as Michael Jordan as they shoot baskets in the school yard, or are Tiger Woods winning the Master's Golf Tournament as they chip shots at a run-down miniature golf course. I think of the thousands on death beds who produce videos of their ends; writers everywhere who dream of making it; everyone everywhere who harbours a fantasy of being famous, of being the object of a gaze, of a lens, of Andy Warhol's scant minutes of fame ('in the future, everyone will be famous for fifteen minutes'). As a writer in the 'zine *Zyzzyva*', reciting the routines of his life put it, 'Two questions constantly occur to me: "What would this look like filmed? What would the sound track be?"' (Shields 1994: 170). This is all fabricated as 'celebrity' in my work.

Celebrity influences life in profound ways – as Walter Benjamin noted, it 'bursts this prison world asunder' (Benjamin 1968: 236). Celebrity is 'the glorious moment continued and absorbed into personality . . . it's a defiance of time and death' (Lahr 1994: 113). In the trope of celebrity that I have described, one obviously doesn't need to be a 'real' celebrity to be in the liminality of celebrity. In the betwixt and between cultural spaces of celebrity and sport, life can be mirrored and restructured without and in spite of prior conditions.

Today we cannot speak of celebrity and sports without thinking of Michael Jordan, the National Basketball Association player who has been called the 'greatest athlete in the history of American sports' (Gates 1998:

48). I now turn to a particular image of Jordan, a bronze statue situated in front of the United Center at 1901 West Madison St, Chicago. Various Chicago tourist officials and the United Center business office tell me that this statue is now the 'number one tourist destination' in Chicago. A virtual on-line tour of Chicago stops at the statue, as do the Gray Line and local tour companies. Their information brochures reassert the status of the Jordan statue as touristic marker:

> From State and Madison Streets: $7.70. The Bulls and Blackhawks play at the new state-of-the-art United Center at 1901 W. Madison, 312-455-4000. The building is a tourist stop if only to view the life sized bronze statue of MichaelJordan.(http://www.ci.chi.il.us/Tourism/ThingsToDo/Sports.html)

and

> The Michael Jordan statue has fast become one of Chicago's favorite tourist attractions. All day long, and both prior to and after United Center events, people from all over the world come to visit and have their picture taken in front of one of Chicago's most famous and recognizable landmarks (http://www.united-center.com/virtual-tour/index.html).

Officially called the Jordan Monument, *Spirit* was created by the husband-wife team of Omri and Julie Rotblatt-Amrany of Highland Park, Illinois in 1994. The statue's 'origin story' goes as follows:

> In late 1993, Bulls Chairman, Jerry Reinsdorf, directed team Vice President, Steve Schanwald, to conduct a search for a sculptor who could craft a statue as tribute to the greatest player in NBA history. In January, 1994 Schanwald hired to design and create a statue of the then retired Bulls superstar which would stand forever at the entrance to the United Center, the Bulls' new home, which was set to open in August of that same year. Schanwald sought a design which would be a realistic depiction of Jordan, illustrate the spectacular nature of his unique skill, and create an illusion of flight. Following a review of submissions by a number of sculptors, the now familiar design submitted by the Amaranys was approved by Jerry Reinsdorf. (http://www.united-center.com/virtual-tour/index.html)

The statue was unveiled before a national television audience by Larry King, Reinsdorf and Jordan in a 1 November 1994 ceremony at which Michael Jordan's number −23 was retired. Sitting on a 5 foot high black granite base inscribed with Jordan's basketball achievements, and the words, 'The best there ever was. The best there ever will be', the statue of Jordan measures 12 feet tall (17 feet from top to bottom of the complete sculpture) and weighs 2,000 pounds. The statue was cast in bronze using the 'lost wax' method at Art Casting of Illinois, a foundry in Oregon, Illinois. Again, the 'origin story' relates:

Figure 10 Typical tourist pose in front of the Jordan monument [Synthia Sydnor]

> Working in secrecy, and putting in 16-hour days, 7 days a week for 4 months, the Amrany's finished work depicts Jordan soaring over an abstract entanglement of opponents, preparing to unleash one of his signature dunks. The airborne Jordan is attached to the base at just one point – the knee. (http://www.united-center.com/virtual-tour/index.html)

Philosophers like Mirceau Eliade (1952) and Martin Heidegger (1971) say that there is a power in the image of a live person made into a statue: Eliade wrote that 'such images bring men together . . . more effectively and more genuinely than any analytical language. Indeed, if an ultimate solidarity of the whole human race does exist, it can be felt and activated only at the level of images' (1952: 17). Jordan's statue certainly packs this essence of celebrity into one void, the now-unarguably universal language of sport. It is common during the summer to see busloads of tourists arriving with cameras to visit the monument. In addition to taking an obligatory photo at the monument, tourists throw pennies and other coins (which are donated to local Chicago charities) to 'make a wish' at the statue, which is 'maintained with a wax coating', guarded by a black iron fence, a 'guard at Gate Four 24 hours a day', and other secreted video surveillance.[6] Unlike other urban statuary, there is virtually no vandalism at this site – some try to climb the fence for a photograph, but otherwise, 'people respect the site so, for they love Michael Jordan' (Brooks Boyer 1998). The fact that the site is 'safe' is also distinguished by those who laud the West Side, legended to be 'not a good neighbourhood', in Chicago, as having changed since the erection of the monument: city buses now frequent the site, and visitors are not fearful.[7]

I began to try to interpret the touristic activity at the statue by first categorizing what people did at the statue (they 'visited'/looked at the statue, were photographed in front of it, and sometimes sang to the statue) by using a treatise of two centuries ago as my guide. In his famous *Reflections on the Imitation of Greek Works in Painting and Sculpture*, Johann Joachim Winckelmann wrote, 'the more tranquil the state of the body, the more capable it is of portraying the true character of the soul' (Winckelmann 1987: 35). In the case of the Jordan monument, this import of the tranquillity of the statue as portraying what is thought to be the 'true character of the soul' shows Jordan – predictably – as towering and of superhuman ability.

People crave to know what others are really all about. We spend our lives trying to figure this out. Statues smack us in the face with 'what life is all about'. At the same time that they seduce with the magnificence of life, statues like the Jordan monument preserve the hegemony of nation, family, work, competitiveness, patriotism, and so forth. Statues are particularly capable of celebrating these hegemonic practices because they are commissioned (formally, informally, subversively, subconsciously and/or unconsciously) by powerful values, ideals and/or administrative bodies. An *avant garde*, uncomplimentary or critical rendition of Jordan would not have sufficed.

Statues of the West (Bieber 1971), among which the Jordan monument is surely included, are part of an invented heritage that hails imaginatively back to antiquity. This philosophical basis of Greek revivalism in Western modernism was the idea, from thinkers such as Winckelmann and much earlier, that 'the only way for us to become great . . .is to imitate the ancients, especially the Greeks' (Winckelmann 1987: 5; see also Clarke 1989: 112; Vance 1989; Vermuele 1981). Such concerted attempts at imitation may be seen as what has been labelled 'selected' or 'invented' 'tradition' (Hobsbawm and Ranger 1983: 1-14; Frow 1991: 133). Invented traditions, such as occur when museums, banks, city streets and places like the United Center are embellished with *faux* ancient friezes and statuary, may also be seen to be continually performed by human bodies. At the 'Rocky' Statue (depicting the boxer played by actor Sylvester Stallone in the *Rocky* films) at the top of the steps of the Art Museum in Philadelphia, tourists recreate the victorious training scene from the first *Rocky* film). (Like the Jordan statue, the statue remains one of the top touristic sites of Philadelphia).

It can be argued that modern/postmodern human bodies are made into classical statuary so as to make viewing these bodies palatable. Historically, the erotic voyeurism of 'naked bodies as ancient athletes' was masked behind what came to be a socially acceptable practice: the visiting of ancient sculpture and forms at museums was articulated as a practice of high culture by non-aristocratic practitioners. This 'museum going' carried over to the use of classical statuary and other motifs at athletic festivals and sport events. Indeed, some adults and teenagers who have seen the Jordan statue alluded to this aspect of high culture at the Jordan statue when they noted things to me about the statue such as 'statues teach us about history'; 'it is good to spend time seeing such fine art'; 'this is an important part of Chicago'.

The body displayed as a statue, most often in poses reminiscent of classical statuary, usually made of white stone, but also of bronze, still,[8] naked-yet-not naked, is a body spectators can gawk at and desire.

At the end of the millennium we are voyeurs to bodies from a past, for statues are always from the past. As Robert Lowenthal says in his work, *The Past is a Foreign Country*, 'the past is a world into which time travelers may pry without embarrassment or fear of rebuff' (Lowenthal 1985: 296). The 'remoteness' of the past enables people to engage with it creatively, to frame it however they want.

Such statues as that of Jordan at the United Center are nostalgically contextualized aesthetically to be patriotic; to hail from 'our' noble past, to pay homage to a team or national hero; and to be historical or commemorative.

Using the ideas of Winckelmann and Eliade, we can interpret such hegemonic formations as involved in a process that evokes emotions – nostalgia, patriotism, joy and sadness – from onlookers because they see the 'soul'. Poseurs in front of Jordan's image sometimes said in so many words that were proud to be American, that their photo commemorated their awe of Jordan's ability and accomplishments, that the photo marked their pilgrimage to 'Jordan's home', that the statue was mecca for them.

But we know as anthropologists that these affects are not innocent – in our times, such emotions are labelled as commodities or signifiers of 'false' or inauthentic desire and experience. Whatever emotions, commodities or invented traditions I can force upon my interpretation of the Jordan statue, the statue does seem to pack the essence of celebrity into its void. So here is yet another way that we can use anthropology to interpret this artifact: borrowing from Giorgio Agamben's *Coming Community*

> the statue[9] is a pure singularity that communicates only in the empty space of the example . . . [it is] expropriated of all identity, so as to appropriate belonging itself . . . Tricksters or fakes, assistants or 'toons, they are the exemplars of the coming community. (1994: 10.1)

Here the statue of Jordan is cliché – an 'assistant', a "toon', an 'exemplar of the coming community', a blank with no clear meaning except to refer to the world as it is.

Games, Sports and Cultures

The spectators' reaction to the Spirit statue is to look, read the inscriptions, then to be photographed. When I asked visitors conversationally about the statue, many said things such as: 'it's huge and magnificent'; 'I haven't thought much about it'; 'I am excited to be here'; 'it's a symbol of this great city'; 'Jordan is the greatest that ever was'; 'it's nice that this will be here forever'; 'since we were in Chicago we wanted to see this'. As noted above, families visiting the statue also sometimes stated that they were proud to be American, that they were happy to be visiting the US/Chicago/the United Center/this neighbourhood. When I was able to extend my conversations to explain that I was writing about the statue and what people did around it, the most common reaction was laughter. Sometimes it seemed to me that onlookers tried their best to help me by telling me something 'academic', 'serious', 'unknown', or 'unusual' about the statue, statues in general, or Jordan. They knew tidbits of the statue's origin story, and would recount them, or they would link the statue to their experiences in viewing other statues such as in a museum in a foreign country ('we've seen lots of statues in Europe, never of a basketball player though'). Most of all though, they revered Jordan.

The statue is experienced in a postmodern way – by feeling and filming in ways that have been practised and introduced to the viewer a thousand times before in other situations in popular culture. On the Internet, I found several of the countless fan pages on Jordan that showcase the obligatory photo in front of the Jordan Monument. One page read, 'Michael Jordan at the United Center. Here I am honing my "blading skilz!"' (of a male teenager in roller blades at the statue) (http://home-page.dave-world.net/~soleiux/chilife.htm); more pages were family vacation poses in front of the Jordan monument; a few home pages were creative such as the man who photographed himself holding a computer game magazine showcasing the soon-to-be-released game Riven 'jamming witt Michael Jordan in Chicago'.
(http://www.riven.com/interest/kodak.html)

The philosopher Giorgio Agamben says that:

> the root of all pure joy and sadness is that the world is as it is. Joy or sadness that arises because the world is not what it seems or what we want it to be is impure or provisional . . . In the highest degree of their purity . . . sadness and joy refer not to negative or positive qualities, but to a pure *being-thus* without any attributes. (1994: Appendix 90.1, emphasis original)

It is this *being-thus* without any attributes, that that I am using to interpret the Jordan Monument.

Walter Benjamin was concerned with things like the Jordan Monument and *being-thus*, with how the 'uniqueness of a work of art is inseparable from its being imbedded in the fabric of tradition' (Benjamin 1968: 223). He forged an approach that we reckon with today when he read tradition as 'thoroughly alive and extremely changeable' (Benjamin 1968: 223). Benjamin explored how new methods of production are interwoven with the old, and 'dialectical images still arise from which it is possible to deduce various collective ideas of wish fulfillment'(Bronner 1994: 143).

But Benjamin claimed that with the increasingly pronounced effect of technology upon art, the ability of an audience to fasten upon the utopian residues of art became weak. He perceived premodern objects and artwork to have an 'aura' that allowed the object to 'look at us in return' (Bronner 1994: 142). As technology made possible new ways of mechanical reproduction, there was a loss of aura, the utopian presence of the past was weakened, the 'quality of presence always depreciated' (Benjamin 1968: 220-2). For Benjamin, when technical reproduction put the copy of the original into situations which would be out of reach for the original itself, the original 'authority' of the object was lost. Yet it seems that a statue such as Jordan's is artwork that still has authority, or even aura, in our times.

The Jordan Monument is a liminal thing; it is human yet it is not, it lives and moves, yet it is still. Kenneth Gross, in *Dream of the Living Statue* describes this aura:

> These things cannot happen: A statue cannot move or speak; it cannot open its eyes, nod, or call out, cannot tell a story, dance or do work; it cannot turn on the viewer, or run away, banishing its solidarity and repose, shedding its silence. A statue is almost by definition a thing that stands still, and what we call its movement is at best a resonant figure of speech. Yet these things happen; we imagine them happening. Our language requires that they happen. The fantasy of a statue that comes to life is as central a fable as we have. Time and again, we find texts in which the statue that stands immobile in temple or square descends from its pedestal, or speaks out of its silence . . . it is one of our oldest images of the work of magic, one of our most primitive metafictions. (1992: xi)

The Jordan Monument behaves in the fantasy of the *tableau vivant* that Gross describes of the moving statue (Virillio 1991: 91; Sontag 1990; Sturzebecker 1996; Annan 1992: 3-6). After attending a Bulls game for the first time in Winter 1998, one man I spoke with about the statue relayed

> the statue was so weird because it is huge and magnificent and Michael Jordan is still alive! It [the monument] says something like 'the greatest athlete that ever lived.' It's as if he already died, but he is alive. When I saw him on the court, it was a very strange feeling. It was as if he was not real – it was very strange – he is everywhere in our society, then all of a sudden you see the real thing and I almost couldn't comprehend what I was seeing.

Such a statue as Jordan's comes to life imaginatively, televisually and through commodification (Andrews 1996a, 1996b). Twenty-eight-inch-high copies of the Monument, also sculpted by Omri and Julie Rotblatt Amrany, are autographed by the artists, and by Jordan. Like the original, the miniatures are cast in bronze and sit on a black granite base, but unlike the original, 123 of these can be purchased for $10,000 each at the United Center. Their publicity office told me that the Chicago Bulls are selling these limited edition reproductions of the statue to partially offset costs associated with the construction of the James Jordan Boys and Girls Club. In the past two years, 43 miniatures have been purchased.

At United Center, the statue freeze-frames for us the human sport endeavour, it museualizes (Huyssen 1995: 14) or captions and publicly displays Jordan's simulacrum as a unique museum, 'the ultimate' person engaged in sport, our hero, our victor. The Jordan monument stands as a souvenir for the busloads of tourists that arrive to stand before it as a way for them to remember what it is to be human, how our form can be divine; the athlete statue shows us how far we can go. On a postcard, hanging in miniature on a Christmas tree, or encased in a snow globe – all that we want to say that is good and noble about humanity is on display. Thus, the Jordan monument is an organ of remembrance; a vehicle of hegemony; and a poststructuralist, apocalyptic way of 'stockpiling' as voiced by Baudrillard, Eco, Boon and Stewart, among others (Huyssen 1995: 25; Baudrillard 1983: 19; Eco 1976; Boon 1991; Stewart 1984).

I have so far exposed the Jordan statue in many many ways, purposefully not encasing my interpretation as a tidy explanation of what the sculpture means culturally. It does serve to legitimate particular ideals in sport culture, or culture at large; it acts as an authentic[10] experience/event for the visitor; as a naïve touristic marker that is collected by visitors; and as a blank, liminal space. It is to my interpretation of the sculpture as a prop-artifact-backdrop that rips liminal spaces for us that I want to turn for the remainder of the essay.

Remember that the liminal can apply not only to rites of passage of individuals or groups, but to the liminal spaces, the 'not here, not there', that are in theory, in writing, in statuary, in culture at large, in our post modern times, all at the same time (Bhabha 1994: 245, 256).

The thought of Henri Bergson from the 1890s might be revisited in conceptualizing liminal spaces in this way. Bergson reminds us that 'space, by definition is outside us; yet the separation between a thing and its environment cannot be absolutely definite and clear-cut; there is a passage by insensible gradations from one to the other' (Bergson 1991: 202, 209). I am interested in these gradations between spaces, things like the Jordan statue, everyday culture and the liminal. There is in thinking of these gradations the paradox of the statue that doesn't come to life, yet at the same time offers the viewer (or the artist creator-designer) the pantomime of a person most alive – the celebrity athlete: a man about to dunk one, Mike flying above abstracted, smaller others.

Perhaps statues, which are on one hand as primal as the history of human community, and on the other hand are among many transformative, liminal features of times of new meaning and cultural creativity, have, in Bhabha's words, the capacity to 'transform' our sense of ourselves in postmodern ways, as epitomized by the words engraved on the Jordan Monument:

Michael Jordan
Chicago Bulls 1984–1993
The best that ever was, the best that ever will be.

We come full circle, back again to Winckelmann's idea that the more static the body, the more it can enact what it is to be human, what the essence of the soul is, being thus, whatever.

I insinuated above that the statue might rip a liminal cultural space for the viewer; that statues are props that float viewers and creators into liminal narratives. Furthermore, things that are associated with sport's cultural formations, artifacts and practices, may be the epitome of third spaces, spaces where we are *whatever*, where *whatever* can happen.

If the Jordan Monument is a space of unmeaning, then it is a liminal realm where there is a certain freedom to juggle with the factors of existence. In this freedom, third spaces are becoming places where the old rules may no longer apply, where identities are fluid, where meanings are negotiated, where what Agamben calls *whatever* can happen, *whatever* can be loved. From Agamben, '*whatever* refers precisely to that which is neither particular nor general, neither individual nor generic' (1994: translator's notes: 1). The epistemological and ontological standpoints offered by *whatever* shown to us in things such as urban sport statuary transport us into liminal spaces and spaces of freedom. *Whatever* is celebrity.

In the spaces of sport celebrity, we are Agamben's *whatever*. These third spaces of celebrity, media, the *whatever* of celebrity, the *whatever* of sport, the *whatever* reproduced by the Jordan statue is an example of the pure *being-thus* that Agamben highlights. Celebrity, *being-thus* and *whatever* are third spaces at the end of the twentieth century where for a few seconds – gazing at the Jordan monument – one may be free, happy, unjudged as Black, White, Asian, rich, poor, ugly, disabled. These *being-thus* spaces sometimes are culture itself.

I gaze at the Michael Jordan statue again. It seems that a statue like this is called a mecca, has an extraordinary role in our culture for some, perhaps because it is a prop to *whatever*, to *being-thus*: it serves not as a way for us to remember, but as a performance that dehistoricizes/creates/prolongs liminality. Possibly, this statue serves to do precisely the opposite of what we say it does: it deforms,[11] not forms. In the everyday sense of the use of the statue, the statue is commissioned to save a moment, a memory, a regime, a person. But performatively, the statue tears a liminal space into everyday space, prolonging the nature of the threshold.

Thresholds' moments are liquid, undefinable, and the memories of thresholds are always in the act of becoming; thresholds are like celebrity: dazzling (Turkle 1995; McCordock 1996: 106, 110, 158, 165) dangerous, wondrous. Perhaps because of this danger, the black iron fence keeps visitors from coming within three feet of the Jordan Monument. If lookers could meld with the statue by touching it, their social and civic practices might become violent, orgiastic, revolutionary.

So, such cultural spaces of celebrity – the Jordan statue – are redemptive, full of great opportunity or joy; but possibly also destructive, tense, painful, made up of extreme reactions (McCorduck 1996: 106-10, 158-65). For instance, during the 1996 Democratic National Convention held at the United Center, overzealous security wonks decided to cover the Michael Jordan statue outside. They were afraid the number of delegates anxious to see it would present 'a security problem'.[12]

In liminal spaces, civility and culture are up for grabs – they can be reshaped and negated. In such spaces, for example, in the sometimes violent crowd behaviour after a big game win, rioters in the streets insert themselves into history performatively, with their bodies, in the way that they can make, as Paul Connerton says, 'society remember' (Connerton 1989). Rioters are in a liminal space, a seductive swirl of celebrity, of sport. Still another sport related example: teenagers who blend music, drug taking and snowboarding are creating liminal spaces of sport and celebrity that might 'normally' be described in negative ways, but that may instead be envisioned in a different light using Agamben's conception of whatever.

Particularly, to interpret both the violent destructive actions (which I briefly overviewed in the paragraph above) that are sometimes homogeneous with present-day/postmodern sport culture, as well as the positive, hegemonic images like the United Center's Jordan monument, we should look again to Agamben's (1994: 49.0)[13] glorification of tricksters and fakes, assistants and 'toons'. To be a trickster, fake, assistant or toon expands the bounds of what can be made, played with and created in the form of cultural capital in the liminal spaces of culture.

These liminal spaces of sport and celebrity are not temporary spaces – everywhere and (al)ways, they script life at the end of the twentieth century. Humans live in liminality, we collect or musealize these spaces all the time. These liminal spaces are not (only) postmodern places of nihilism or complicity, but are also visual, virtual, written, oral, imaginary, sites where it is possible to get outside the construction of difference, or, at least, of the difference of our times, and to move (un)toward Agamben's coming community or to Homi Bhabha's 'location of culture', where it is possible to always be in the act of becoming. 'Becoming what?' you might ask. I cannot answer that question. I can only comment that this liminal becoming, celebrity like, at the end of this millennium seems to have a lot to do with sport.[14] To explore these liminal spaces in our sport anthropology projects might allow us to provocatively view sport in manifestations not usually studied within the anthropology canon in academe.

Notes

1. Huyssean (1995: 14-15), uses this word. See also Baudrillard 1983; Bruner 1994: 397-415; Bruner and Kirshenblatt-Gimblett 1994: 435-70; Boon 1991: 255-78; Clifford 1992: 96-116; Eco 1976.
2. For the theoretical and methodological foundations of my work, see

for example Schechner 1989, 1993a, 1993b: 296-320; Agamben 1994; Van Gennep 1960; Bhabha 1994; Denzin 1992; Fiske 1993; Denzin 1995; Huyssean 1995; Boon 1991; Bruner 1993; Clifford 1988, 1992; Connerton 1989; Culler 1988; Eco 1976; Denzin 1994; Richardson 1994; Denzin 1994; Turkle 1995.

3. 'About five years ago, a revolution took place in the sports world . . . As a result, you can either watch the Indians play or stroll through the park's palatial food court, which includes two delis, an in-house bakery, a chicken and rib stand, Beers of the World, Kids Land, a Tex-Mex plaza serving four flavors of margaritas, and more than 65 other varieties of nouvelle ballpark fare' (Spitz 1996: 83).

4. I have modified Bhabha's Third Space, a singular capitalized entity into 'third spaces', lowercase plural, in my work.

5. As theorized by Benjamin (1968: 236): 'the film responds to the shriveling of the aura with an artificial build-up of the "personality" outside the studio. The cult of the movie star, fostered by the money of the film industry, preserves not the unique aura of the person, but the "spell of the personality", the phony spell of a commodity.'

6. Much of the detailed information about the Jordan monument's security, upkeep and touristic activities in this essay came from Brooks Boyer, Chicago Bulls administration office. I am indebted to him for help on my project.

7. For example, 'Tour 4: 1998: January 10, March 14, May 16. On Chicago's West Side, we will tour a neighborhood that has undergone many waves of change. This tour includes: A visit and reception at the young artist workshops located at the Duncan YMCA Arts and Education Center. A photo opportunity in front of the Michael Jordan statue, 'The Spirit' at the United Center . . . and a tour of other cultural and historical sites along the way' (http://www.ci.chi.il.us/Tourism/NeighborhoodTours/3and4.html).

8. On 'stillness' of statues, Renaissance writers like Winckelmann pointed out the general and most distinctive characteristics of Greek masterpieces are, finally, a noble simplicity and quiet grandeur, both in posture and expression. Just as the depths of the sea always remain calm however the surface may rage, so does the expression of the figures of the Greeks reveal a great and composed soul even in the midst of passion (1987: 33).

9. Agamben never refers to statues – I have appropriated his words to apply to statues.

10. On authenticity, see Bruner 1994: 397-415, and Bruner and Kirshenblatt-Gimblett 1994: 435-70. These pieces, however, go far beyond the trope of musealization as quest for authenticity, and instead highlight the creative, unique experiences that individuals and groups may encounter in their travels for authenticity.

11. On the idea of 'deforming' and Benjamin's thought, see Bullock and Jennings 1996: 280-2.

12. Bob Collins, 'Postcard from Chicago: A daily report from the Democratic Convention August 27, 1996' (http:// www.news.mpr.org/features/199611/05_newsroom_ election/postcards/cpc0827.htm).

13. Agamben tells us:

What was technologized was not the body, but its image. Thus the glorious body of advertising has become the mask behind which the fragile, slight, human body continues its precarious existence, and the geometrical splendor of the "girls" covers over the long lines of the naked, anonymous bodies led to their death in the Lagers (camps), or the thousands of corpses mangled in the daily slaughter on the highways.

To appropriate the historic transformations of human nature that capitalism wants to limit to the spectacle, to link together image and body in a space where they can no longer be separated, and thus to forge the whatever body, whose physics is resemblance – this is the good that humanity must learn to wrest from commodities in their decline. Advertising and pornography, which escort the commodity to the grave like hired mourners, are the unknowing midwives of this new body of humanity (1994:49.0)

14. I have also aimed in this essay to use specific conceptions of celebrity and liminality to interpret sport culture for another reason: to weaken boundaries between the cultural spaces of sport – spaces of theory, the academy, celebrity, sport-product consumption, transnational selling and street sport. Weakening the boundaries makes the definitions of sport fluid, and the production, theorization and circulation of sport studies (by which I mean sport history, sociology, philosophy, anthropology, Olympic studies, and so forth) are shoved into popular culture.

References

Abbas, A. (1990), 'Disappearance and Fascination: The Baudrillardian Obscenario', in Ackbar Abbas (ed.), *The Provocation of Jean Baudrillard*, Hong Kong: Twighlight.

Agamben, G. (1994), *The Coming Community* (Michael Hardt, trans.), Minneapolis: University of Minnesota Press.

Andrews, D. L. (1996a), 'The Fact(s) of Michael Jordan's Blackness: Excavating a Floating Racial Signifier', *Sociology of Sport Journal*, 13: 125-8.

Andrews, D. L. (1996b), 'Deconstructing Michael Jordan: Reconstructing Postindustrial America', *Sociology of Sport Journal*, 13: 315-18.

Annan, G. (1992), 'A Moral Tale', (Review of Susan Sontag, The Volcano Lover: A Romance), *New York Review of Books*, August 13: 3-6.

Baudrillard, J. (1983), *Simulations* (Paul Foss, Paul Patton, Philip Beitchman, trans.), New York: Semiotext(e) Inc.

Baudrillard, J. (1996), *Cool Memories II: 1987-1990* (Chris Turner, trans.), Durham: Duke University Press.

Baudrillard, J. (1988), *The Ecstasy of Communication* (Bernard and Caroline Schultze, trans.), New York: Semiotext(e).

Benjamin, W. (1968), 'The Work of Art in the Age of Mechanical Reproduction', in W. Benjamin (H. Arendt, ed., H. Zohn, trans.), *Illuminations*, New York, Schocken Books (original work published 1936).

Benjamin, W. (1973), *Charles Baudelaire: A Lyric Poet in the Era of High Capitalism* (Quintin Hoare, trans.), London: Verso.

Bergson, H. (1991), *Matter and Memory* (N. M. Paul and W.S. Palmer, trans.), New York: Zone Books (original work published 1896).

Bhabha, H.K. (1994), *The Location of Culture*, London and New York: Routledge.

Bieber, M. (1971), *Ancient Copies: Contributions to the History of Greek and Roman Art*, New York: New York University Press.

Boon, J. (1991), 'Why Museums Make Me Sad', in I. Karp and S.D. Levine (eds), *Exhibiting Cultures: The Poetics and Politics of Museum Display*, Washington and London: Smithsonian Institute.

Bronner, S. E. (1994), *Of Critical Theory and Its Theorists*, Oxford: Blackwell.

Bruner, E.M. (1993), 'Epilogue: Creative Persona and the Problem of Authenticity', in S. Lavie, K. Narayan and R. Rosaldo (eds), *Creativity/Anthropology*, Ithaca and London: Cornell University Press.

Bruner, E. M. (June 1994), 'Abraham Lincoln as Authentic Reproduction: A Critique of Postmodernism', *American Anthropologist*, 96: 397-415.

Bruner E.M. and Kirshenblatt-Gimblett, B. (1994), 'Maasai on the Lawn: Tourist Realism in East Africa', *Cultural Anthropology*, 9: 435-70.

Bullock, M., and Jennings, M.W. (eds), (1996), *Walter Benjamin: Selected Writings. Volume 1 1913-1926*, Cambridge, MA: The Belknap Press of Harvard University Press.

Cady, E.H. (1986), 'Pop Art and the American Dream', in David Vanderwerken and Spencer K. Wertz (eds), *Sport Inside Out: Readings in Literature and Philosophy*. Fort Worth: Texas Christian University Press.

Clarke, G.W. (ed.), (1989), *Rediscovering Hellenism: The Hellenic Inheritance and the English Imagination*, Cambridge: Cambridge University Press.

Clifford, J. (1988), *The Predicament of Culture: Twentieth-Century Ethnography, Literature and Art*, Cambridge Mass and London: Harvard University Press.

Clifford, J. (1992), 'Traveling Cultures', in L. Grossberg, C. Nelson and P. Treichler (eds), *Cultural Studies*, New York and London: Routledge.

Connerton, P. (1989), *How Societies Remember*, Cambridge: Cambridge University Press.

Culler, J. (1988), *Framing the Sign: Criticism and Its Institutions*, Norman and London: University of Oklahoma Press.

Csikszentmihalyi, M. (1981), 'Some Paradoxes in the Definition of Play', in A. T. Cheska (ed.), *Play as Context*. West Point: Leisure Press.

Csikszentmihalyi, M. (1990), *Flow: The Psychology of Optimal Experience*. New

York: Harper & Row.

Denzin, N.K. (1992), *Symbolic Interactionism and Cultural Studies: The Politics of Interpretation,* Oxford UK and Cambridge: Blackwell.

Denzin, N.K. (1995), *The Cinematic Society: The Voyeur's Gaze,* London: Sage Publications.

Denzin, N.K. (1994), 'The Art and Politics of Interpretation', in N. K. Denzin and Y. S. Lincoln (eds), *Handbook of Qualitative Research,* Thousand Oaks, CA: Sage Publications.

Denzin, N.K. (1994), 'The Fifth Moment', in N.K. Denzin and Y.S. Lincoln (eds), *Handbook of Qualitative Research,* Thousand Oaks, CA: Sage Publications.

Eco, U. (1976), *Travels in Hyperreality* (William Weaver, trans), San Diego and New York: Harcourt Brace Jovanovich.

Eliade, M. (1952), *Images and Symbols: Studies in Religious Symbolism,* New York: Sheed and Ward.

Fiske, J. (1993), *Power Plays, Power Works,* London and New York: Verso.

Frow, J. (1991), 'Tourism and the Semiotics of Nostalgia', *October,* 57: 123-51.

Frueh, J. (1991), 'The Fear of Flesh that Moves', *High Performance,* 55: 70-1.

Gates, H.L. Jr., (1998), 'Net Worth: How the Greatest Player in the History of Basketball Became the Greatest Brand in the History of Sports', *The New Yorker,* June 1: 48-61.

Gross, K. (1992), *The Dream of the Moving Statue,* New York: Cornell University Press.

Hobsbawm, E. and Ranger, T. (1983), *The Invention of Tradition,* Cambridge and New York: Cambridge University Press.

Huyssean, A. (1995), *Twilight Memories: Making Time in a Culture of Amnesia,* New York and London: Routledge.

Jordan, M. (1998), *For the Love of the Game: My Story,* Mark Vancil (ed.), New York: Crown Publishers, Inc.

Lahr, J. (1994), 'The Voodoo of Glamour', *The New Yorker.* March 21: 113.

Lowenthal, D. (1985), *The Past is a Foreign Country,* Cambridge: Cambridge University Press.

McCorduck, P. (1996), 'Sex, Lies and Avators', *Wired:* April: 106-10, 158-65.

Novak, M. (1976), *The Joy of Sports: End Zones, Bases, Baskets, Balls and the Consecration of the American Spirit,* New York: Basic Books.

Parker, A. and Kosofsky Sedgwick, E. (eds), (1995), *Performativity and Performance,* New York and London: Routledge.

Prebish, C.S. (1993), *Religion and Sport: The Meeting of the Sacred and the Profane. Contributions to the Study of Popular Culture,* No. 36. Westport, Connecticut and London: Greenwood Press.

Richardson, L. (1994), 'Writing: A Method of Inquiry', in N.K. Denzin and Y.S. Lincoln (eds), *Handbook of Qualitative Research,* Thousand Oaks, CA: Sage Publications.

Schechner, R. (1989), *Between Theater and Anthropology,* Philadelphia: University of Pennsylvania Press.

Schechner, R. (1993a), *The Future of Ritual: Writings on Culture and Performance*, London and New York: Routledge.

Schechner, R. (1993b), 'Ritual, Violence, Creativity', in S. Lavie, K. Narayan and R. Rosaldo (eds), *Creativity/Anthropology*, Ithaca and London: Cornell University Press.

Shields, D. (1994), 'Information Sickness', *Utne Reader*. March/April: 170. (Originally published in *Zyzzyva*, Spring: 1993).

Sontag S. (1990), *On Photography*, New York: Anchor Books.

Sontag, S. (1992), *The Volcano Lover*, New York: Farrar, Strauss & Giroux.

Spitz, B. (1996), 'Chez Stadium: Which American Arena Will Be the First to Get a Michelin Star?' Sky, (March): 81-4.

Springwood, C.F. (1996), *From Cooperstown to Dyersville: A Geography of Baseball Nostalgia*, Boulder: Westview Press.

Stewart, S. (1984), *On Longing: Narratives of the Miniature, the Gigantic, the Souvenir, the Collection*, Baltimore and London: The Johns Hopkins University Press.

Sturzebecker, R. (1996), *Gymnastic Circuses, Dance Festivals, Athletic Exhibitions: West Chester University*, 1871-1991, West Chester PA: Russell Sturzebecker.

Turkle, S. (1995), *Life on the Screen*, New York: Simon & Schuster.

Turner, V. (1967), *The Forest of Symbols: Aspects of Ndembu Ritual*, Ithaca: Cornell University Press.

Van Gennep, A. (1960), *The Rites of Passage*, (M.B. Vizedom and G.L. Caffee, trans), Chicago: The University of Chicago Press. (original work published 1909).

Vance, W. L. (1989), *America's Rome*, New Haven and London: Yale University Press.

Vermuele, C.C. (1981), *Greek and Roman Sculpture in America*, Berkeley: University of California Press.

Virillio, P. (1991), *The Lost Dimension* (Daniel Moshenburg, trans), New York: Semiotext(e).

Winckelmann, J. J. (1987), *Reflections on the Imitation of Greek Works in Painting and Sculpture* (E. Heyer and R. C. Norton, trans.), La Salle IL: Open Court. (original work published 1755).

Index

DATE DUE

DEMCO, INC. 38-2931